The Case for Non-Sovereignty

Territories like American Samoa, Anguilla, Aruba, Bermuda, the British Virgin Islands, the Cayman Islands, the Cook Islands and the Faeroes are sub-national island jurisdictions (SNIJs). They all share some measure of autonomous government, and are easily construed as independent states-in-waiting. Yet most of these territories exhibit no urgency to become independent. Instead, they appear to have decided that there are political and economic benefits accruing today when island territories are autonomous but not sovereign. In an uncertain world, a substantial degree of autonomy, respect and protection for local culture and identity, reasonable provision of employment opportunities, welfare and security by a larger and benign metropolitan state, have collectively weakened most local thrusts for independence. In spite of the mandate of the United Nations Committee on Decolonization, there is a strong case to be made today for non-sovereignty, and it is the SNIJs that provide clear evidence.

Most of the papers in this volume were previously published as a special issue of *The Round Table: Commonwealth Journal of International Affairs*, Vol. 95, Issue No. 386, September 2006.

Godfrey Baldacchino is Canada Research Chair (Island Studies) at the University of Prince Edward Island, Canada; Visiting Professor of Sociology at the University of Malta, Malta; and Executive Editor of *Island Studies Journal*.

David Milne is an expert in federalism and Emeritus Professor of Political Studies at the University of Prince Edward Island, Canada. His research interests include public policy for small jurisdictions and Canadian constitutional politics and law.

The Case for Non-Sovereignty

Lessons from sub-national
island jurisdictions

Edited by Godfrey Baldacchino and
David Milne

Routledge
Taylor & Francis Group

LONDON AND NEW YORK

First published 2009
by Routledge
2 Park Square, Milton Park, Abingdon, Oxon, OX14 4RN

Simultaneously published in the USA and Canada
by Routledge
270 Madison Avenue, New York, NY 10016

Routledge is an imprint of the Taylor & Francis Group, an informa business

Typeset in Sabon Roman by KnowledgeWorks Global Limited, Chennai, India
Printed and bound in Great Britain by MPG Books Ltd, Bodmin, Cornwall

British Library Cataloguing in Publication Data
A catalogue record for this book is available from the British Library

ISBN10: 0–415–45550–2 (hbk)
ISBN13: 978–0–41–45550–3 (hbk)

This volume is dedicated to **Peter H. Lyon** OBE, in grateful acknowledgement of his generous support and service to the Island Studies programme, its faculty and students at the University of Prince Edward Island, Canada, over many years. Peter's contribution to the development of the Institute of Island Studies and to the interdisciplinary graduate programme in Island Studies at UPEI has been exceptional, as has been his unfailing support and enthusiasm for our research and publications in Commonwealth outlets, including *The Round Table*.

Contents

Contributors

Godfrey Baldacchino is Canada Research Chair (Island Studies) at the University of Prince Edward Island, Canada, Visiting Professor of Sociology at the University of Malta, Malta, and Executive Editor of *Island Studies Journal*. His latest publications include *A World of Islands* (2007); and *Bridging Islands: The Impact of Fixed Links* (2007). His recent articles have appeared in *Asia Pacific Viewpoint, Canadian Geographer, Journal of Small Business & Entrepreneurship* and *World Development*.

Barry Bartmann is Professor of Political Studies at the University of Prince Edward Island, Canada, and the founding coordinator of its Island Studies programme. His fields of interest include the international relations of small (often island) states and comparative politics. He has made submissions to various governments and international organizations on issues regarding small states. His articles have appeared in such journals as *The Round Table* and *Island Studies Journal*.

John Connell is Professor of Geography, School of Geosciences, University of Sydney, Sydney, Australia. His key research interests are concerned with political, economic and social development in less developed countries, especially in the South Pacific region and in other small island states. His publications include *Urbanisation in the South Pacific: Towards Sustainable Development* (2002).

Bob Conrich is a retired arbitrator with a background in law, business, construction, government, history, journalism and politics. A resident of Anguilla, British West Indies, for over twenty years, he does *pro bono* consulting work in the British Overseas Territories.

Megan Davies was formerly Research Assistant at the Institute of Development Studies, University of Sussex, UK. She has interests in disaster risk reduction, particularly volcanic eruptions and risk communication and perception. Her main experience is in volcanic disaster management in the Caribbean. Her research interests include the use of education as a disaster management tool.

Yash Ghai was born in Kenya. He is currently Head of the Constitution Advisory Support Unit, UNDP Nepal. He retired at the end of 2005 from the University of Hong Kong after teaching there for seventeen years. Before then, he was Professor at the University of Warwick, UK. He has written on constitutional law, human rights, ethnicity and sociology of law. His books include *Autonomy and Ethnicity: Negotiating Claims in Multi-ethnic States* (2001) and *Hong Kong's New Constitutional Order: The Basic Law and the Resumption of Chinese Sovereignty* (1999). He has advised on the drafting or reform of constitutions in many countries: he was Chair of the Kenya Constitution Review Commission and Kenya National Constitutional Conference (equivalent to a constituent assembly). He is Special Representative of the UN Secretary General for human rights in Cambodia.

Ilan Kelman is involved in research and advocacy work that relates to two areas: understanding and reducing island vulnerability, which aims to build safe and healthy communities on islands and in other isolated areas; and disaster diplomacy, examining how and why disaster-related activities do and do not reduce enmity. Ethical research and practical approaches are of particular interest along with connections between disaster research and disaster risk-reduction practice.

Sandy Kerr is a Lecturer in Environmental Management at the International Centre for Island Technology (ICIT), Orkney Islands campus of Heriot-Watt University, Scotland, UK. His interests include the sustainable management of coastal and island resources, particularly fisheries, conservation and energy. His articles have appeared in journals such as *Ocean and Coastal Management*, *Fisheries Research* and *Town Planning Review*.

Jerome L. McElroy is Professor of Economics, Department of Business Administration and Economics, St Mary's College, Notre Dame, Indiana, USA. His current research interests in small islands include sustainable tourism, Caribbean tourism after Castro, the impact of political status on tourism development, and the contrasts between tourist-driven (SITE) and aid/remittance-driven (MIRAB) small island economies. His articles have appeared in such journals as *Annals of Tourism Research*, *Asia Pacific Viewpoint* and *The Round Table*.

David Milne is Emeritus Professor of Political Studies at the University of Prince Edward Island, Canada. Research interests include public policy for small jurisdictions and Canadian constitutional politics and law. His publications include the co-editing of *Lessons from the Political Economy of Small Islands: The Resourcefulness of Jurisdiction* (2000) with Godfrey Baldacchino and the co-authoring of the chapter on Island governance in *A World of Islands: An Island Studies Reader* (2007) with Edward Warrington.

Tom Mitchell is a Research Fellow at the Institute of Development Studies, University of Sussex, UK. He is a geographer working on climate change, disaster management, participatory processes and governance. Practical experience includes conducting deliberative processes for improving disaster resilience and working with small island developing states to assess disaster policy. Other interests include volcanoes, livelihoods, education and social vulnerability. He has extensive experience in the Caribbean and shorter assignments in the Indian Ocean.

Gert Oostindie is Director of the Royal Netherlands Institute of Southeast Asian and Caribbean Studies (KITLV), and Professor of Caribbean History, both at Leiden University, The Netherlands. He has published extensively on the colonial history and decolonization of the Dutch Caribbean; on history, ethnicity and migration in the Caribbean and Latin America in general; and on the significance of colonial history to Dutch national identity. Recent books include *Paradise Overseas: The Dutch Caribbean* (2005) and *Decolonising the Caribbean: Dutch Policies in a Comparative Perspective* (2003, with Inge Klinkers).

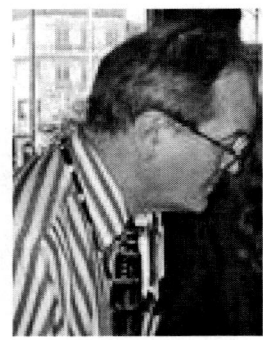

Iain Orr worked in the United Kingdom's Foreign and Commonwealth Office (FCO) from 1968 to 2002, mostly dealing with China (including being Consul-General in Shanghai, 1987–1990). He negotiated Environment Charters with the UK's Overseas Territories (OTs), and managed an FCO fund for environmental work in the OTs. He is a founder partner of the Global Islands Network and a consultant to the World Land Trust.

Kara B. Pearce has a BA in Economics from St Mary's College, Notre Dame, Indiana, USA. She currently serves as a Research Coordinator for the CB Richard Ellis office in Charlotte, North Carolina. Her research interests focus on the correlates of small island tourist economies.

Anthony J. Regan is a constitutional lawyer specializing in constitutional development as part of conflict resolution. He has lived and worked in Papua New Guinea (PNG) for some fifteen years where he taught at the U-PNG Law Faculty, and has served as adviser to Bougainville parties in the Bougainville peace process since 1994. He has also been involved in the Solomon Islands and Sri Lanka peace processes, and in the constitution-making process in East Timor. His current research includes: conflict resolution and civil society in Melanesia; and ombudsman institutions and leadership codes as constitutional accountability and anti-corruption mechanisms.

Elaine Stratford is Associate Professor in Geography at the School of Geography and Environmental Studies, University of Tasmania, Australia. Her work focuses on cultural geography and the geopolitics of islands; sustainability and community; the sense of identity in place. Her research interests deal with the interstices of cultural geography and political ecology, with particular emphasis on island studies, sustainability and community, and the use of qualitative research methods. She has published articles in such journals as *Australian Geographical Studies*, *Cultural Geographies* and *Geoforum*.

Kathleen Stuart completed an MA degree in Island Studies in 2006, after a long career in the private sector during which she earned degrees in sociology, dietetics and business. She has assisted Dr Godfrey Baldacchino on the Jurisdiction Project since its inception in 2004, and began teaching Island Studies to undergraduates at the University of Prince Edward Island in 2007. Her research interests include public policy, entrepreneurship, sustainable development and jurisdiction. Her recent articles have appeared in *Sustainable Development* and *Journal of Small Business and Entrepreneurship*.

Ronald L. Watts is Principal Emeritus, Professor Emeritus of Political Studies, and Fellow of the Institute for Intergovernmental Relations at Queen's University, Kingston, Ontario, Canada, where he has been a member of the academic staff since 1955. He has worked for over forty years on the comparative study of federal systems and Canadian federalism, subjects on which he has written or edited some twenty books, monographs and reports, as well as over eighty journal articles and book chapters. He has received five honorary degrees, and became a Companion of the Order of Canada in 2000. His books include *Comparing Federal Systems*, third edition (2008) and *The Spending Power in Federal Systems* (1999).

Acknowledgements

The support of the Social Sciences and Humanities Research Council of Canada (SSHRC) to the proposals 'Patterns of Sub-National Autonomy amongst the World's Islands' (SRG Application No. 410-2004-0397) and 'Offshoring Strategies from Sub-national Island Jurisdictions' (SRG Application No. 410-2007–0577) is gratefully acknowledged. We are indebted to colleagues and friends who have helped us structure this book's themes and arguments, amongst them Harvey W. Armstrong, Barry Bartmann, Geoff Bertram, Christian Depraetere, Norman Girvan, Rob Greenwood, Mark P. Hampton, Hiroshi Kakazu, Will Kymlicka, Bjarne Lindström, Peter Lyon, Jerome L. McElroy, Iain Orr, Stephen A. Royle, Mark Shrimpton, Henry F. Srebrnik, Paul K. Sutton, Edward Warrington and Ronald L. Watts. Special thanks to Doug Brown, Harvey Lazar and (again) Ronald L. Watts at the Institute of Intergovernmental Relations, Queen's University, Kingston, Ontario, Canada, for the opportunity to discuss relevant issues during October 2004. We thank Timothy M. Shaw, former Director of the Institute for Commonwealth Studies (ICS) at the University of London, for co-organizing a workshop on the theme of this book at the ICS in London, UK, in April 2005, and again as an integral part of the Commonwealth People's Forum at the Commonwealth Heads of Government Meeting (CHOGM) held in Malta in November 2005. We also thank Dr Andrew J. Williams as Editor-in-Chief of *The Round Table: Commonwealth Journal of International Affairs* (TRT), for accepting to run a thematic issue of TRT on the subject of sub-national island jurisdictions in September 2006. Along with the new Director of the ICS, Dr Richard Crook, and the sponsorship of Taylor and Francis, Dr Williams supported the hosting of a launch of the TRT special at the ICS Offices in London in October 2006.

We also acknowledge the input of graduate students following the Master of Arts Programme in Island Studies at the University of Prince Edward Island (UPEI), Canada, for sub-national island jurisdictional data collation: Faiz Ahmed, Jean-Louis Arsenault, Ryan Boulter, Hans Connor, Douglas Deacon, Crystal Fall, Barbara Groome Wynne, Laura Fanning, Heather Gushue, Margaret Mizzi, Ryan O'Connor, Janice Pettit, Ariana Salvo – and Kathleen Stuart, who acted as overall graduate student coordinator.

The map of sub-national island jurisdictions around the world has been expertly drawn by Gill Alexander, Dept of Geography, Archaeology and Palaeoecology, Queen's University Belfast, Northern Ireland, UK.

At Taylor and Francis, we are grateful for the support and assistance of Richard Delahunty, Ygraine Cadlock, Brian Guerin and Vicky Claringbull, who shepherded the text through to final publication.

We remain grateful to all the contributors to this volume for their willingness to share their work and to comply with rigorous editorial demands and deadlines. Full responsibility for any shortcomings remains, of course, only our own.

Godfrey Baldacchino
Prince Edward Island, Canada

David Milne
Malta

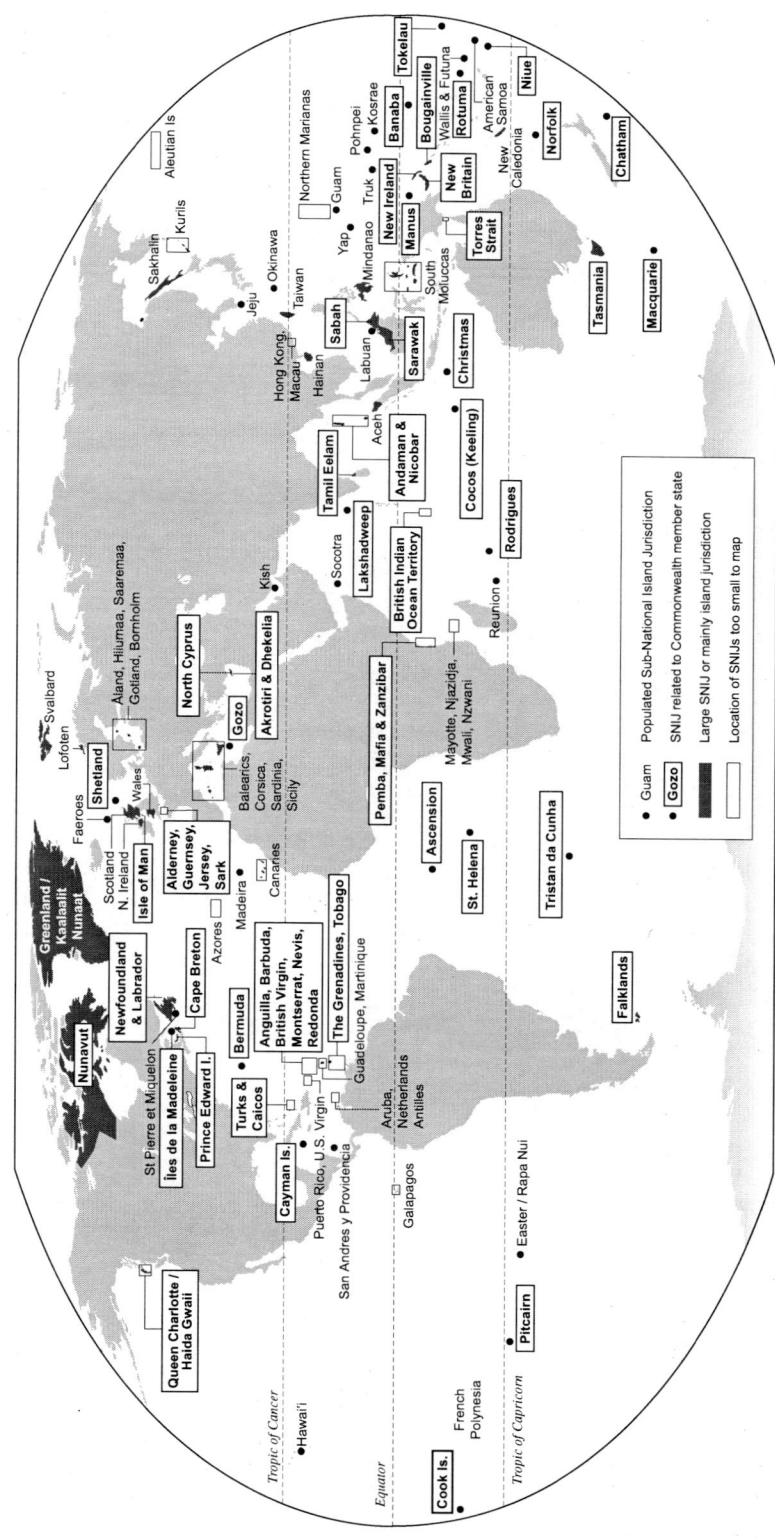

The World's Sub-national Island Jurisdictions (2008).

Source: Compiled by Gill Alexander (Queen's University Belfast, Northern Ireland).

1 Success without sovereignty: exploring sub-national island jurisdictions

Godfrey Baldacchino and David Milne

KISH ISLAND: FACT OR FICTION?

From the palm-lined road nearby, the mountains of Iran's southern coast are visible. But any shadow cast by Iran's repressive regime barely seems to reach Kish's gentle sand. On this small island, 18 km off the southern coast of the Islamic Republic of Iran, it is far easier to find a five-star hotel than a mosque. That's because Iran's dictatorial government is trying to showcase Kish not as a strict Islamic haven, but as an earthly paradise designed to win over the international community.

(Roston, 2005, p. 21)

Kish Island is one of three 'industrial free trade zones' approved by the Majlis (Iran's Islamic Consultative Assembly) in August 1993. Kish may be small: just 5 km wide and 17 km long. Still, it is administered semi-autonomously by 'an Authority organized as a company with autonomous legal status, whose capital shall belong to the government' (Law on Administration of Free Trade-Industrial Zones, Article 5). Its very smallness and islandness lets Kish get away with such a departure from fundamentalist theocratic rule.

Many readers can be excused for thinking that the above example is a purely fictional one. For how could the most puritanical, hard-line and anti-Western of contemporary states – the Iran of the mullahs and the ayatollahs, member of 'the axis of evil' widely believed to be developing a nuclear arsenal – tolerate shopping malls, hyper-markets, theme parks, women in high heels and pool tables on part of its territory, an island which runs its own (semi-private) airline and has plans for an 18-hole PGA golf course and a Formula One race track (Roston, 2005; Watson, 2004)?

Yet Kish Island is very real and its *modus vivendi* is not hard to understand. Iran, like other states, is keen to attract international capital: hence, the conversion to a visa-free trade zone and booming business hub. Kish's insignificant, remote and peripheral island status provides a tolerable and convenient diversion from the required austere life of the mainland. Here, Iran can profitably experiment with a site that is small and bounded, with no danger of destabilizing spillovers. Kish serves as an informal market for an international trade in avionics where Iran's air force fleet of ageing US-made F-15s, F-5s and F-4s (bought during the reign of the Shah), now under a US embargo, can access desperately needed maintenance parts and expertise.

MAINLAND–ISLAND RELATIONS

This 'Mainland Iran–Kish Island' dialectic is not unique. There are many similar examples of 'mainland-island relations' in the contemporary world which, from a surface glance, do not seem to make sense. Yet their logic becomes clearer when seen in the context of states requiring unique offshore spaces outside the strait-jacket of the increasingly restrictive, 'level playing field' rules of global commerce among sovereign states. Islands then provide bounded space for the emergence of ingenious new species of asymmetrical economies and governance.

The pattern repeats itself again and again where states make creative use of their small, far-flung and remote island jurisdictions to facilitate activities that would be simply anathema on home ground. Take Batam Island, located close to Singapore, that acts as the exclusive economic zone of Indonesia (Royle, 1997). Or consider Labuan Island, an integrated international offshore finance centre for neighbouring Malaysia (e.g. Fields, 2002). The Maldives, with its small population and convenient archipelagic geography, is another fundamentalist Islamic state that tolerates a vibrant tourism industry via a scrupulous zoning policy (Baldacchino, 2004a).

Even developed metropolitan powers play the same game, if in a somewhat more cynical fashion. The United Kingdom, for example, appeals for curbing low/no-tax regimes via the OECD and the G7, while encouraging British investment to benefit from the very same low/no-tax regimes of the Isle of Man, the Channel Islands, Bermuda and the Cayman Islands, for whose 'good government' the same United Kingdom remains ultimately responsible. Though a self-professed unitary state, China treats Hong Kong (since 1997) and Macao (since 1999) as 'special administrative regions', where 'the socialist system and policies shall not be practised ... and the previous capitalist system and way of life shall remain unchanged for 50 years' (Ministry of Justice, People's Republic of China). Kinmen Island for its part acts as a relatively safe clearinghouse for China–Taiwan relations: particularly appreciated at times of tension (Hung-Ta, 2004).

The rationale for these metropolitan–island arrangements, however, is scarcely one-sided. From the perspective of small island territories, there are quite plausible reasons to aspire to an 'arm's-length' relationship with a larger, 'mainland' benevolent patron. McElroy and Mahoney (2000) explain how the smaller players in these unequal dyads derive substantial economic advantages from the arrangement. These include: free or concessionary trade with, and export preference from, the parent country; social welfare assistance; ready access to external capital through special tax concessions; availability of external labour markets through migration; aid-financed infrastructure and communications; higher-quality health and educational systems; natural disaster relief; and provision for costly external defence. Autonomy without sovereignty may also facilitate tourism development because of easier terms of access and security.

Most of these special conditions have emerged in the context of a history of a relatively benign colonial relationship – typically one dominated by strategic rather than economically exploitative interests. *The Economist* (2003) has claimed that the island citizens of Aruba, Bermuda and French Polynesia are amongst the world's top ten richest peoples: these three territories are non-sovereign island jurisdictions, benefiting from customized linkages with the much larger states of the Netherlands, the United Kingdom and France respectively. Various other sub-national island jurisdictions partake of some form of profitable asymmetrical federalism with(in) a typically larger state (Stevens, 1977; Baldacchino, 2004b).

Of course, it is important to recognize that the arrangements for many of the islands cited above vary enormously in nature and character. Typically, those like Kish Island – which have been constructed from above for profit or strategic convenience – lack the elements of genuine jurisdictional autonomy and historic entitlement that arise in many enduring island federacy arrangements. Kish Island cannot presume, for example, to claim a distinct status akin to the Isle of Man or the Åland Islands; these are 'autonomies' of a totally different order and character. The Isle of Man draws upon centuries of convention and practice to fortify its distinct constitutional status as a separate crown dependency from the UK mainland, while the Åland Islands have enjoyed international protection for its autonomy since 1920. Moreover, since there is often so little sociological or ideological substance or drive in Kish and other such island autonomies created from above, these do not exhibit anything like the claims to distinct 'nation' status that may arise in autonomies like the Faeroe Islands (e.g. Ackren, 2006), or even a struggling and constitutionally constrained Corsica (e.g. Lauwers, 2003).

It is when the conditions of island identity are strong, and when there are powerful constitutional precedents to sustain the claim to self-rule, that island autonomies truly come into their own as partners in a genuine bilateral federal covenant. Constitutional arrangements here are truly 'federal', that is, contractual, the products of free consent between the parties, and not merely autonomies that are devolved from a central government and can be taken away as quickly as they were intially granted (Elazar, 1987, pp. 5–12). Such vigorous examples of federal 'self-rule' and 'shared-rule' arrangements between islands and their metropoles are set out below in all their luxuriant variety. Most are a continuing testament to the rich governance systems, with all of their anomalies and asymmetry, that remain with the European retraction of Empire. Moreover, these delicate arrangements between European metropoles and their maritime dependencies have in turn been absorbed and 'grandfathered' at the supranational level within the European Union.

In their vast majority, then, these examples from the world's sub-national (mainly island) jurisdictions show a remarkable pattern of mutual accommodation and convenience between large (often metropolitan) states and their offshore islands. It is usually in the interests of *neither* party to push these islands into straightforward sovereignty, as was so often the case in the decades following the Second World War. Now, both prefer a negotiated bilateral partnership that can take its place within the highly variegated 'federal' landscape of governance within the modern world. Of course, there may also be in the metropolitan state an evident embarrassment over these remnants of empire and the continuing burden that they may present, so well reflected in the Netherlands' ongoing tug-of-war with its Caribbean island dependencies, or of New Zealand with its Pacific equivalents (see Oostindie and Connell, Chapters 9 and 11 respectively, this volume) So, the patterns and motivations on each side for current non-sovereign constitutional arrangements are complex and do not always move in the same direction or remain constant from one case to the next.

In any event, we have to confront the fact that the contemporary global political and legal geometry is more complex than it has ever been and obliges us to rethink older notions of sovereignty and the international state system. Upholding and distinguishing strict 'sovereign' from 'non-sovereign' entities in international practice was never consistently followed in the past and is even less tenable today, as power is increasingly pooled among and across states, and reconfigured and redistributed from within national territories. This practical spirit increasingly animates the arrangements of many offshore islands with their metropolitan partners, where non-sovereign island jurisdictions will wish to preserve, or even enhance, their asymmetrical status and autonomous powers, rather than take the risk of joining the ranks of sovereign states themselves. In short, life in the 'antechamber' of the state system (see Bartmann, Chapter 5, this volume) may look a good deal more attractive to these jurisdictions than the romantic advocates of sovereign self-determination had ever supposed.

Such a position, of course, looks timid and self-defeating from the perspective of those who grew up in the heady days of colonial emancipation following the Second World War; but it is no longer so. Opting for non-sovereign jurisdictional status may be a highly rational, strategic choice that can result in substantial net material and security gains for the jurisdiction. As Oostindie's Chapter (9) in this collection so ably demonstrates, these judgements should not be lightly or ideologically dismissed, particularly at a time when security concerns are real and when sovereignty for most islands has largely *not* delivered relatively high levels of economic prosperity. The grant of *sub-national island jurisdictional* status (SNIJ) typically confers a solid safety net supported by a metropolitan power, while permitting enough discretion to safeguard national identity, local culture and the general exercise of local power. McElroy and Pearce (Chapter 4, this volume) refer to a 'superior level of performance' by SNIJs. The metropolitan player can meanwhile exercise 'soft imperialism' (which does not typically raise eyebrows amongst the members of the UN Committee on Decolonization), keep a watchful eye for potential geo-strategic military or economic rents, and lavish its munificence upon its small island beneficiaries.

Within this framework, islands may therefore be wise to ignore the siren call of sovereignty and cut their arrangements more pragmatically and creatively. Such a pragmatism manifests itself clearly, for example, in the muddy and treacherous waters of para-diplomacy (see Kelman *et al.*, Chapter 6, this volume). Of course, there are many circumstances where sovereignty will show itself to be the most logical or compelling course of action: such would explain the independence of East\rquote Timor in 2002 and of Montenegro in 2006, and Kosovo in 2008 (e.g. Bahcheli *et al.*, 2004). And there are many examples where (often small) island sovereign states have succeeded beyond all expectations and where the tools of sovereignty have been a vital part of the explanation for their success. A good case study would be Iceland; but, even here, as Kristinsson (2000) argues, the continued utility of undiminished sovereignty, together with non-membership of the European Union, will depend on circumstances. Surely, this is the point: the appropriate political architecture and jursidictional status for any island can only be known after careful review of all its current and likely future options undertaken in a clearsighted pragmatic spirit (e.g. Le Rendu, 2004). And, certainly for our purposes here, there appears to be every reason to expect islands in that kind of review to continue to opt for contoured, negotiated, non-sovereign, constitutional arrangements in the future (e.g. Dodds, 2002).

AN 'ISLAND STUDIES' HOLISTIC PERSPECTIVE

We now move to a panoramic vantage point from which to observe and to understand how small islands – as parts of larger, multi-layered systems – have adapted and sustained themselves historically and how they now address current pressures of globalization and environmental threats. Indeed, sub-national island autonomies span all oceanic basins and boast all manner of diversities of size, climate, topography, ecology, history, economy, politics and jurisdiction (see the map on page xvii).

These islands are the rich breeding grounds for unique adaptations of governance in the modern world, just as surely as islands have provided, ever since the days of Darwin and his contemporaries, bounded territories for study of biological and ecological systems in nature. A case study of an island such as Tasmania (see Stratford, Chapter 7, this volume) can sensitively explore some of these dimensions and properties of islandness – isolation and distinctiveness – as island 'resources'. As the work of comparative federal scholar Ronald Watts (Chapter 3, this volume) so powerfully illustrates, islands are an excellent lens through which to understand unique variations in federal governance arrangements. Watts' taxonomy of islands borrows its language and ideas about island federal relationships from evolutionary biology with its talk of variations or 'species' within a genus of self- and shared-rule arrangements. Watts arranges many *de jure* islands into various constitutional groupings, while avoiding problematic cases (like the Turkish Republic of Northern Cyprus). The evidence also shows two kinds of physical determinism: (1) a high logistical inclination for islands to enjoy some powers of self-rule, with different kinds of shared-rule arrangements with metropolitan states; and (2) a tendency for islands to be run as single jurisdictions, as if there were something abhorrent about splitting that which nature had defined as unitary (e.g. Baldacchino, 2002).

In fact, while there are some 30,000 islands with a land area larger than 0.1 km^2 (Dahl and Depraetere, 2007, pp. 60–61), only nine (at most) today are split between two or more different countries (Baldacchino, 2006, p. 854). Small island territories have been 'decolonizing without disengaging' (Houbert, 1986), particularly since the\rquote 1940s, starting with the departmentalization of four French overseas island territories in 1946; followed by the setting up of the Netherlands Antilles in 1954, and dramatized by the secession of Anguilla from St Kitts-Nevis in 1979. Historical practice and/or international provisions have secured over time the autonomy of such locations as Åland, Svalbard, the Channel Islands and the Isle of Man. Military interventions and/or sectarian strife has led to *de facto* autonomous jurisdictions in Northern Cyprus, Mindanao, Sri Lanka and Taiwan (though the latter is somewhat unique in being recognized by a number of states). Constitutionally or legally entrenched provisions secure and frame the autonomy of island provinces like Hawai'i, Mwali, Prince Edward Island and Tasmania. First nations enjoy self-determination in locations such as Nunavut, Haida Gwaii/Queen Charlotte Islands, Rotuma and the Torres Strait. There are the various former colonies, not interested in independence (as stubbornly confirmed in various plebiscites), and engaged in evolving binary relations with Amsterdam, Copenhagen, London, Paris, Sydney, Washington or Wellington. Specific sub-national arrangements treat Kish, Labuan, Madeira, Corsica, Sicily, Nevis, Scotland and Zanzibar differently from the rest of their nation-state, often in respect of cultural differences and distinct histories, or as an outcome of deliberate, central government strategy. There are also special island (or mainly island) regions which enjoy a specific autonomy portfolio, *de jure* or *de facto*: Hong Kong, Macao, Shetland and Sakhalin – thanks to a recognition of the prudent management of resourcefulness (investment finance, human capital, fossil fuels) that may be threatened in the loss of autonomy. The Galápagos Islands, featured in this collection, are another example of distinct autonomy arrangements, this time aimed at preserving an island's unique ecosystem and its legendary place as Darwin's laboratory for pioneering evolutionary thought (see Kerr, Chapter 10, this volume).

ISLANDS IN FLUX

Of course, the relationship of most 'island–mainland' dyads is far from smooth or settled. Asymmetrical federalism is by definition in perpetual negotiation: in 2005, Jeju Island become a 'special administrative province' of South Korea, enjoying even more autonomous powers (Chosun Ilbo, 2005); and the Bermuda Independence Commission visited London for high-level talks (Sanders, 2005). In 2006, Åland – now with its own top-level internet domain (.ax) – threatened to scuttle the renewed attempt to get the European Constitution endorsed (Rennie, 2006); Tokelau rejected a move to independence in free association with New Zealand following a referendum (see Connell, Chapter 11, this volume); while China and Taiwan continued their – so far verbal and diplomatic – confrontation. Also in 2006, the UK High Court ruled that the Chagossians were entitled to return to the Chagos Archipelago; the UK government's subsequent appeal was dismissed by the Court of Appeal in May 2007 (http://www.chagossupport.org.uk/). Also in 2007, Saint Barthélemy and Saint Martin became distinct *collectivités d'outre mer* as part of the latest reforms to the French overseas territories. Then, in 2008, the Netherlands Antilles break up: Bonaire, Saba and St Eustatius becoming muncipalities of the Netherlands; while Curaçao and Sint Martin join Aruba, each in *status aparte* within the Kingdom of the Netherlands.

The fluidity of the 'mainland–island' arrangement is enhanced precisely because it is *both* federal (and thus involving multi-level governance, which presents competing claims for legitimacy and policy competence) *and* asymmetrical (where the striking of *idiosyncratic* or special deals and outcomes is often preferred). The relationship is liable to change (e.g., in Canada, see IIGR, 2005); and 'full sovereignty' (whatever that phrase may imply in the twenty-first century) remains a viable option and vision, should it be impossible to work out decent terms for a sub-national solution. We could scarcely find a better example of this critical fluid nature of governance than that of Bougainville (see Ghai and Regan, Chapter 8, this volume) with the recent changing nature of that island's status towards autonomy either within, or possible independence from, Papua New Guinea. The issue of re-negotiation in these cases may be fractious: the terms of the relationship may be the subject of civil strife, guerrilla movements or other forms of internal warfare and diplomatic tension. This can take the guise of 'infra-nationalism' which is a political and institutional structure beyond the constitution, a *de facto* island (or sub-island) state apparatus existing in taunting defiance of the main state, with which relations are *not* harmonious – as has occurred in recent decades in such diverse places as

Aceh, Bougainville, Corsica, Cyprus, New Caledonia, Mindanao and Sri Lanka (Weiler, 1991).

This state of variability is often represented in an expression of ambivalent, 'love-hate' nationalism. The smaller (island) player is often demonstrably proud of its own (sub-?) national identity, captured also by explicitly showcased cultural differences (in language, religion, history, ethnic composition, political ideology and other identity symbols like flags, anthems, currency, monuments, emblems and top-level internet domains) from its larger player. Yet it may refer to a benign, special relationship with the larger player for the purpose of defending its prized autonomy and self-determination (from the threat of international piracy, general insecurity or irredentist neighbouring states). If the relationship lies in discord, then local political movements and the public at large are likely to see, and play upon, the image of the larger player in a colonial or imperialist light, unfairly and insensitively pushing its weight around, and frustrating their legitimate rights to self-determination. The larger player, in contrast, would tend to react (if at all) by invoking obligations towards order and regional stability and against renegade, destabilizing and quirky politics. The situation 'on the ground' is usually far more complex, with different political parties, social classes and other social groupings on the island, on the mainland and in between (the influential island diaspora) championing and expressing their preference for one or more of what could be a bewildering range of relational solutions (e.g., for the Caribbean, *see* Ramos and Rivera, 2001, pp. 1–21). We capture something of these intricate dynamics in this volume's study of two island archipelagos linked to South American states, the Galápagos Islands in relation to Ecuador, and the Caribbean islands of San Andrés and Old Providence in relation to Colombia (see Kerr, Chapter 10, this volume).

These case studies illustrate how contingent and varied are the experiences of many island communities as they seek to navigate towards more autonomous patterns of governance and economy within a bilateral arrangement with a mainland state. The patterns can vary sharply from case to case in response to the particular circumstances of the geography and history of islands. In some cases, islands like San Andrés and Old Providence have been consigned to a near fief-like condition; others, like the Galápagos Islands, to a slightly more elevated status, and yet others have navigated far more independently. There is much variability and contingency too in the patterns of island economies. This has presented a very serious challenge to thinkers in the field who have begun to do comparative study and reflection on these different patterns and to generate *typologies* of island governance and economy that\rquote warrant further study (e.g. Warrington and Milne, 2007; Bertram and Poirine, 2007).

CONCLUSION

Back in the mid-1980s, riding a significant wave of reflection triggered by the 1983 US-led invasion of Grenada, the overriding issue of debate was *security* for those islands still enamoured of decolonization (e.g. Alford, 1984; Commonwealth Consultative Group, 1985; Diggines, 1985; Harden, 1985; Lyon, 1985). There was no 'small is beautiful' rhetoric here, but, rather, dark talk of extreme vulnerability – even non-viability – for such small island states. Their economies were often dimmised in a similarly scathing manner. In a journal editorial, the *raison d'être* for small states and the motley 'left-overs' of empire was reduced half-humorously to: 'casino countries, tax havens, sheep stations, bauxite plants, air bases, tourist traps, oilwells with surrounds, banana plantations and nutmeg groves' (Editorial, *The Round Table,* 1984, p. 124). This colourful representation was even then an unfair and incorrect characterization, and it has become increasingly so. Almost as an act of vengeance, many small sub-national island jurisdictions now show enviable *per capita* levels of prosperity, even higher than those for small sovereign island states (Armstrong *et al.*, 1998; Armstrong and Read, 2002; Bertram, 2004; Easterly and Kraay, 2000; Poirine, 1998).

To be sure, islands can still be used and valued principally for *strategic* metropolitan purposes. Japan, for example, maintains its only large and contentious US military base on the outlying island prefecture of Okinawa, recently the subject of a resiting agreement (Kakazu, 2000). Britain summarily deported the entire island population of the Chagos Archipelago and leased the islands to the USA, which in turn built the ultra-sophisticated Indian Ocean military base at Diego Garcia (Winchester, 2004). Of course, the USA meets another strategic purpose in the questionable practice of detaining suspected terrorists in 'legal limbo' on its island base at Guantánamo Bay in Cuba (Supreme Court of the United States, 2004; Greenhouse, 2008). The Australian government 'excised' Christmas Island, Cocos (Keeling) Islands and the Ashmore Reef from the nation's territory for the purposes of immigration, deeming that persons who had arrived there had not effectively entered the country (Connell, 2006, p. 55).

But this unflattering portrait of sub-national islands as weak and subordinate containers purely at the mercy of outside metropolitan powers is scarcely the norm in this new age of globalization and multi-level governance. Island jurisdictions customarily defy that caricature, whether as fully fledged states or increasingly as sub-national actors working out their own pragmatic responses to the challenges of a changing global system in concert with their partners. Of course, the patterns vary enormously, as do the constitutional choices and options. Sovereignty is still a powerful dream for many peoples, whether living on islands or not, and in many circumstances it may be the best of all options. But we also now live in a world where there is less certainty about the merits of sovereignty than was once the case, and less arrogance about the ultimate choices that island jurisdictions ought to take. We welcome this more pragmatic and tolerant spirit respecting constitutional arrangements, along with the confidence and flexibility it engenders among island peoples worldwide. Now islands can get on with making their choices, and crafting their futures with less fear and ridicule than in the past.

References

Ackren, M. (2006). The Faeroe islands: options for independence, *Island Studies Journal*, 1(2), pp. 223–238.

Alford, J. (1984). Security dilemmas of small states, *The Round Table: Commonwealth Journal of International Affairs*, 73(292), pp. 377–382.

Armstrong, H. W. and Read, R. (2002). The phantom of liberty? Economic growth and the vulnerability of small states, *Journal of International Development*, 14(3), pp. 435–458.

Armstrong, H. W., De Kervenoael, R. J., Li, X. and Read, R. (1998). A comparison of the economic performance of different micro-states, and between micro-states and larger countries, *World Development*, 26(4), pp. 639–656.

Bahcheli, T., Bartmann, B. and Srebrnik, H. F. (eds) (2004). *De Facto States: The Quest for Sovereignty* (London: Routledge).

Baldacchino, G. (2002). Jurisdictional self-reliance for small island territories: considering the partition of Cyprus, *The Round Table: Commonwealth Journal of International Affairs*, 92(365), pp. 349–360.

Baldacchino, G. (2004a). Sustainable user practices on/for Islands, *Insula: International Journal of Island Affairs*, 13(1–2), pp. 5–10.

Baldacchino, G. (2004b). Autonomous but not sovereign? A review of island sub-nationalism, *Canadian Review of Studies in Nationalism*, 31(1–2), pp. 77–90.

Baldacchino, G. (2006). Innovative development strategies from non-sovereign island jurisdictions: a global review of economic policy and governance practices, *World Development*, 34(5), pp. 852–867.

Bertram, G. (2004). On the convergence of small island economies with their metropolitan patrons, *World Development*, 32(2), pp. 343–364.

Bertram, G. and Poirine, B. (2007). Island political economy, in G. Baldacchino (ed.) *A World of Islands: An Island Studies Reader*, pp. 323–378 (Charlottetown, Canada, and Luqa, Malta: Institute of Island Studies and Agenda Publishers).

Chosun Ilbo (2005). Jeju Island to become special autonomous province, 22 May, http://english.chosun.com/w21data/html/news/200505/200505220011.html

Commonwealth Consultative Group (1985). *Vulnerability: Small States in the Global Society* (London: Commonwealth Secretariat).

Connell, J. (2006). Nauru: the first failed Pacific state?, *The Round Table: Commonwealth Journal of International Affairs*, 95(383), pp. 47–63.

Dahl, A. L. and Depraetere, C. (2007). Island locations and classifications, in G. Baldacchino (ed.) *A\rquote World of Islands: An Island Studies Reader*, pp. 57–106 (Charlottetown, Canada, and Luqa, Malta: Institute of Island Studies and Agenda Publishers).

Diggines, C. E. (1985). The problems of small states, *The Round Table: Commonwealth Journal of International Affairs*, 74(295), pp. 191–205.

Dodds, K. (2002). *Pink Ice: Britain and the South Atlantic Empire* (London: IB Tauris).

Easterly, W. and Kraay, A. C. (2000). Small states, small problems? Income, growth and volatility in small states, *World Development*, 28(11), pp. 2013–2027.

Economist, The (2003). On the world's rich list, London, *The Economist Magazine*, 17 May, p. 33.

Editorial, The Round Table(1984). Small states and left-overs of Empire, *The Round Table: Commonwealth Journal of International Affairs*, 73(290), pp. 122–129.

Elazar, D. J. (1987). *Exploring Federalism* (Tuscaloosa, AL: University of Alabama Press).

Fields, B. (2002). Labuan: the undiscovered pearl of the South China Sea, *Escape from America Magazine*, no. 32, http://www.escapeartist.com/efam32/labuan.html

Greenhouse, L. (2008). 'Justices, 5–4, Back Detainee Appeals for Guantánamo', *New York Times*, June 13.

Harden, S. (1985). *Small Is Dangerous: Micro States in a Macro World* (New York: St Martin's Press).

Houbert, J. (1986). Decolonizing without disengaging: France in the Indian Ocean, *The Round Table: Commonwealth Journal of International Affairs*, 75(298), pp. 145–166.

Hung-Ta, C. (2004). The cultural landscape in the island with the status of borderland, paper presented at the eighth 'Islands of the World' Conference, International Small Islands Studies Association (ISISA), Kinmen Island, Taiwan, November.

Institute of Intergovernmental Relations (IIGR) (2005). Special discussion papers on 'asymmetric federalism' (Kingston ON, Canada: Queen's University), www.iigr.ca/iigr.php/site/browse_publications?section=43

Kakazu, H. (2000). *The Challenge for Okinawa: Thriving Locally in a Globalized Economy* (Okinawa Development Finance Corporation, March).

Kristinsson, G. H. (2000). From home rule to sovereignty: the case of Iceland, in G. Baldacchino and D. Milne (eds) *Lessons from the Political Economy of Small Islands: The Resourcefulness of Jurisdiction*, pp.rquote 141–155 (Basingstoke: Macmillan).

Lauwers, G. (2003). Discussing autonomy and independence for Corsica, in B. Coppieters and R. Sakwa (eds) *Contextualizing Secession*, pp. 49–71 (Oxford: Oxford University Press).

Law on Administration of Free Trade-Industrial Zones, www.kishfreezone.org/investment/rules2.htm

Le Rendu, L. (2004). *Jersey: Independent Dependency? The Survival Strategies of a Microstate* (Wiltshire, UK: ELSP).

Lyon, P. (ed.) (1985). *Small States and the Commonwealth* (London: Butterworth).

McElroy, J. L. and Mahoney, M. (2000). The propensity for political dependence in island microstates, *Insula: International Journal of Island Affairs*, 9(1), pp. 32–35.

Ministry of Justice, People's Republic of China, www.legalinfo.gov.cn/english/LegalKnowledge/LegalKnowledge1.htm

Poirine, B. (1998). Should we hate or love MIRAB?, *The Contemporary Pacific*, 10(1), pp. 65–106.

Ramos, A. G. and Rivera, A. I. (eds) (2001). *Islands at the Cross Roads: Politics in the Non-independent Caribbean* (Jamaica: Ian Randle Publishers).

Rennie, D. (2006). Tiny island that's ready to stop Europe in its tracks, *Daily Telegraph* (UK), 15\rquote February, http://telegraph.co.uk/core/Content/displayPrintable.jhtml?xml=/news/2006/02/15/waland15.xml&site=5

Roston, A. (2005). Iran's bizarre military bazaar, *The Walrus*, 2(4), pp. 21–24.

Royle, S. A. (1997). The benefits of insularity on development: the case of Batam island, Indonesia, paper presented to Development Studies Association Conference, Norwich, University of East Anglia, September.

Sanders, R. (2005). Bermuda: independence or not?, *Caribbean Net News*, 8 March, www.caribbeannetnews.com/2005/03/08/sanders.shtml

Scoop Independent News (2006). Tokelau referendum does not produce a 2/3 majority, 16 February, http://www.scoop.co.nz/stories/PA0602/S00232.htm

Stevens, R. M. (1977). Asymmetrical federalism: the federal principle and the survival of the small republic, *Publius: The Journal of Federalism*, 7(4), pp. 177–204.

Supreme Court of the United States (2004). Rasul *et al.* v. Bush, President of the United States *et al.*, www.supremecourtus.gov/opinions/03pdf/03-334.pdf (Decided: 28 June).

Warrington, E. and Milne, D. (2007). Island governance, in G. Baldacchino (ed.) *A World of Islands: An Island Studies Reader*, pp. 379–428 (Charlottetown, Canada, and Luqa, Malta: Institute of Island Studies and Agenda Publishers).

Watson, I. (2004). 'Iran island resort is an experiment in free trade', *NPR News*, 7 December, audio, www.npr.org/templates/story/story.php?storyId=4206243; www.kishisland.com/

Watts, R. L. (2000). Islands in comparative constitutional perspective, in G. Baldacchino and D. Milne (eds) *Lessons from the Political Economy of Small Islands*, pp. 17–37 (Basingstoke: Macmillan).

Watts, R. L. (2003). *Comparing Federal Systems,* 2nd edition (Kingston and Montreal: McGill-Queen's University Press).

Weiler, J. H. H. (1991). The transformation of Europe, *The Yale Law Journal*, 100, pp. 2403–2483.

Winchester, S. (2004). *Outposts: Journeys to the Surviving Relics of the British Empire*, 2nd edition (London: Penguin Academic Books).

2 A listing of the World's populated sub-national island jurisdictions

Kathleen Stuart

The development of a global database of sub-national island jurisdictions (SNIJs) began in 2004. The initial list compiled consisted of post-colonial 'overseas territories' which were known to exhibit significant legislative competence and executive governance beyond simply that of a commune, ward, county or municipality with delegated powers. These islands, often locked in federal relationships of one kind or another, conform closely to the listing and categorization in the chapter by Ronald Watts in this volume. It soon became apparent, however, that the arrangements in many other islands also warranted attention, particularly where islands as sub-national territories had been selected for distinctive asymmetrical treatment. These islands – whether recognized as UNESCO World Heritage sites, as territories requiring national Ministries, or some other distinct political status – have been added to the list which follows as Table 2.1. No sufficient rationale for capping island size, either by geography or population, could be found; and so, only unpopulated islands were excluded.

Three sets of graduate students in Island Studies at the University of Prince Edward Island, Canada, were tasked to develop factual dossiers on each SNIJ in the on-line database. Primary data were assembled from expert resource persons and reliable contacts, often within the jurisdictions, and were corroborated by secondary data gleaned from other reliable sources (like news agencies) via web-based search engines. These dossiers are available in the public domain as research tools, and offers for their revision and updating are welcome.

The following list of SNIJs (Table 2.1) is my compilation. It is intended to be both illustrative and widely inclusive. It reflects selected information from the dynamic SNIJ database now available through the Island Studies website at: www.island-studies.ca. SNIJs exhibit a broad range of jurisdictional capacities, from extremely limited to full sovereignty in everything but name. The table also includes some island territories which have been difficult to classify. Although they may be *de jure* municipalities or equivalent forms of local government, they exhibit some *de facto* capacity for self-governing autonomy, even if only in a single dimension. For example, the Norwegian archipelago of Lofoten, made up of six municipalities within a county, has been declared a petroleum-free zone due to the lobbying efforts of a resident non-governmental organization. Another example is Macquarie Island, part of Huon Municipality in the State of Tasmania, Australia, but declared a UNESCO World Heritage Site, and run by scientists.

In Table 2.1, SNIJs are arranged by associated power. Additional columns provide (a) a very brief description of the nature of the autonomy, (b) the date at which

Table 2.1 Key indicators for the world's Sub-national Island Jurisdictions

	Associated power/ federation	SNIJ	General description of autonomy	Year of autonomy	Population
1	Antigua and Barbuda	Barbuda	Special status (local council 11 members)	1981	1,500
2	Australia, Commonwealth of	Macquarie Island	UNESCO World Heritage Site; run by Australian Antarctic Division	1997	30
3	Australia, Commonwealth of	Norfolk Island	Legislative assembly (9 seats)	1979	2,114
4	Australia, Commonwealth of	Christmas Island	Territory (unicameral shire council – 9 seats)	1958	396
5	Australia, Commonwealth of	Cocos (Keeling) Islands	Territory (unicameral shire council – 7 seats)	1955	627
6	Australia, Commonwealth of	Tasmania	State (province) within Commonwealth	1901	456,652
7	Australia, Commonwealth of	Torres Strait Islands	Torres Strait Regional Authority, admin. by Queensland for 18 Torres Strait local and island councils	1994	8,089
8	British Crown	Guernsey, Bailiwick of	Crown dependencies (not in EU) Alderney, Guernsey, Herm, Sark, sm islets	1254, 1948	65,031
9	British Crown	Isle of Man	Crown dependency – (not in EU but free access to mkt)	1765	72,000
10	British Crown	Jersey, Bailiwick of	Crown dependency (not in EU), largest of Channel Islands	1945	90,502
11	Canada	Haida Gwaii (Queen Charlotte Islands)	Council of the Haida Nation (CHN) to protect, assert aboriginal title and land claims; in British Columbia	1980	5,000
12	Canada	Newfoundland and Labrador	Province within federation	1949	586,000
13	Canada	Nunavut (Islands and mainland)	Self-governing territory; Inuit homeland	1999	23,000
14	Canada	Prince Edward Island	Province	1873	138,000

(continued)

Table 2.1 (Continued)

	Associated power/ federation	SNIJ	General description of autonomy	Year of autonomy	Population
15	Chile	Rapa Nui (Isla de Pascua/Easter I)	1st governor (1984); council of elders (1988); World Heritage Site (1996)	1999	3,500
16	China, People's Republic of	Hong Kong	Special admin. region, semi-autonomous (intl agreement) (more than 200 islands)	1997	6,855,000
17	China, People's Republic of	Hainan	Province	1912, 1988	8,180,000
18	China, People's Republic of	Macao	Special admin. region, semi-autonomous entity pursuant to international agreement	1999	520,400
19	Colombia	San Andrés y Providencia	Department dominated by executive branch of government; disputed by Nicaragua	1810, 1991	59,500
20	Comoros, Union of the	Anjouan (Nzwani)	Island sub-jurisdiction within union (federation)	2002	189,000
21	Comoros, Union of the	Moheli (Mwali)	Island sub-jurisdiction within union (federation)	2002	24,000
22	Comoros, Union of the	Grande Comore (Ngazidja)	Island sub-jurisdiction within union (federation)	2002	234,000
23	Denmark, EU	Bornholm	Regional municipality, single-tier local government	2007	43,000
24	Denmark, EU	Faeroe Islands	Federacy (17 inhabited islands of 21), not in EU	1948	46,000
25	Denmark, EU	Greenland (Kalaallit-Nunaat)	Autonomous dependency (not in EU)	1979 home rule	56,000
26	Ecuador	Galápagos	Province of Republic	1822	17,000
27	Equatorial Guinea	Annobon	Island province in a republic (dictatorship with govt in exile)	1968	5,000
28	Equatorial Guinea	Bioko (Eri, Fernando Poo)	2 provinces (North and South Bioko)	under dictatorship	101,000

(continued)

Table 2.1 (Continued)

	Associated power/ federation	SNIJ	General description of autonomy	Year of autonomy	Population
29	Estonia, UK	Saaremaa	Saaremaa county council	1992	40,000
30	Estonia, UK	Hiiumaa	Hiiumaa county council	1992	11,087
31	Fiji	Rotuma	Administered by district officer; Rotuma council	1992	2,600
32	Finland, EU	Åland Islands	De-militarised federacy	1921	26,200
33	France, EU	Corsica	Regional government, the Collectivité Territoriale de Corse (CTC)	1975, 1982	279,000
34	France, EU	Fr. Polynesia (Tahiti, Society Is.)	Overseas collectivity (5 admin. divisions, 130 islands); own president, legislative assembly	1946, 2003	259,800
35	France, EU	Guadeloupe	Overseas department: (Guadeloupe/ La Désirade/Les Saintes/Marie-Galante)	1946	422,500
36	France, EU	Martinique	Overseas department	1946	381,400
37	France, EU	New Caledonia (Kanaki, Kanaky)	'Sui generis collectivity' (overseas territory): 3 provinces (includes autonomous Kanak region–2 provs)	1988	213,679
38	France, EU	Réunion	Overseas department (site of administration for 5 islands)	1946	766,153
39	France, EU	Saint Barthélemy	Territorial collectivity; has unicameral territorial council with president; laws of France	2007	6,852
40	France, EU	Saint Martin	Territorial collectivity; has unicameral territorial council with president; laws of France	2007	33,102
41	France, EU	Saint-Pierre and Miquelon	Territorial collectivity (two main islands + 6 islets) (2 communes)	1985	6,125
42	France, EU	Wallis and Futuna	Territorial collectivity; two island groups, 3 traditional chiefdoms; territorial council and President	1959, 1961	15,480

(continued)

Table 2.1 (Continued)

	Associated power/federation	SNIJ	General description of autonomy	Year of autonomy	Population
43	France, EU (claimed by Comoros)	Mayotte	Territorial collectivity (two main islands + 30 islets)	1946, separate 1974	186,026
44	Hellenic Republic, EU	Greek Islands	7 main island groups: Ionian, Saronic, Cyclades, Dodecanese, Sporades, Aegean, Crete	various 1985–98	499,000
45	Independent; unrecognized	Taiwan (Formosa)	Dispute: Republic of China; claimed by People's Rep. of China	1949	21,336,000
46	India	Andaman and Nicobar	Union territory admin. by national government	1950	356,152
47	India	Lakshadweep	Union territory admin. by national government	1956	60,600
48	Indonesia	Aceh	Special autonomous district (in Sumatra) of unitary state (archipelago)	1949, secess movement	3,799,000
49	Indonesia	Maluku	Province (archipelago of South Moluccas); has militant separatist movement since 1999	1999	1,313,022
50	Indonesia	North Maluku	Province (archipelago); formerly one province with Maluku; religious and ethnic unrest	1999	870,000
51	Indonesia	West Papua (Irian Jaya)	Province	war, indep. movement mid-1990s	1,958,000
52	Iran	Kish	Kish free zone organization, a company with an autonomous legal status		20,000
53	Italian Republic, EU	Sardinia	Autonomous region – cultural (4 provinces) (Sard language legalized in 1991)	1948	1,677,000
54	Italian Republic, EU	Sicily	Autonomous region – cultural (9 provinces)	1948	5,151,000
55	Japan (US military base)	Okinawa (Ryuku Islands)	Prefectures (Sakashima Islands/Okinawa Islands); (Amami Islands) Kyushu	1972	1,292,000
56	Japan/Russia (disputed)	Ho'aido (Japan Northern Terr.)	Etorofu, Kunashiri, Shikotan, Habomai; claimed by Japan (1945) and Ainu nationalists	dispute, 1947, 1991	11,000

(continued)

Table 2.1 (Continued)

	Associated power/federation	SNIJ	General description of autonomy	Year of autonomy	Population
57	Kiribati	Banaba/Ocean Island	Municipal administration by Rabi council of leaders and elders on Rabi in Fiji	1942–1983	300 + 5,000 in Rabi
58	Korea, Republic of (South Korea)	Jeju (Cheju-do)	Special self-governing province	1917	543,000
59	Malaysia	Labuan	International offshore finance centre; federal territory of Malaysia admin. by fed. govt	1984	78,000
60	Malaysia	Sabah (North Borneo)	State	1963	1,760,000
61	Malaysia	Sarawak (North Kalimantan)	State	1963	1,846,000
62	Malta, EU	Gozo	Ministry for Gozo	1987, 1998	23,800
63	Mauritius	Rodrigues	Autonomous island region of Mauritius; agitation for full sovereignty	2002	36,000
64	Netherlands, EU	Aruba	Autonomous part of kingdom of Netherlands	1986	71,218
65	Netherlands, EU	Netherlands Antilles	Autonomous federation (5 islands – Bonaire, Curaçao, Saba, Sint Eustatius and Sint Maarten), Part of Kingdom of the Netherlands. Dismantled in 2008	1954	218,126
66	New Zealand	Chatham Islands	Local council	1995	760
67	New Zealand	Cook Islands	Associated state in free association	1965	21,200
68	New Zealand	Niue	Self-governing in free association with NZ at request of Niue	1974	2,156
69	New Zealand	Tokelau	Self-administered territory (3 atolls)	1925	1,405
70	Norway, Kingdom of	Jan Mayen	Administration shared between Nordland Company and Norwegian armed forces	1995	18
71	Norway, Kingdom of	Lofoten Islands	Archipelago of 6 municipalities, part of Nordland county; declared temporary petroleum-free zone (2003)	Traditional	24,500

(continued)

Table 2.1 (Continued)

	Associated power/ federation	SNIJ	General description of autonomy	Year of autonomy	Population
72	Norway, Kingdom of	Svalbard (Spitzbergen)	Territory admin. by Norwegian polar dept of ministry of justice; governor in territory	1920	2,756
73	Papua New Guinea	Bougainville (North Solomons)	Autonomous province (4 reps to parliament) in transition (peace treaty 2001)	2001	185,000
74	Papua New Guinea	Manus (Admiralty Islands)	Province (2 representatives to PNG parliament)	1975	32,840
75	Papua New Guinea	New Britain (Western and Central)	Province (3 representatives to PNG parliament)	1975	130,190
76	Papua New Guinea	New Ireland	Province (3 representatives to PNG parliament)	1975	87,000
77	Philippines, Republic of the	Autonomous Region in Muslim Mindanao	6 provinces in Mindanao and Sulu Archipelago; autonomous regional govt	1989	2,803,805
78	Portugal, EU	Azores	Autonomous region (9 islands), regional legislative assembly	1976	232,000
79	Portugal, EU	Madeira	Autonomous region (Madeira, Porto Santo and two groups of barren islets)	1976	284,000
80	Russian Federation	Novaya Zemlya (Severny, Yuzhny)	Part of Arkhangel'skaya oblast (region); site of nuclear testing, Russian army base	1950s	100 Nenet
81	Russian Federation	Sakhalin and Kuril Islands	Part of Sakhalin regional duma (includes Sakhalin Island and Kuril Islands)	1947	608,000
82	Russian Federation	Hasava (islands and mainland)	Nenets autonomous region, Yamalo-Nenets, Taimyr (Dolgano-Nenets)	no status	161,000
83	São Tomé e Príncipe	Príncipe	Province with political and admin. autonomy; 7-member regional assembly	1995	5,700
84	Spain, EU	Balearic Islands	Autonomous province; 4 island councils: Majorca, Minorca, Ibiza, Formentera	1978; 2007	842,000
85	Spain, EU	Canary Islands	Autonomous region (13 islands)	1983	1,643,000

(continued)

Table 2.1 (Continued)

	Associated power/ federation	SNIJ	General description of autonomy	Year of autonomy	Population
86	Sri Lanka	Tamil Eelam (unrecognized state)	Tamil separatist movement in north and eastern Sri Lanka	2002/ceasefire	1,871,500
87	St Kitts and Nevis	Nevis	State within federation (secession pressure, abated in 2004)	1983	38,836
88	Sweden, EU	Gotland	Single-tier local government (municipality); pilot project on decentralization (1996–2002)	1996	58,000
89	Tanzania, United Republic of	Mafia Island	Province (Chole, Jibondo, Juani Islands and coastal mainland)	1979	40,800
90	Tanzania, United Republic of	Zanzibar (Unguja) and Pemba	Autonomous province (Zanzibar, Pemba and number of small islands)	1979	641,000
91	Trinidad and Tobago, Republic of	Tobago	Ward of republic, 15-member house of assembly	1962	58,400
92	Turkey, Republic of	Turkish Republic of Northern Cyprus	*De facto* state only recognized by Turkey	1974	264,172
93	United Kingdom, EU	Akrotiri and Dhekelia	Sovereign British – 2 military bases on Cyprus; admin. by UK base commander	1960	3,500 mil/ 5,000 civil
94	United Kingdom, EU	Anguilla	Overseas territory	1980	13,008
95	United Kingdom, EU	Bermuda	Overseas territory	1968	64,935
96	United Kingdom, EU	British Indian Ocean Territory (BIOT)	Overseas territory (inhabitants expelled); Diego Garcia leased to US military	1965	1,500 mil/ 2,000 civil
97	United Kingdom, EU	British Virgin Islands	Overseas territory	1977	22,187
98	United Kingdom, EU	Cayman Islands	Overseas territory	1962	43,100
99	United Kingdom, EU (claimed by Argentina)	Falkland Islands (Islas Malvinas)	Overseas territory	1998 amended	2,967
100	United Kingdom, EU	Montserrat	Overseas territory (extensive UK aid due to volcano)	1989	9,245
101	United Kingdom, EU	Northern Ireland	Home nation	1999; susp till 2007	1,685,000

(continued)

Table 2.1 (Continued)

	Associated power/ federation	SNIJ	General description of autonomy	Year of autonomy	Population
102	United Kingdom, EU	Orkney	UK's smallest local authority; island council: 6 wards, 21 councillors; one rep in Scottish parliament	1974	20,000
103	United Kingdom, EU	Pitcairn Islands	Overseas territory	1904, 1940	46
104	United Kingdom, EU	Saint Helena	Overseas territory (includes Ascension, Tristan da Cunha as dependencies)	1989	7,415
105	United Kingdom, EU	Scotland	Home nation; part of United Kingdom; own parliament	1999	5,116,900
106	United Kingdom, EU	Shetland	Island council: 22 wards/councillors; two reps to devolved Scottish parliament	1974	43,000
107	United Kingdom, EU	Turks and Caicos Islands	Overseas territory (40 islands, 8 inhabited)	1976	19,956
108	United Kingdom, EU	Wales	Home nation; part of United Kingdom; own assembly	1999	2,958,600
109	USA	Aleutians	Unorganized borough of Alaska; strong US military presence; fed. natural resource mgt	1867	8,200
110	USA	American Samoa	Unincorporated and unorganized territory admin. by Office of Insular Affairs	1966	57,902
111	USA	Hawaii	State (8 major islands and numerous smaller islands); homeland compact with US govt	1959	1,210,000
112	USA	Northern Marianas	Self-governing commonwealth in political union with USA (14 islands, 3 main)	1986 covenant	78,252
113	USA	Puerto Rico	Self-governing commonwealth in free association with USA	1952	3,676,000
114	USA	US Virgin Islands	Organized, unincorp. territory admin. by Office of Insular Affairs (3 islands)	1917, 1954	108,775
115	USA (US military base)	Guam	Organized, unincorporated territory admin. by Office of Insular Affairs	1944	166,090
116	Yemen, Republic of	Socotra	Part of Aden governorate (province); special conservation and development programme	1990	44,000

arrangements for self-rule first became operative, and (c) a ballpark estimate of recent population size. Where more than one date for self-rule is specified, the first entry may reflect legitimate constitutional authority followed by a second entry showing recent changes that may be more relevant to the current level of autonomy. No attempt has been made to define the quality or extent of autonomy that is enjoyed by each jurisdiction.

Acknowledgement is particularly made to the CIA *World FactBook* (various editions) and the *Island Jurisdictions* website moderated by attorney-at-law Dan MacMeekin at: http://macmeekin.com/Library/Jurisds/aaaindex.htm. No copyright to the reproduced SNIJ information is asserted. Moreover, while information is believed to be accurate, neither such accuracy nor currency of information is warranted, especially because circumstances can and do change. Inclusion in this dynamic list is also not to be construed as an act of acknowledging the legitimacy or otherwise of any jurisdictional powers, *de jure* or *de facto*. Effective date of compilation of this SNIJ database is: 25 August 2007.

3 Island jurisdictions in comparative constitutional perspective

Ronald L. Watts

BALANCING SELF-RULE AND SHARED RULE

Island jurisdictions, even more than their mainland counterparts, are gripped by dual and seemingly contradictory pressures for both autonomous self-government, on the one hand, and for political partnership on the other. The need to balance these two sets of pressures is an ever-present fact of life for island communities, whether sovereign or not.

In surveying the international scene, it is worth noting that pressures for island autonomy have expressed themselves in the acceptance by the United Nations of 14 individual island states among its 192 members, some quite large, but a number quite small:

> Barbados, Cuba, Cyprus, Dominica, Grenada, Iceland, Jamaica, Madagascar, Malta, Mauritius, Nauru, Singapore, Sri Lanka, St Lucia.

The UN also has 25 sets of islands (unions or federations) among its members:

> Antigua and Barbuda, Bahamas, Cape Verde Islands, Comoros, Federated States of Micronesia, Fiji, Indonesia, Japan, Kiribati, Maldives, Marshall Islands, New Zealand, Palau, Philippines, São Tomé and Príncipe, Samoa, Seychelles, Solomon Islands, St Kitts and Nevis, St Vincent and the Grenadines, Tonga, Trinidad and Tobago, Tuvalu, United Kingdom, Vanuatu.

This accounts for a total of 39 sovereign island members in the UN. In addition, five other UN members represent significant portions of islands: the Dominican Republic and Haiti (sharing the island of Hispaniola), the Republic of Ireland (shared with Northern Ireland), and East Timor and Papua New Guinea (both sharing islands with Indonesia). Papua New Guinea itself includes a number of dependent islands (one of which, Bougainville, may itself emerge as an independent sovereign state within the next decade). One other island jurisdiction – Taiwan – has been and could be considered an independent state, although it is regarded by the Republic of China as a renegade province. (Indeed, Taiwan was a member of the United Nations, and even of the Security Council, until 1971, when 'mainland' China replaced Taiwan in the organization.)

At the same time, there are many other islands that possess various degrees of self-government but are linked in formal political partnerships with other territories or islands. Some 18 other islands, or groups of islands (some of them larger than islands that are sovereign units and members of the UN), are states, provinces or territories in eight different federations:

> In Argentina 1: Tierra del Fuego (shared with Chile); in Australia 1: Tasmania; in Canada 3: Prince Edward Island, Newfoundland and Labrador, and Nunavut (an archipelago with some mainland territory); in Comoros 3: Njazidja, Mwali and Nzwani (this federation has been torn by serious secession pressures); in Federated States of Micronesia 4: Kosrae, Pohnpei, Truk and Yap; in Malaysia 3: Penang, Sabah and Sarawak; in Spain 2: Balearics and Canary Islands; and in the USA 1: Hawai'i.[1]

In addition, a variety of autonomy arrangements link small islands to larger states. Ten islands or groups of islands form federacy relationships with a larger polity, and three islands or sets of islands have developed associated-state relationships with a larger polity. Moreover, 18 other islands, or groups of islands, though having a measure of constitutional home rule, are directly administered by a larger polity. (Federacy, associated state, confederal and other arrangements are defined and examined later in this chapter.)

Since 1946, the United Nations has been keeping a controversial list of 'non-self-governing territories' which the UN, often following its own ideological agenda, sees as deserving of 'graduation' to sovereign status (see Connell, Chapter 11, this volume). Yet most of the citizens of these territories have democratically opted to maintain their associated-state status, and have rejected independence (Baldacchino, 2004). There were 16 jurisdictions on this UN list in 2007, of which all but two were island units:

> American Samoa, Anguilla, Bermuda, British Virgin Islands, Cayman Islands, Falklands/Malvinas, Guam, Montserrat, New Caledonia, Pitcairn Islands, St Helena and its dependencies, Tokelau, Turks and Caicos Islands, the US Virgin Islands, and the two non-island units of Gibraltar and Western Sahara.

Several international regional associations include a significant number of island members. Some 16 of the sovereign island states that are UN members are linked in a confederal partnership in the Caribbean Community and Common Market (CARICOM) (17 full and associate island members). The 12 full island members of CARICOM are:

> Antigua and Barbuda, the Bahamas, Barbados, Dominica, Grenada, Haiti, Jamaica, Montserrat, St Kitts and Nevis, St Lucia, St Vincent and the Grenadines, and Trinidad and Tobago. In addition, there are five associate island members: Anguilla, Bermuda, the British Virgin Islands, the Cayman Islands and the Turks and Caicos. The three non-island members are Belize, Guyana and Suriname. A number of other islands (Dominican Republic, Netherlands Antilles, Puerto Rico and Cuba) maintain observer status, as do Mexico and Venezuela.

Moreover, there are four island members in the European Union, namely the United Kingdom and Ireland (which joined the then European Economic Community in 1973), and Cyprus and Malta (which joined the European Union in 2004).

Yet another four islands or groups of islands are members of the Nordic Council, namely:

> Iceland, Greenland, Faeroe Islands, and Åland Islands. (The Nordic Council also includes Denmark, Finland, Norway and Sweden.)

The South Asian Association for Regional Cooperation (SAARC) includes two island members, Sri Lanka and Maldives;[2] while the Association of South East Asian Nations (ASEAN) in addition to Brunei Darussalam, Cambodia, Laos, Malaysia, Myanmar, Thailand and Vietnam, also includes Indonesia, the Philippines and Singapore.

Of the 53 freely associated members of the British Commonwealth, 27 are islands or groups of islands:

> Antigua and Barbuda, the Bahamas, Barbados, Cyprus, Dominica, Grenada, Jamaica, Kiribati, Maldives, Malta, Mauritius, New Zealand, Papua New Guinea, Samoa, Seychelles, Singapore, Solomon Islands, Sri Lanka, St Kitts and Nevis, St Lucia, St Vincent and the Grenadines, Tuvalu, Tonga, Trinidad and Tobago, United Kingdom and Vanuatu. Fiji, a long-time member, was suspended from the Commonwealth in December 2006 following a military coup. Nauru was declared a special member of the Commonwealth in January 2006.

Thus, altogether at least 89 islands or sets of islands are involved in some combination of autonomous self-government combined with formal collaboration in a wider political partnership. These comprise:

- 22 islands as fully fledged constituent units in federations,
- 10 island federacies,
- three island associate states,
- 18 islands with some form of constitutional home rule,
- 36 islands involved in one or more of CARICOM, the Nordic Council, SAARC, ASEAN and the Commonwealth not already included in the preceding categories.

Although much has been written elsewhere about federal and autonomy arrangements and about international collaborative relations, little of that literature has focused specifically on islands as participating members. This chapter therefore sets out to map in a general comparative way the various types of federal and autonomy arrangements and international collaborative relationships involving islands today.

The 89 different island 'units' identified for further analysis in this chapter comprise a considerably shorter list than the over 100 SNIJs (sub-national island jurisdictions) that Stuart treats in her contribution to this volume. This notable discrepancy arises principally because Stuart admits examples of islands undergoing actual or imminent constitutional change, as in the Netherlands Antilles, and of other island territories having either:

- formal (but non-constitutional) or otherwise informal 'special' or asymmetrical arrangements for elements of self-rule struck with central powers (such as Kish Island in Iran; Jeju Island Autonomous Province in South Korea; Rotuma in Fiji;

Gozo in Malta; Hong Kong and Macau Special Autonomous Regions in the People's Republic of China); or

- indigenous island-based communities with some sovereignty within another state (such as Haida Gwaii/Queen Charlotte Islands in Canada; Aleutians in Alaska, USA; and the Torres Strait Islands in Australia); or
- *de facto* island powers sometimes in open confrontation or contestation with a central state (such as the Turkish Republic of Northern Cyprus, Tamil Eelam in Sri Lanka, Southern Mindanao in the Philippines).

In a sense, all of these examples, illustrating complex *de facto* and *de jure* features, disclose once again the tensions between autonomy and partnership that arise with special force in island relationships. It remains to be seen how these various arrangements of SNIJs are resolved and what ultimate constitutional form they may take, but in all cases, these islands too wrestle with the same contemporary conditions as follows:

- the simultaneous pressures upon political units for both autonomy and political collaboration;
- the search for formal political and institutional arrangements within the variety of combinations of self-rule and shared rule;
- and within each of these forms, the selection and sharing of jurisdiction within the variety of forms actually exercised by islands in such constitutional arrangements.

CONTEMPORARY CONDITIONS INDUCING PRESSURES BOTH FOR AUTONOMY AND PARTNERSHIP

A notable trend affecting not only islands but all polities at the turn of the twenty-first century is the growing constraints upon the sovereignty of nation-states. Indeed, the concept of the sovereign nation-state itself has become regarded as increasingly obsolete. Accordingly, some scholars have pointed to the emergence of a fundamental paradigm shift from a world of nation-states to a world of constrained state sovereignty and increased inter-state linkages of a constitutionally confederal or federal character (Elazar, 1994, pp. x–xii). Thus, for example, there are at present some 25 polities that in practice operate as federations containing some two billion people or 40% of the world population and encompassing some 510 constituent or federated states. This can be compared to some 168 other politically sovereign member states in the United Nations. Moreover, a variety of forms of looser political partnerships and collaborative intergovernmental functional agencies have also been developing.

In addition, there have emerged some new variants of the federal idea. These include the European Union, in which individual federations, unions and unitary states have 'pooled their sovereignty' in a hybrid structure involving elements of confederation and of federation. The 2007 edition of the *CIA World Factbook*, an authoritative collection of 'country' data, justifies the inclusion of the European Union in its compendium as follows:

Although the EU is not a federation in the strict sense, it is far more than a free-trade association such as ASEAN, NAFTA, or Mercosur, and it has many of the attributes associated with independent nations: its own flag, anthem, founding date, and currency, as well as an incipient common foreign and security policy in its dealings with other nations. In the future, many of these nation-like characteristics are likely to be expanded.

(CIA, 2007)

There are several reasons for this international trend towards various forms of pooling of sovereignty among states. First, modern developments in transportation, social communications, technology and industrial organization have produced pressures at one and the same time both for larger political organizations and for smaller ones (Geertz, 1963, p. 108; Watts, 1981, pp. 3–4; Simeon and Swinton, 1995, p. 3). The pressure for larger political units has been generated by the goals shared by most societies today: a desire for progress, a rising standard of living, social justice, and influence in the world arena. Furthermore, these have been reinforced by a growing awareness of world-wide interdependence in an era when advancing technology has made both mass destruction and mass production possible. This has led to the pressures for various forms of supranational organizations, confederations and federations.

At the same time, the motivation for smaller, self-governing political units has been accentuated by the desires to make government more responsive to the individual citizen and to give expression to primary group attachments such as linguistic, ethnic and cultural ties, religious connections, historical traditions and social practices, which provide the distinctive basis for a community's sense of identity and yearning for self-determination. As a result, the world has seen the rise of many microstates. Indeed, the late 1960s has been referred to as a period "not only of miniskirts but of ministates" (Duchacek, 1970, p. 2). In part, this motivation for political autonomy has arisen at least as a reaction to the growth of large supranational organizations with their tendency to submerge the sense of identity, to be remote from the influence of the individual citizen, and to create a sense of powerlessness and political impotence (Friedman, 1994, p. 1143). Such pressures have been reinforced in island communities where their geographical location and specificity have emphasized the sense of distinctiveness.

Given these dual pressures, more and more peoples throughout the world have come to see the need for some form of federal political partnership that would combine elements of shared rule for specified common purposes with autonomous self-government for purposes related to maintaining regional or island distinctiveness (Elazar, 1995). Indeed, such a combination of shared rule and self-rule would appear to provide the closest institutional approximation to the multinational reality of the contemporary world (Boeckelman, 1996, p. 3).

A second closely related factor encouraging heightened interest in various forms of federal relationships is the recognition that an increasingly global economy has itself unleashed economic and political forces strengthening both international and local pressures at the expense of the traditional nation state (Ohmae, 1995, 1999). Cheaper transportation, information technology and communications costs have led to materials and components being acquired separately in several different countries, assembled in yet another by an international business, and marketed by still more firms under product mandates or other arrangements (Vernon, 1990, p. 24; Norrie, 1995, p. 24; Saxenian, 1994, p. 7; Storper, 1995). Furthermore, global communications and consumerism have wakened desires in the smallest and most remote villages around the world for access to the global marketplace of goods and services. As a result, governments have been faced increasingly with the desires of their citizens to be both global consumers and local citizens at the same time, a trend which Tom Courchene, in his typically picturesque labelling, has called 'glocalization' (Courchene, 1995; see also sociologist Roland Robertson, 1995). In such a situation, the sovereign nation-state is simultaneously proving both too small and too large to serve all the desires of its citizens. Furthermore, in such a context, federal or confederal relationships with their different interacting levels of government appear to provide a way of mediating citizen preferences.

Third, the spread of market-based economics is creating socioeconomic conditions conducive to political partnerships embodying the broadly interpreted federal idea (Kincaid, 1993, pp. 4–5). Among these are the emphasis upon contractual relationships, the recognition of the non-centralized character of a market-based economy, entrepreneurial self-governance and consumer-rights consciousness, the thriving of markets on diversity rather than homogeneity, and the requirement of inter-jurisdictional mobility and competition as well as cooperation. The realization that people do not have to like each other in order to benefit each other in market relationships, the emphasis in market competition upon individual and group talent and merit, and the inherently anarchic character of a market economy which resists centralization and institutional immortality also encourage political relationships of a loose and horizontal, non-hierarchical character.

Fourth, changes in technology have been generating new and more federal models of industrial organization with decentralized flattened hierarchies involving non-centralized interactive networks (Kincaid, 1993, pp. 5–6). This in turn has influenced the attitudes of people to non-centralized forms of political organization. The industrial revolution of the nineteenth and early twentieth centuries spawned models of large, hierarchical, bureaucratic organizations. However, the inefficiencies and alienation produced by such organizations, whether the General Motors Corporation in Michigan or the Kremlin in Moscow, created demands in the later twentieth century for decentralization and flattened hierarchies. The emergence of cybernetic technology such as personal computers, the internet, cell (or mobile) phones, digital photography, fax machines, satellite television, and fibre optics has spawned models of organization – ranging from the Wikipedia to web blogs – that emphasize non-centralized interactive networks. The increasingly pervasive extent of such relationships has, not surprisingly, influenced public attitudes in favour of non-centralized forms of political organization.

A further factor encouraging a renewed interest in federal relationships has been the example of the classical modern federations: the USA (1789), Switzerland (1848), Canada (1867), Australia (1901) and Germany (1949) have shown a remarkable resilience to changing conditions and have all consistently been placed within the top 20 of the some 174 sovereign states in the annual United Nations ranking in terms of economic welfare, respect for rights and quality of life (UNDP, 2006). Indeed, in 2006 Australia ranked third, Canada ranked sixth, the USA eighth, Switzerland ninth, Belgium thirteenth, Austria fourteenth, Spain nineteenth and Germany twenty-first as 'the world's most livable countries'. The example of the European Union with its progressive widening and deepening has also provided an influential confederal model for closer collaboration among sovereign states (Hesse and Wright, 1995; Jones and Keating, 1995; Keating, 2004).

The issue of balancing political collaboration and autonomy is one that has had a particular cogency for political entities that are islands. The geographical character of islands accentuates their distinctiveness as communities, to the extent that they may even find it difficult to co-habit the same political structure as adjacent islands.[3] 'Islandness' has been a major factor in their cases in accentuating the pressures for significant autonomy, both substantively and symbolically. But even islands find it difficult in the contemporary globalized world to be totally self-sufficient. They have felt the need, therefore, for forms of political partnership with other political entities that would at the same time respect adequately their desires for autonomy.

This raises the issue of whether a single meaningful threshold for island political autonomy can be identified. The answer would seem to be that there is no simple formula. The degree of political autonomy that can be realistically sustained will depend on the circumstances and relate to a variety of factors. Particularly important will be both the material and human resources (in terms of both education and critical mass) necessary to sustain autonomous economic and political policies, the degree of remoteness and the transportation links available, affecting the realistic possibilities of useful collaboration, and the extent of interdependence or self-dependence characterizing the island's relations with neighbouring states. The example of the island of Nauru in the central Pacific Ocean which in 1968 became an independent republic with a population just over 6,000 (and subsequently increased to 9,000) is sometimes cited as an example of how small an island can sustain sovereign independence. But it was the royalties from its rich phosphate mining resources that made Nauru one of the richest per capita countries in the world, enabling relative self-sufficiency. This situation has been undergoing significant change, however, with the exhaustion of its phosphate mines and gross mismanagement of its accumulated revenues, forcing large numbers of its residents to settle abroad. The country has been referred to as the first 'failed state' in the Pacific (Connell, 2006). This illustrates how the ability to sustain self-dependence is affected by particular circumstances and how these may change significantly over time, for better and/or for worse.

Often, the choice between dependent or independent 'sovereign' status is the only obvious one, and this is how it is often presented. There is another alternative, however: that of mutual interdependence. Where dependence is not merely one-sided, but mutual and based on genuine collaboration and partnership, a relationship may be established where neither partner is dominant or subordinate. Given the complex nature of relationships in the increasingly global economy referred to earlier, such collaborative forms of interdependence would appear to express better the character of the contemporary world than either total dependency or independence. If that is the preferable objective, then the task is to find the appropriate collaborative institutions and processes that take account of the particular circumstances of the participating polities, and to make possible an interdependence surmounting the limitations of pure dependence or independence.

It is precisely this practical spirit that has inspired contemporary island communities increasingly to move away from the former post-war obsession with simple 'sovereignty' in order to explore other useful, broadly 'federal' patterns of autonomy and interdependence. Hence the relevance of this volume. But, to grasp the meaning of these choices, as explored in various case studies in this book, requires a deeper immersion in the architecture of these forms of governance.

FORMS OF POLITICAL RELATIONS COMBINING AUTONOMY AND PARTNERSHIP

Recent scholarly work has been engaged in mapping out the different forms and relations of autonomy and collaboration, based on a convergence of the traditions of political science (analysing federal and confederal relationships) and international relations scholars (studying international intergovernmental structures and processes). As a result of this work, the term 'federal' has been extended to a broadened category of political relationships combining self-rule and shared rule (Elazar, 1987; Watts, 1994, 2008). While formerly the term 'federal', as used by political scientists, was based on a fairly strict and precise definition derived from the model of the United States of America as the first modern federation, now there is a growing recognition that there is a wide range of federal solutions embodying the combination of self-rule and shared rule. There is, in short, no single pure model that is appropriate everywhere.

To understand this broader concept of federal relationships it is helpful to use a taxonomy borrowed from biology. In biology, the term 'genus' refers to a category of living things closely related in structure and evolutionary origin. Within a genus are a variety of 'species', each with distinctive characteristics. The term 'federal' is increasingly being taken by political scientists as a broad genus referring to a whole variety of political relationships combining elements of 'self-rule' (autonomy) and 'shared rule' (collaborative partnership). This genus encompasses a broad spectrum of species, ranging through unions, constitutionally decentralized unions, federations, confederations, federacies, associated states, condominiums, leagues and intergovernmental functional agencies. There may also be hybrids of these specific forms aimed at creating practicable workable arrangements. The notion of a spectrum is appropriate for this range of species, since at the margins of each specific category particular examples may shade into one another, just as the various colours of a spectrum shade into their neighbouring colours.

The various species of federal partnership arrangements, with references to particular examples involving islands, and some of the major advantages and disadvantages of each specific form, are outlined below. These represent a broad menu of constitutional choices, with each species nonetheless incorporating considerable variety within its class.

Unions

Unions are polities compounded in such a way that the constituent units preserve their respective integrities primarily or exclusively through their participation in the common organs of general government rather than through dual government structures. Examples of islands in this category are New Zealand, St Vincent and the Grenadines, and Trinidad and Tobago. The advantage of this specific form is that it maximizes 'shared rule' and cohesion, but does so substantially at the expense of the autonomy of the constituent islands or communities.

Constitutionally decentralized unions

These unions are basically unitary in form but incorporate constitutionally protected sub-national units of government which have some functional jurisdiction and autonomy. Examples involving constitutionally decentralized unions of islands are:

> Antigua and Barbuda, Fiji, Indonesia, Japan, Papua New Guinea, Solomon Islands and Vanuatu.

Examples of islands given a measure of constitutional home rule within unions with mainland territories are:

> Corsica, French Polynesia, New Caledonia, and Wallis and Futuna Islands (with France); Sicily and Sardinia (with Italy); Tokelau (with New Zealand); Zanzibar and Pemba (with Tanzania); Anguilla, Bermuda, the British Virgin Islands, Cayman Islands, Falklands, Gibraltar, Montserrat, Pitcairn, St Helena and its dependencies, and Turks and Caicos Islands (with the UK); American Samoa, Guam and the US Virgin Islands (with the USA).

Constitutional home rule combines an emphasis upon unitary cohesion with some self-rule, although ultimately the central government retains the potential for control.

Federations

Federations are compound polities, combining strong constituent units and a strong general government, each government possessing sovereign powers delegated to it by the people through a constitution, each government empowered to deal directly with the citizens in the exercise of its legislative, administrative and taxing powers, and each government elected directly by its citizens. There are currently 26 federations in the world:

> Argentina, Australia, Austria, Belgium, Bosnia and Herzegovina, Brazil, Canada, Comoros, Ethiopia, Federated States of Micronesia, Germany, India, Malaysia, Mexico, Nigeria, Pakistan, Palau, Russia, São Tomé and Príncipe, South Africa, Spain, St Kitts and Nevis, Switzerland, United Arab Emirates, United States of America, and Venezuela.

Although South Africa and Spain do not label themselves as federations, in practice they meet the criteria for federations. Some of these federations are experiencing considerable instability, particularly the Comoros, Ethiopia and Pakistan.

Federations encompassing islands as full-fledged constituent units (with the number of such island units indicated in brackets) are:

> Argentina (1), Australia (1), Canada (3), Comoros (3), Federated States of Micronesia (4), Malaysia (3), São Tomé and Príncipe (2), Spain (2), St Kitts and Nevis (2), and USA (1) (*see page 22 for the names of these units*).

It should also be noted that the short-lived West Indies Federation (1958–62), which was composed of ten island units, was the most decentralized of modern federations.

Among the advantages of federation as a form of political partnership is that it permits a relatively decisive form of shared rule able to carry out redistributive policies. Furthermore, because the federal institutions are based on direct election by the citizens, in contrast with confederations, associated states and some federacies, this form provides all citizens with an opportunity to participate fully through democratic processes in the legislative and executive operations of shared rule. The political autonomy of the constituent units is limited to those powers assigned to them by the constitution, but these are fully safeguarded by a supreme constitution not unilaterally amendable by the federal government. The main disadvantage of federations is their tendency to constitutional complexity, legalism and rigidity.

Confederations

Confederations occur where several pre-existing polities join together to form a common government for certain limited purposes such as foreign affairs, defence or a common trade policy, but the common government is dependent upon the will of the constituent governments. By contrast with federations in which shared rule is carried out by a directly elected government, decision-making in the areas of shared rule in confederations is primarily intergovernmental in character, the central institutions being composed of delegates from the constituent governments. Thus the common institutions in a confederation have only an indirect electoral and fiscal base. Among historical examples of confederations have been Switzerland (1291–1798, 1815–48) and the United States (1781–9), both subsequently abandoned for federation as a preferred form of union. In the contemporary world, the European Union is predominantly an economic confederation, although it has increasingly incorporated some features of a federation. CARICOM is another example of an economic confederation. The former includes two island members (Republic of Ireland and the United Kingdom), and in the latter 12 of the 14 members are islands. Eight of the members of CARICOM are currently negotiating with a view to establishing an even closer confederal union with a monetary union that would involve Barbados and the nine members of the Organization of Eastern Caribbean States (OECS). The latter are:

> Antigua and Barbuda, Dominica, Grenada, Montserrat, St Kitts and Nevis, St Lucia, and St Vincent and the Grenadines. Anguilla and the British Virgin Islands are associate members.

The advantage of this form, compared with federations, is that the governments of the constituent units directly participate in the decision-making of the common institutions. Since these institutions are dependent on the endorsement of the constituent units, the autonomy of the latter is better protected against encroachment. The disadvantage of this form, compared with federations, is that a 'democratic deficit' in the basis of the common institutions tends to weaken their public legitimacy, and the redistribution of resources to reduce disparities within the confederation is made more difficult by the requirement of the assent of all the constituent units.

Federacies

The term federacies was coined by Daniel Elazar for asymmetrical federal relationships where a smaller unit or units are linked to a larger polity, often a former colonial power, but retain considerable autonomy, and have a minimal role in the government of the larger, and the relationship can be dissolved only by mutual agreement (Elazar, 1987, pp. 7, 54–7; Elazar, 1994, pp. xvi, xix, 349–59). Elazar identified eleven current federacies, all but Jammu and Kashmir (India) being islands (Elazar, 1987, pp. 55–6). The island examples are:

> The relationship of the Faeroe Islands and Greenland to Denmark, the Åland Islands to Finland, the Azores and the Madeira Islands to Portugal, the Isle of Man, Guernsey and Jersey to the United Kingdom, and the Northern Marianas and Puerto Rico to the United States.

Rather than seeking full independence, these island units have established an asymmetrical federal association with the larger polity on the basis of internal autonomy and self-government. This has enabled them to share in the benefits of association with a greater state without being incorporated within it as fully fledged constituent units.

Since in the case of federacies mutual agreement is required for dissolution, federacy relationships provide a more stable linkage than associated states, where a similar asymmetrical relationship may be dissolved unilaterally by either polity (see below). Federacies provide a considerable measure of island autonomy, although compared with full-fledged constituent units in a federation or confederation, this autonomy carries the price of limited influence over the policies of the larger polity. Hence, they do not compare favourably in this respect to islands like Prince Edward Island and Newfoundland (and Labrador) that as units in a federation enjoy guarantees (by law or convention) of representation in the House of Commons, Senate and federal Cabinet in Canada. Nevertheless, some islands in a federacy relationship – such as the Faeroe Islands, Greenland, the Åland Islands, the Azores and Madeira – elect a small number of members to the parliament of the larger polity, though others – such as the Northern Marianas, Puerto Rico, the Channel Islands and Isle of Man – do not.

Generally, in federacy relationships the larger polity is exclusively responsible for foreign affairs, defence and security and usually also for currency, while the smaller polities have autonomy over all domestic matters. There is considerable variation, however, within federacies, in both their institutional and jurisdictional arrangements.

Associated states

Associated states, involving radically asymmetrical relationships, are similar to federacies, but differ in that they can be dissolved by either of the units acting alone on prearranged terms established in the constituting document or a treaty. Examples are:

> The Cook Islands and Niue in relation to New Zealand; and the Netherlands Antilles in relation to the Netherlands (although the latter is now breaking up after a series of referenda in 2005 and 2006).

Among non-island examples are some independent states which are members of the United Nations but which by treaty have an associated state relationship with a larger state. These are:

> Monaco in relation to France, San Marino in relation to Italy, Liechtenstein in relation to Switzerland, and Bhutan in relation to India.
>
> (Elazar, 1994: p. xix)

In most associated states, the larger polity is responsible for foreign relations and defence, but often the exercise of this power requires consultation with or the consent of the smaller associated state. Since either side of the associated state relationship may dissolve the relationship acting alone, these relationships tend to be looser and less stable than federacies.

Condominiums

Condominiums are arrangements which govern relatively small political units which function under the joint rule of two or more external states in such a way that the inhabitants have substantial internal self-rule. A non-island example was Andorra which functioned under a joint French-Spanish responsibility for its international relations for over 700 years until 1993. Among island examples have been Vanuatu which operated under a British-French condominium during 1906–80 until it became an independent republic, and Nauru, which was under a joint Australia-New Zealand-United Kingdom condominium during 1947–68, prior to becoming an independent republic in 1968.

Leagues

Leagues are linkages of politically independent polities acting together for specific purposes and functioning through a common secretariat rather than a government and from which members may unilaterally withdraw. Among examples involving islands are:

> The Nordic Council (including Iceland, Greenland, Faeroe Islands and Åland Islands), SAARC (including Sri Lanka and Maldives), ASEAN including Indonesia, the Philippines and Singapore, and the Commonwealth including the United Kingdom and 26 other islands or groups of islands among its 53 members.

Leagues provide a loose form of intergovernmental collaboration but their ability to take decisive collaborative action is extremely limited.

Intergovernmental functional agencies

These agencies are organizations or agencies established by two or more polities for the joint implementation of a particular task or tasks. First developed in the nineteenth century, there are now more than 100 functional intergovernmental agencies on the international scene. Examples which have involved islands are the

North Atlantic Fisheries Organization and the International Whaling Commission. Like confederations and leagues, these are intergovernmental in character but are limited to much more specific functions serving their member governments. They are usually served by a secretariat and to the extent that they go beyond their very limited functional mandates, they are usually empowered only to submit recommendations to their member governments.

Hybrids

Some political partnerships have combined characteristics of different kinds of partnership relationships. Examples including island members have been Canada which initially in 1867 was basically a federation, but for half a century or more included some quasi-unitary constitutional elements that were actively employed, and the European Union after Maastricht which is basically a confederation but now includes some features of a federation (for example, qualified majorities in the Council of Ministers and the co-decision-making roles of the European Parliament). Hybrids occur because statesmen are often more interested in pragmatic political solutions than in theoretical purity. The development of further new innovative forms of partnership and collaboration may therefore be expected.

In considering forms of political partnership and collaboration, there is another recent trend. This is the tendency for federations, confederations, federacies and associated states themselves to become constituent members of even wider federations, confederations or supranational organizations. Examples are:

> Austria, Belgium, Germany and Spain, themselves each federations, being members of the European Union; and Canada, Mexico and the United States, all federations, joining together in the North American Free Trade Agreement (NAFTA).

These examples illustrate an emerging trend towards multiple levels (not just two) of federal relationships to reconcile local, regional, national and supranational impulses in order to maximize the realization of citizen preferences.

VARIATIONS IN THE SCOPE OF JURISDICTION

While differences in the forms of political partnership identified above are important in determining the character of the collaboration, cooperation and coordination on the one hand and the extent of island self-rule and autonomy on the other, it needs to be emphasized that, within each of those categories of political partnership, there is considerable room for variation in the range of matters assigned for shared rule and the range of matters assigned for self-rule.

Taking federations as an example, there is enormous variation in the degrees of centralization or decentralization, in the legislative authority assigned to each level of government, in the relationship of executive responsibilities to legislative powers, in the tax- and revenue-raising powers of the levels of government, and in the scope of expenditure responsibilities (Watts, 2008, pp. 171–8). For example, federal government expenditures after intergovernmental transfers as a percentage of total (federal-state-local) government expenditures in 2000–4 ranged among federations from 84.3% in Malaysia to 37.0% in Canada and 32.0% in Switzerland (Watts, 2008, p. 103, Table 10). Federations have also varied in terms of the degree of symmetry or asymmetry in the powers of their constituent units, the character of the federal legislative and executive institutions, the institutional arrangements for facilitating intergovernmental collaboration, the judicial arrangements for umpiring internal conflicts, and the procedures for constitutional amendment (Watts, 2008, pp. 117–30, 157–70).

Similarly, within each of the other categories of political partnership identified above, such as constitutionally decentralized unions, confederations, federacies and so on, there have been variations in the specific powers allocated to the shared institutions and those assigned to the constituent units, in the symmetry or asymmetry of jurisdiction allocated to the federating units, and also variations in the precise structure and processes of their institutions established for shared decision-making.

Among federacies, for example, there are significant variations in the allocation of jurisdiction. While the jurisdiction of the larger polity has generally applied mainly to foreign affairs, defence and currency, in some cases, but by no means all, the jurisdiction of the larger polity has extended to a number of domestic matters. Examples are the sharing of taxation in the Faeroe Islands, the Åland Islands, the Azores, and Madeira, the shared role relating to criminal and most civil law, social insurance, navigation, aviation and communications in the Åland Islands, responsibility for the judiciary in the Åland Islands and the Faeroe Islands, and a shared role in land-use control in the Faeroe Islands. Other examples are the role of Portugal in education in the Azores and Madeira, the provision by the United Kingdom of common services in the Isle of Man, and the regulation by the United States of customs, interstate commerce, postal services, coast guard, and licensing of radio and television in Puerto Rico (Elazar, 1994, *passim*). On the other hand, under some federacy relationships, while the larger polity has had general jurisdiction over foreign affairs, defence, security and currency, the smaller federated polity has sometimes been empowered to conduct negotiations in realms related to foreign affairs. Examples are the Faeroe Islands and Greenland in relation to foreign trade and fishery agreements, the Azores and Madeira in relation to international treaties and agreements which concern them, the Isle of Man in relation to levying customs duties, reaching special arrangements with the European Union and issuing its own currency, and Puerto Rico, which does not have diplomatic or consular representation in other countries but does maintain direct contacts with its Caribbean neighbours (Elazar, 1994, *passim*). It is worth noting too that, where a larger polity has a federacy relationship, these relationships are not always identical or symmetrical for each federacy linked to it. For instance, the federacy relationships of Denmark with the Faeroe Islands and with Greenland differ in the allocations of jurisdiction, the arrangements between the United Kingdom and the Isle of Man and the Channel Islands differ in some respects, and those between the United States and Puerto Rico and the Northern Marianas involve differences. These variations often relate to their different colonial past and to their geographic location and economic circumstances.

While considering the varied allocation of jurisdiction within each form of political partnership, there are overlaps among the specific categories in the degree of centralization or devolution. For example, the European Union, a confederation, is in some respects, notably in the field of regulating internal trade, more centralized than the Canadian federation. Another example of a federation more decentralized than a confederation was the West Indies Federation compared with the East African Common Services Organization (but both are now defunct). Similarly, some of the more centralized federations, such as Malaysia, are marked by less devolution than the relatively decentralized unitary systems such as Japan.

These variations suggest that, in understanding the relationship between political partners, one needs to take account both of the form of the particular partnership and of the specific allocation of jurisdiction to each government within the particular form that has been adopted. The appropriate assignment of responsibilities and functions within the partnership will depend on a number of factors. Among these are the primary purposes for participation in the partnership, the nature of the local society and economy in each constituent unit, and the particular aspects of the identity of the constituent communities considered most significant to their inhabitants. Also important are the degree of economic complementarity, the geographical proximity or remoteness, and the facilities for inter-unit transportation, communications and access. Where the association is with a former imperial centre, as in the case of many federacies, the nature of the historical linkages and role of that former imperial power can also be significant.

In the case of small islands, the degree of autonomous jurisdiction that is appropriate may depend not only upon their size but upon their location in relation to the other jurisdictions, and the extent to which material resources are limited and provide little opportunity for diversification. Other relevant factors are, on the one hand, the degree to which autonomous environmental sustainability is made possible by geographic remoteness, and on the other, the possibility of telecommunications as a means of countering smallness and remoteness. Particularly important is the quality of education of the populace, enabling them to exercise their own jurisdiction in particular matters. At the same time the degree to which islands may be willing to see responsibilities transferred to the institutions of partnership or exercised by them may depend on the extent to which the particular institutions and processes of the partnership make possible a sensitive handling of shared powers. It is not simply a matter of reassigning jurisdiction. Often in effecting change and development, the real issue may not be whether an alternative form of political partnership should be adopted or additional powers or sovereignty should be granted to the constituent islands, but whether those islands can organize their material and human resources to use their existing jurisdiction more effectively. Indeed, that is one of the major themes running through this volume.

There are other notable points concerning allocation of jurisdiction in various regimes. First, at one time it was thought that economic policy was most appropriately handled in an integrated manner, while cultural and social policy was best devolved to recognize the distinctive identity of different constituent units. Indeed, that was a major theme in the establishment of the Canadian federation in 1867: economic, security, and international matters were centralized; cultural and social matters were essentially decentralized. But Canadian experience and experience elsewhere has shown that economic policy and social and cultural issues are closely interrelated. Consequently, constituent units in political partnerships have a very real interest in economic policy issues. This has resulted in the need to identify within the realm of economic policy those aspects requiring integrated or coordinated action and those aspects where autonomous constituent unit action may be beneficial both economically and in terms of ensuring maintenance of identity.

Second, fiscal resources have a major importance in determining the realistic scope of jurisdiction. Whatever the legislative or administrative jurisdiction assigned, the availability of fiscal resources to the constituent units will in large part determine their real degree of dependency or genuine autonomy. However, where the organs of shared rule lack adequate resources, this will undermine their ability to provide benefits from a common jurisdiction or from the redistribution of resources. The collapse of the West Indies Federation, the central institutions of which had a very limited jurisdiction accentuated by inadequate fiscal resources, provides a classic illustration of this point (Watts, 2008, p. 182). The effectiveness of the federal government was limited by its lack of significant powers, and this contributed to its lack of appeal and prestige in the eyes of both the political leaders and the electorates.

Third, it needs to be reiterated and emphasized that the allocation of jurisdiction within a political partnership must be related to the particular circumstance and real needs of the situation. As noted earlier, among the factors that need to be taken into account in determining the appropriate jurisdiction are the size of the constituent units, their problems, and the extent and diversity (or lack of diversity) of their resources and products. Size is clearly a determinant in the sustainability of political autonomy, but as also noted earlier there is no simple threshold for determining this since it depends on a variety of factors.

Fourth, in any partnership regime it is important to embody processes enabling flexibility to adjust the balance of jurisdictions as conditions change. Such factors as the non-renewability of certain resources, changes in the world demand for products and in the terms of trade, and the growth of regional economic organizations will over the long term have an important bearing. Consequently, there need to be processes in place making possible the adjustment of jurisdictional allocations to meet changing conditions.

CONCLUSION

Two themes have emerged from this international overview. One is the wide variety in the forms of political partnership and in the scope of shared and autonomous jurisdictions within these partnerships arising from differences in their circumstances. The second is the degree to which these have evolved and changed over time as conditions and circumstances have altered.

The taxonomy of political forms for combining autonomy and partnership presented here has identified their distinctive characteristics, the existence of variations in jurisdiction within each, and the basic advantages and disadvantages of each form. This raises the seemingly obvious question about which are the 'best models' for islands wishing to deal effectively with both their internal and external problems. The first response is that there is no single universal 'best model' that is applicable to all islands. The circumstances and requirements of the 89 islands referred to in the introduction to this chapter vary enormously. The appropriateness of the arrangements is, therefore, affected by a number of factors. These include the number of polities involved in the partnership, the population size and resources of the island entities, the relative sizes of the partners in relation to each other and whether the association is with a continental federation or with a relatively small nation-state, and whether the partnership is inter-island (as in the Caribbean) or in relation to a mainland or continental polity. Also significant are the complementary or competitive character of economies, historical or past colonial relationships, whether the tradition of the larger polity is unitary or federal, the degree of community or distinctiveness of culture, language, social organization and legal traditions of the polities involved, and whether the relationship involves entities which are members of even wider supranational bodies such as the EU or NAFTA. Depending on the particular set of circumstances, different models are likely to be appropriate. Furthermore, as comparative political studies have frequently indicated, identical political institutions applied in different circumstances have frequently operated in very different ways (Watts, 2008, pp. 1–2). The fallacy of assuming that there is a single universal 'best model' for all islands must, therefore, be avoided.

What comparative studies can beneficially do, however, is draw attention to the variety of possible options worth considering in a given situation. Such studies also help to identify the general characteristics of each form of political partnership, and hence the particular circumstances and objectives for which such a model, or a variant of that model, is likely to be appropriate. For example, of the current 26 federations, some have been highly successful in terms of longevity and their ranking on the UN Human Development Index (UNDP, 2006). Yet others have failed or experienced severe stress because federation, or the particular form of federation adopted, has been inappropriate to their particular circumstances (Watts, 1977; 2008, pp. 179–88). Similarly, among federacies, some have been more successful than others. As a confederation, the European Union has proved a relatively successful example; but it has found it increasingly necessary to adopt features more typical of federations, and its attempts to ratify a constitution incorporating these features have so far floundered. A major empirical task yet to be undertaken, therefore, is the in-depth analysis of the various attempts to apply these different models to island situations.

There is one further question which arises in any attempt to evaluate the various ways of combining autonomy and partnership for islands. That is, what are the appropriate criteria for judging which alternative is appropriate in a given situation? Is the judgement to be based on economic criteria, social welfare, or the sort of multiple criteria employed by the United Nations Development Programme to rank countries in terms of the human development of their citizens (UNDP, 2006)?

Despite the variety of circumstances and of arrangements in which political partnerships of autonomous islands have been developed, there is one fundamental common underlying theme. That is, in the contemporary world neither pure dependence nor pure independence has proved fully satisfactory. Even a sovereign state as powerful as the United States has found the need for association with other polities in order to meet economic and security needs. Given the wide variety of island relationships identified in this chapter, the case studies of sub-national island jurisdictions examined elsewhere in this volume should contribute to our broader general understanding of the actual and potential character of island relationships within the world and of the ways in which allocations of jurisdiction can be most fruitfully and strategically employed.

Acknowledgements

I appreciate very much the enormous help that was given to me by Godfrey Baldacchino and David Milne in updating this chapter. An earlier version had appeared as 'Islands in Comparative Constitutional Perspective', in G. Baldacchino and D. Milne (eds) *Lessons from the Political Economy of Small Islands: The Resourcefulness of Jurisdiction*, Basingstoke, Macmillan, in association with the Institute of Island Studies, Canada, 2000, pp. 17–37. Reproduced with permission of Palgrave Macmillan.

Notes

1. Contrary to the impression given by its name, Rhode Island, while a fully fledged state of the USA, is a mainly mainland state. Note also that Venezuela includes 72 islands, but none are fully fledged states in the federation.
2. Other states represented in SAARC are Afghanistan, Bangladesh, Bhutan, India, Nepal and Pakistan.
3. There are various examples of islands refusing to join, or stay within, the same political unit as their island neighbours. Tuvalu and Mayotte are good examples, while Anguilla actually seceded from St-Kitts-Nevis-Anguilla. A 1998 referendum to have Nevis secede from St Kitts failed by a whisker. This dynamic has been described as the 'Tuvalu Effect' (Baldacchino, 2002, p. 353).

References

Baldacchino, G. (2002) 'Jurisdictional Self-reliance for Small Island Territories: Considering the Partition of Cyprus', *The Round Table: Commonwealth Journal of International Affairs*, 365, pp. 349–60.

Baldacchino, G. (2004) 'Autonomous But Not Sovereign? A Review of Island Sub-nationalism', *Canadian Review of Studies in Nationalism*, 31, pp. 77–90.

Boeckelman, K. (1996) 'Federal Systems in the Global Economy: Research Issues', *Publius*, special issue on 'Federal Systems in the Global Economy', 26, pp. 1–11.

CIA (Central Intelligence Agency) (2007) *CIA World Factbook* (Washington, DC: CIA). Also, https://www.cia.gov/cia/publications/factbook/geos/ee.html

Connell, J. (2006) 'Nauru: The First Failed Pacific State?', *The Round Table: Commonwealth Journal of International Affairs*, 383, pp. 47–63.

Courchene, T. J. (1995) 'Glocalization: The Regional/International Interface', *Canadian Journal of Regional Studies*, 18(1).

Duchacek, I. (1970) *Comparative Federalism: The Territorial Dimension of Politics* (New York: Holt, Rinehart and Winston).

Elazar, D. J. (1987) *Exploring Federalism* (Tuscaloosa, AL: University of Alabama Press).

Elazar, D. J. (ed.) (1994) *Federal Systems of the World: A Handbook of Federal, Confederal and Autonomy Relationships*, 2nd edition (Harlow: Longman).

Elazar, D. J. (1995) 'From Statism to Federalism: A Paradigm Shift', *Publius*, 25, pp. 5–18.

Friedman, B. (1994) 'Federalism's Future in the Global Economy', *Vanderbilt Law Review*, 47, pp. 1441–1483.

Geertz, C. (ed.) (1963) *Old Societies and New States: The Quest for Modernity in Asia and Africa* (London: Collier-Macmillan).

Hesse, J. J. and Wright, V. (eds) (1995) *Federalizing Europe? The Cost, Benefits and Preconditions of Federal Political Systems* (Oxford: Oxford University Press).

Jones, B. and Keating, M. (eds) (1995) *The European Union and the Regions* (Oxford: Clarendon Press).

Keating, M. (2004) 'European Integration and the Nationalities Question', *Politics and Society*, 31(1), pp. 367–388.

Kincaid, J. (1993) 'The Relevance of the Federal Idea in the Contemporary World', outline prepared for the Salzburg Seminar, 22–28 May.

Norrie, K. (1995) 'Is Federalism the Future?', in K. Knop, S. Ostry, R. Simeon and K. Swinton (eds), *Rethinking Federalism: Citizens, Markets and Governments in a Changing World*, pp. 135–153 (Vancouver: UBC Press).

Ohmae, K. (1995) *The End of the Nation State. The Rise of Regional Economics* (New York: Free Press).

Ohmae, K. (1999) *The Borderless World: Power and Strategy in the Interlinked Economy* (New York: Harper Collins).

Robertson, R. (1995) 'Glocalization: Time-Space and Homogeneity-Heterogeneity', in M. Featherstone, S. Lash and R. Robertson (eds), *Global Modernities*, pp. 25–44 (London: Sage).

Saxenian, A. (1994) *Regional Advantage* (Cambridge, MA: Harvard University Press).

Simeon, R. and Swinton, K. (1995) 'Rethinking Federalism in a Changing World', in K. Knop, S. Ostry, R. Simeon and K. Swinton (eds), *Rethinking Federalism: Citizens, Markets and Governments in a Changing World*, pp. 3–11 (Vancouver: UBC Press).

Storper, M. (1995) 'The Resurgence of Regional Economics, Ten Years Later: The Region as a Nexus of Untraded Interdependencies', *European Urban and Regional Studies*, 2, pp. 191–221.

United Nations Development Programme (2006) *Human Resources Report* (New York: Oxford University Press).

Vernon, R. (1990) 'Same Planet, Different Worlds', in W. Brock and R. Hormats (eds), *The Global Economy*, pp. 15–40 (New York: W. W. Norton).

Watts, R. L. (1977) 'Survival or Disintegration', in R. Simeon (ed.), *Must Canada Fail?*, pp. 42–60 (Montreal: McGill-Queen's University Press).

Watts, R. L. (1981) 'Federalism, Regionalism, and Political Integration', in D. Cameron (ed.), *Regionalism and Supranationalism*, pp. 3–19 (Montreal: Institute for Research on Public Policy).

Watts, R. L. (1994) 'Contemporary Views on Federalism', in B. de Villiers (ed.), *Evaluating Federal Systems*, pp. 1–29 (Cape Town: Juta and Co.).

Watts, R. L. (2008) *Comparing Federal Systems*, 3rd edition (Montreal and Kingston: McGill-Queen's University Press).

4 The advantages of political affiliation: dependent and independent small-island profiles

Jerome L. McElroy and Kara B. Pearce

INTRODUCTION

It appears that the independence candle for islands has been snuffed, at least for the moment. The current status is regarded as the best of both worlds. Island jurisdictions wield many of the benefits associated with political sovereignty while they are delegating responsibilities to, and enjoying the security and reaping the material benefits of remaining in association with, a larger, and typically richer, patron (Baldacchino, 2004).

The recent refusal by residents of Tokelau in a February 2006 referendum to opt for full independence from New Zealand and decision to retain their colonial links is no surprise to island scholars (Taitt, 2006). Conservative legislative caution for small sub-national island jurisdictions (SNIJs) and their consistent adherence to the status quo have been hallmarks of the vestiges of empire, particularly in small islands scattered across the globe (Baldacchino, 2006a). The Tokelauan decision to hew to traditional arrangements appears doubly reasonable given the steadily mounting volume of research emphasizing the substantial and enduring socioeconomic and jurisdictional benefits associated with affiliation. The intersection of this research is surfacing from three distinct but tangential niche literatures of the small-island genre: in economic development, political economy and tourism.

Perhaps taking their clues from the natural scientists, early development researchers sought to carve out a special island demography and economy. In the first case Dommen (1980) and others argued for a special island demography based on the propensity of working-age cohorts to migrate for livelihood purposes and a resulting early demographic transition. In the second case the pioneering work of Seers (1964) and Demas (1965) – based principally on the Caribbean – with its emphases on small market size, capital goods constraints and export propulsion was followed by the MIRAB (MIgration – Remittances – Aid – Bureaucracy) model of Bertram and Watters (1985), drawn mainly from Pacific experience. This construct assumed embedded emigration mobility and posited that small islands subsist primarily on migrant remittances, foreign aid and public employment (bureaucracy). It has become the dominant paradigm in the development literature and, according to Bertram's recent (2006) assessment based on descriptive statistics and case studies, can be applied in varying degrees to some two dozen island societies.

However, a second strand of writing between the borders of development and political economy is challenging the MIRAB orthodoxy. This stream argues that, far from being subsidized rentier outposts, small island economies including SNIJs on average possess a private-sector dynamism in their own right. According to Armstrong and Read (2002; 2000), small countries (mainly islands) out-perform larger states and SNIJs outdo their sovereign neighbours. Although Poirine (1998) suggests this latter result is mainly thanks to high levels of per capita aid, this new wave of research, first articulated by Baldacchino and Milne (2000) from North Atlantic experience, argues that much of the insular advantage derives from three factors: (1) domestic policy, namely the deliberate restructuring of the colonial economy of export staples primarily towards international services (tourism and offshore banking); (2) favourable geography (Armstrong and Read, 2006); and (3) the judicious use of jurisdiction and autonomy to manipulate metropolitan linkage for local benefit (Baldacchino and Milne, 2000). A specific example of this so-called PROFIT model (Baldacchino, 2006b) is the creation of island tax havens to attract offshore finance, insurance and foreign sales corporations (Hampton and Abbott, 1998).

Parallel to these currents, an expanding tourism literature has consistently emphasized the increasing importance of the visitor industry in small islands in general (Apostolopoulos and Gayle, 2002; Briguglio *et al.*, 1996; Beller *et al.*, 1990), and in the Caribbean (McElroy and de Albuquerque, 1998), the Mediterranean (Tsartas, 1992), and the Pacific (Milne, 1992) in particular. Recent studies have indirectly linked insular tourism success with the assumed favourable economic advantages of affiliation. These include ease of trade with and travel from affluent metropolitan visitor origin markets (no passport, same language, currency, customs, etc.), ready access to private investment capital and off-island managerial/marketing expertise, aid-financed transport and communications infrastructure, special tax and duty-free gift/souvenir/liquor concessions and the like (McElroy, 2003). In fact, Bertram (2004) contends that the superior performance of SNIJs is directly linked to their degree of centre–periphery trade, aid and investment dependence and the affluence achieved by their respective metropolitan patrons. Finally, McElroy (2006) argues primarily from Caribbean and Northern Pacific experiences that the unique synergy between political dependence and insular tourism success is suggestive of a distinct development case, embracing small-island tourism-driven economies (SITES).

SCOPE AND METHOD

Most studies examining the advantages of affiliation have concentrated mainly on a small range of economic indicators (per capita income, growth, aid, structure). One exception is McElroy and Sanborn's (2005) construction of comprehensive socio-economic and demographic profiles contrasting 16 SNIJs and 19 independent islands in the Caribbean and Pacific. Among other things, this study concluded that the former were significantly more affluent and tourist-driven, with higher life expectancy and literacy rates, and lower fertility, and natal and infant mortality than their sovereign neighbours. In short, the SNIJs had more successfully restructured their colonial economies towards international services and achieved greater progress along the demographic transition. The present article expands this effort to determine whether the same advantages obtain across a considerably larger global sample of small islands.

To construct distinct socioeconomic and demographic profiles, 25 variables were selected. Eight were employed to measure macroeconomic performance and structure: per capita GDP, a standard of living proxy; per capita electricity consumption; the labour force participation rate (LFPR) and unemployment rates; share of GDP in agriculture, and in industry and services; and land area as a proxy for general resource availability. To gauge tourism's importance two aggregate measures were used: per resident visitor expenditure and the gross ratio of visitors to the resident population. Since the average length of visitor stay for overnight tourists is roughly seven days, day-trippers (mainly cruise ship passengers) were weighted one-seventh, i.e. by a factor of 0.14. To measure social and health differences, four standard indicators were used: life expectancy, adult literacy, infant mortality and the number of land phone lines per 1000 population. Finally, 11 variables were employed to monitor demographic differences: population size, growth and density, median age, and the distribution into young (0–14 yrs), working-age (15–64 yrs) and old (65+ yrs) cohorts. In addition, birth, death, migration and fertility rates were used.

The two tourism indicators were developed from the *Compendium of Tourism Statistics* (WTO, 2005). All other variables were taken from the *World Factbook* (CIA, 2005). To construct distinct statistical profiles of the SNIJs and independent islands, average values across the 25 variables were calculated for each respective group, and statistical differences were determined using a two-sample means test. To operationalize the test, 55 small islands were selected of less than one million in population, with two exceptions – Mauritius (1.2 million) and Trinidad and Tobago (1.1 million) – for which nearly complete data were available. Because of the heavy data requirements necessary to construct the comprehensive profiles, as well as the need to use comparable indicators from a unitary standard source(s), many (especially small) SNIJs were excluded from the analysis. The resulting sample comprised 25 non-sovereign and 30 independent islands spanning all major oceanic regions. They comprised 19 in the Caribbean, 17 in the Pacific, nine in the Atlantic, seven in the Indian Ocean, two in the Mediterranean (Cyprus and Malta) and Bahrain in the Persian Gulf. Given previous research, it was hypothesized that the dependent islands would exhibit higher levels of socioeconomic performance, tourism development and demographic maturity than their sovereign counterparts.

RESULTS

The Appendix contains the basic data for the 55-island sample (see Appendix 4.1), while Table 4.1 displays average values of the 25 indicators for the two island groupings classified by political status. P-values are provided to assess statistical significance based on the two-sample means test. In general results conform to expectations. In all cases the average values of the SNIJ profile contrast with those of the independent profile in the hypothesized directions. Basically the outcomes of this global comparison confirm results from the smaller-scale, Caribbean–Pacific pilot study (McElroy and Sanborn, 2005). There are empirically verifiable and distinct socioeconomic and demographic differences among small islands dichotomously stratified according to political status.

According to the data, the SNIJs clearly differ in size, economic behaviour and structure from the sovereign countries. To illustrate, with respect to basic resource

Table 4.1 Dependent versus independent island profiles

Variable	Dependents	Independents	P-Values (1)
Area (Km^2)	1 390	3 680	0.133
Population	142	318	0.016*
GDP per capita (US$)	17 416	8 463	0.014*
Electricity/pop (2)	4 188	1 994	0.010*
Labour force/pop	44.0	40.7	0.281
Unemployment rate	11.6	15.0	0.415
% Agriculture/GDP	7.0	14.5	0.014*
% Industry/GDP	18.4	20.6	0.412
% Services/GDP	77.6	64.9	0.000*
Visitor spending/pop ($US)	6 044	1 207	0.001*
Visitors/pop	4.6	1.5	0.008*
Life expectancy	76.8	70.0	0.000*
Literacy rate	94.9	90.5	0.058
Infant mortality rate	11.5	24.0	0.003*
Population density	363	307	0.651
Phones/pop	473	248	0.002*
% 0–14 yrs	24.3	30.8	0.002*
% 15–64 yrs	66.8	63.2	0.019*
% 65+ yrs	9.0	5.7	0.003*
Median age	32.2	25.5	0.000*
Crude birth rate	16.3	21.7	0.009*
Crude death rate	6.3	6.8	0.347
Total fertility rate	2.2	2.8	0.018*
Population growth	1.2	1.1	0.683
Net migration rate	1.9	−3.8	0.003*

Sources: See Appendix.
Notes
1 Asterisk denotes statistical significance at the 0.05 level or better.
2 Iceland was excluded from this analysis since it is a major producer of electricity and the indicator would measure more about larger-scale industrial production than general economic activity.

availability, the independents are between two and three times larger on average in both area and population. This subgroup contains the largest islands in the total sample in area (Iceland, Solomons) as well as in population (Mauritius, Trinidad, Fiji, Cyprus). Only the latter characteristic, however, is statistically significant. On the other hand, the SNIJs' superior economic performance tends to compensate for their relative resource scarcity. Most importantly, they average twice the level of per capita GDP – $17,416 compared with $8463 – the most common indicator for measuring standard of living differences. Likewise, in comparison with the sovereign countries, SNIJs average over twice the annual per capita electricity consumption – 4188 to 1994 KWh – another standard proxy indicator for living levels. In similar fashion the means of the two labour utilization variables are in the hypothesized directions. For example, LFPR – the labour force divided by the population – is higher for the SNIJs, at 44% versus 41%, indicating a more economically active citizenry. In addition, their unemployment rate is lower, 11.6% versus 16%. In both cases, however, the differences are not statistically significant.

According to Table 4.1, there are also sharp differences in economic structure between the two groups. The economies of the SNIJs are considerably less reliant on primary production and more oriented towards services. In the first case primary activity (mainly agriculture) absorbs only 7% of GDP, whereas it averages over 17% in the independents. This is not surprising since the independents include a number of low-income, remote agricultural/subsistence economies: Comoros, Kiribati, Micronesia, Solomons and Vanuatu. In the second case service activity predominates in the SNIJs, nearly 78% compared with 65%. These statistically different structural contours in combination with their associated differences in levels of affluence indicate that the SNIJs have more successfully diversified away from income-inelastic colonial staples (sugar, copra, etc.) towards income-elastic services like tourism and offshore finance. This is evident in the five-fold discrepancy in visitor spending per resident in favour of the SNIJs, $6044 versus $1207, and in the nearly three-fold advantage they exhibit on average against the sovereign islands in the ratio of gross visitors to resident population (4.6 to 1.5). It is expected that the SNIJs are more tourism-intensive, since this sub-sample contains many of the most popular destinations in the Caribbean, the most tourism-penetrated region in the world (McElroy, 2004): Aruba, British and American Virgin Islands, Caymans, and Turks and Caicos. It also contains the two Northern Pacific US SNIJs of Guam and Northern Marianas, which are highly developed resort areas catering mainly to the Asian market. In addition, this SNIJ group also includes many successful offshore tax and finance havens in the Caribbean (British Virgins and Caymans), Atlantic (Bermuda) and North Atlantic (Isle of Man, Guernsey and Jersey).

Social patterns also differ between the two profiles. This is particularly true in health standards. For example, life expectancy averages almost seven years higher for the SNIJs (76.8 v. 70 yrs), and their infant mortality averages half the rate of their sovereign neighbours, at 12 versus 24 deaths per 1000 live births. Among other things, these more favourable health indices for the SNIJs may in part reflect better access to medical care given their smaller geographic size and relatively higher average population density (363 v. 307/km^2). In addition, the SNIJs' higher average adult literacy rate of 95% exceeds the independents' rate by nearly 5 points (90.5%) although the difference is statistically significant only at the 6% level. This advantage may be partly a result, or a reflection, of differential information and media access. As a proxy for these influences, telephone usage (excluding cellular) per 1000 population is significantly higher among the SNIJs (473) than among the independents (248). However, it is perhaps their relative affluence and closer adherence to and institutional support for metropolitan standards and regulations that explain most of the their superior health and educational performance.

As hypothesized, the two demographic profiles diverge markedly across almost every indicator. While the sovereign islands exhibit a decidedly young population structure with over 30% younger than 15 years old, the more affluent SNIJs, with their higher labour force participation rates and more dynamic economies, boast an older age profile with a considerably higher median age (32.2 to 25.5 yrs). This is the result of their larger share of retirees (65+ yrs), 9.0% to 5.7%, and working-age cohorts (15–64 yrs), 66.8% to 63.2%, swollen by a heavy influx of migrants to service the labour-intensive requirements of expanding tourism, related construction and offshore activities. The different net migration patterns are also clearly evident in Table 4.1. For example, SNIJs average net *immigration* of roughly two persons per 1000 population in contrast to average net *emigration* from the independents of nearly four per 1000. Some rather extreme examples highlight this contrasting pattern. Net emigration from two stagnant independents, Micronesia and Grenada, was 21 per 1000 and 13 per 1000, respectively, indicating a population loss of between 1% and 2% per annum. Just the reverse case is the net immigration experience of two of the fastest-growing Caribbean tourist SNIJs, the Cayman Islands and the Turks and Caicos Islands (18 per 1000 and 11 per 1000, respectively). Aside from the wide per capita GDP differences noted earlier, perhaps no other variable better captures the structural divide between the profiles than these differential migration experiences, which discriminate between the dynamic, labour-importing SNIJs and their slower-growing, labour-exporting sovereign counterparts.

Finally, the dependencies also demonstrate greater progress through the demographic transition from higher to lower birth and death rates – a common index of development. They average considerably lower crude birth rates than the independents, 16 v. 22 births per 1000 population, and slightly lower crude death rates than the independents, six v. roughly seven per 1000 population. Similarly their total fertility rates average fewer children (2.2 v. 2.8) per woman of child-bearing age. As a result of these patterns, the SNIJs' average rate of natural increase (birth minus death rates) is noticeably lower, as expected (1% v. 1.5%). On the other hand, average annual population growth is slightly higher in the SNIJs (1.2% to 1.1%) because of their heavy net immigration. In comparison with the independent islands these demographic contours are partly a reflection of the SNIJs' relative affluence, older age structure and better health standards. In general these small non-sovereign islands exhibit higher levels of demographic maturity and modernization.

DISCUSSION

This study has argued that the expanding research on small island economies is emerging on three legs: the dominant MIRAB model with roots in the Pacific, the so-called PROFIT or jurisdictional model first developed in the North Atlantic, and the tourism-driven SITES model originally conceived in the Caribbean. Where all three constructs intersect is their common emphasis, in varying degrees, on the flexible and enduring advantages of political affiliation. The present analysis has attempted to strengthen this common thread by establishing in comprehensive detail the superior socioeconomic and demographic performance of SNIJs over their independent counterparts. On the basis of this body of evidence, it further argues, albeit indirectly, that this favourable performance derives partly from metropolitan political and economic ties and partly from the SNIJs' creative use of jurisdiction. According to Baldacchino (2004, p. 9), these sub-national island jurisdictions should be seen "as political innovators, testing out the limits of possibility which insularity, small size, location, and a measure of administrative autonomy may offer". In brief, conscious of the substantial benefits and policy autonomy associated with affiliation, non-sovereign islanders like the Tokelauans have repeatedly opted over the past two decades to retain the status quo (Hintjens, 1997; McElroy and de Albuquerque, 1996).

In this study a global sample of 55 small islands with roughly less than a million in population was broken down into two groups comprising 25 dependencies and 30 sovereign islands. Profiles were constructed using two-sample means analysis across 25 variables. Results clearly and comprehensively demonstrated the favourable performance of the SNIJs over the independents. Though smaller in size, the former economies were considerably more affluent, and were diversified towards the most sustained growth engine in the world economy, international tourism, and to a lesser extent offshore finance. In addition, the SNIJs enjoyed higher life expectancy, adult literacy and communication access (phone lines per 1000 population) and lower infant mortality, natal and fertility rates than their sovereign neighbours.

What about the future? Whereas the tourism viability of these service-oriented SNIJs is anchored to the sustained growth of the global visitor industry, the situation is less assured for offshore finance. Growing concerns about overseas money laundering and tax evasion among the OECD countries in 1997 prompted their Financial Action Task Force (FATF) to publish a list of some 15 so-called 'non-cooperative' countries and territories in 2000. The latter included SNIJs in the Caribbean (Cayman Islands) and the Pacific (Cook Islands, Marshall Islands). Their various weaknesses included excessive secrecy, regulatory loopholes, and inadequate reporting and international cooperation. Although many islands have since made significant institutional and regulatory reforms, and some have achieved de-listing, the damage has been done and a stigma is attached to offshore activity. Because of intensifying global competition, increased international scrutiny and the high cost-burden of setting up the required best-practice financial framework to maintain compliance, Suss *et al.* (2005, p. 602) caution insular policy makers "to evaluate carefully a decision to establish, or to expand any existing, offshore sector". In other words, the future expansion of offshore activity in SNIJs is projected to be less buoyant than in the past.

CONCLUSION

In summary, this study has shown that the SNIJs are more economically developed, socially advanced and demographically progressive than the independent island countries. This differential performance is perhaps best encapsulated in the disparate migration experiences characteristic of the two distinct profiles. On the one hand, the average independent island is typically an emigrant society experiencing slow growth, labour surplus and chronic emigration. On the other hand, the average SNIJ is typically an immigrant society that had passed through the migration transition from labour exporter to labour importer largely thanks to the labour-intensive imperatives of a dynamic international service economy. Further research will test whether these differences obtain in the longer run. In the meantime, the research provides a detailed look at the contours associated with the more successful tourist-driven SNIJs, i.e. the so-called SITES (McElroy, 2006), favoured by geography, close metropolitan ties, and an endogenous policy of export service promotion. It may also provide a springboard for future case studies more directly linking the SNIJs' socioeconomic and demographic advantages to the islands' various exercises of autonomy, and specific status and jurisdictional arrangements.

References

Apostolopoulos, Y. and Gayle, D. J. (Eds) (2002) *Island Tourism and Sustainable Development: Caribbean, Pacific and Mediterranean Experiences* (Westport, CT: Praeger).

Armstrong, H. and Read, R. (2000) Comparing the economic performance of dependent territories and sovereign micro-states, *Economic Development and Cultural Change*, 48, pp. 285–306.

Armstrong, H. and Read, R. (2002) The phantom of liberty? Economic growth and the vulnerability of small states, *Journal of International Development*, 14(3), pp. 435–458.

Armstrong, H. and Read, R. (2006) Geographical 'handicaps' and small states: some implications for the Pacific from a global perspective, *Asia Pacific Viewpoint*, 47(1), pp. 79–92.

Baldacchino, G. (2004) Autonomous but not sovereign? A review of island sub-nationalism, *Canadian Review of Studies in Nationalism*, 31, pp. 1–13.

Baldacchino, G. (2006a) Innovative development strategies from non-sovereign island jurisdictions? A global review of economic policy and governance practices, *World Development*, 34(5), pp. 852–867.

Baldacchino, G. (2006b) Managing the hinterland beyond: two ideal-type strategies of externality management for small island territories, *Asia Pacific Viewpoint*, 47(1), pp. 45–60.

Baldacchino, G. and Milne, D. (Eds) (2000) *Lessons from the Political Economy of Small Islands: The Resourcefulness of Jurisdiction* (Basingstoke: Macmillan).

Beller, W., d'Ayala, P. and Hein, P. (Eds) (1990) *Sustainable Development and Environmental Management of Small Islands* (Paris: UNESCO).

Bertram, G. (2004) On the convergence of small island economies with their metropolitan patrons, *World Development*, 32(2), pp. 343–364.

Bertram, G. (2006) Introduction: The MIRAB model in the twenty-first century, *Asia Pacific Viewpoint*, 47(1), pp. 1–13.

Bertram, G. and Watters, R. F. (1985) The MIRAB economy in South Pacific microstates, *Pacific Viewpoint*, 26(3), pp. 497–519.

Briguglio, L., Archer, B., Jafari, J. and Wall, G. (Eds) (1996) *Sustainable Tourism in Islands and Small States*, Vol. 1, *Issues and Policies* (London: Pinter).

Central Intelligence Agency (2005) *The World Factbook 2005* (Washington, DC: CIA), at http://www.odci.gov/cia/publications/Factbook/index.html, accessed 15 February 2006.

Demas, W. G. (1965) *The Economics of Development in Small Countries with Special Reference to the Caribbean* (Montreal: McGill University Press).

Dommen, E. (1980) Some distinguishing characteristics of island states, *World Development*, 8(12), pp. 931–943.

Hampton, M. P. and Abbott, J. P. (Eds) (1998) *Offshore Finance Centres and Tax Havens: The Rise of Global Capital* (Basingstoke: Macmillan).

Hintjens, H. M. (1997) Governance options in Europe's Caribbean dependencies, *The Round Table*, 344, pp. 535–547.

McElroy, J. L. (2003) Tourism development in small islands across the world, *Geografiska Annaler*, 85 B(4), pp. 231–242.

McElroy, J. L. (2004) Global perspectives on Caribbean tourism, in D. T. Duval (Ed.), *Tourism in the Caribbean: Trends, Development, Prospects*, pp. 39–56 (London: Routledge).

McElroy, J. L. (2006) Small island tourist economies across the life cycle, *Asia Pacific Viewpoint*, 47(1), pp. 61–77.

McElroy, J. L. and De Albuquerque, K. (1996) The social and economic propensity for polical dependence in the insular Caribbean, *Social and Economic Studies*, 44(1), pp. 167–193.

McElroy, J. L. and De Albuquerque, K. (1998) Tourism penetration index in small Caribbean islands, *Annals of Tourism Research*, 25(1), pp. 145–168.

McElroy, J. L. and Sanborn, K. (2005) The propensity for dependence in small Caribbean and Pacific islands, *Bank of Valletta Review*, 31(spring), pp. 1–16.

Milne, S. (1992) Tourism and development in South Pacific microstates, *Annals of Tourism Research*, 19, pp. 191–212.

Poirine, B. (1998) Should we love or hate MIRAB?, *The Contemporary Pacific*, 10(1), pp. 65–105.

Seers, D. (1964) The mechanisms of an open petroleum economy, *Social and Economic Studies*, 13(2), pp. 233–242.

Suss, E., Williams, O. and Mendis, C. (2005) Caribbean offshore financial centers: past, present and possibilities for the future, in D. Pantin (Ed.), *The Caribbean Economy: A Reader*. pp. 590–616 (Kingston: Ian Randle).

Taitt, M. (2006) Tokelauans say no to self-determination, *Fairtax New Zealand Ltd*, 17 February, at http://www.co.n2/stuff/0,2106,3574530a12,00.html, accessed 17 February 2006.

Tsartas, P. (1992) Socioeconomic impacts of tourism on two Greek isles, *Annals of Tourism Research*, 19, pp. 191–212.

World Tourism Organization (2005) *Compendium of Tourism Statistics 2005* (Madrid: WTO).

Appendix Table 4.1 Island indicators

Island	Area (km²)	Pop. (000)	Age 0–14	Age 15–64	Age 65+	Median Age	Pop. Growth	Pop. Density	CBR	CDR	NMR	IMR	TFR	LE	LIT %	GDP/Pop. (U.S.$)	%GDP Agr.	%GDP Ind.	%GDP Ser.	LFPR	% UN	Elect. Millions	# Phones (000)	Spend/Pop. (US $)	Visitors/Pop. (2)	Status (4)
Amer. Samoa	199	57.9	36	61	3	22.8	-0.11	291	23.1	3.3	-20.90	9.3	3.3	75.8	97.0	8 000	-	-	-	24	6.0	120.9	259.1	450	0.7	0
Anguilla	102	13.3	23	70	7	30.8	1.77	131	14.3	5.4	8.80	21.0	1.7	77.1	95.0	7 500	4.0	18.0	78.0	45	8.0	42.6	466.2	4662	4.1	0
Aruba	193	71.6	20	68	12	38.0	0.47	371	11.3	6.6	-	5.9	1.8	79.1	97.0	28 000	1.0	15.0	84.0	58	0.6	716.1	518.2	11900	10.0	0
Bermuda	50	65.4	19	69	12	39.8	0.64	1 308	11.6	7.6	2.50	8.5	1.9	77.8	98.0	36 000	1.0	10.0	89.0	57	5.0	580.3	856.3	5658	4.4	0
British V.I.	150	22.6	21	74	5	31.0	2.06	151	15.0	4.4	10.00	18.1	1.7	76.5	97.8	38 500	1.8	6.2	92.0	45	3.0	32.1	517.7	15797	14.1	0
Caymans	260	44.3	21	71	8	36.8	2.64	170	12.9	4.8	18.25	8.2	1.9	80.0	98.0	32 300	1.4	3.2	95.4	45	4.1	411.0	857.8	11693	12.4	0
Cook Islands	240	21.4	-	-	-	-	-	89	-	-	-	-	-	-	95.0	5 000	17.0	7.8	75.2	52	13.0	26.0	289.7	2337	3.6	0
Faeroe Islands	1399	46.9	21	65	14	35.1	0.62	34	14.0	8.7	0.94	6.2	2.2	79.0	-	22 000	27.0	11.0	62.0	52	1.0	242.0	490.4	-	-	0
Guadeloupe	1706	448.7	24	67	9	31.8	0.92	263	15.4	6.1	-0.15	8.6	2.1	77.9	90.0	7 900	15.0	17.0	68.0	28	27.8	1100.0	468.0	892	1.0	0
Guam	541	168.6	29	64	7	28.4	1.46	312	19.0	4.4	0.00	6.9	2.6	78.4	99.0	21 000	7.0	15.0	78.0	36	15.0	781.3	498.8	12041	5.4	0
Guernsey	78	65.2	15	67	18	41.0	0.29	836	9.0	9.9	3.83	4.7	1.4	80.0	-	40 000	3.0	10.0	87.0	50	0.5	-	843.6	-	-	0
Isle of Man	572	75.0	17	66	17	39.5	0.52	131	11.2	11.3	5.33	5.9	1.7	78.3	-	28 000	1.0	13.0	86.0	53	0.6	-	680.0	-	-	0
Jersey	116	90.8	18	67	16	40.9	0.32	783	9.7	9.2	2.80	5.2	1.6	79.2	-	40 000	5.0	2.0	93.0	58	0.9	630.1	813.9	561	1.1	0
Martinique	1060	439.9	22	67	11	33.6	0.76	415	14.1	6.4	-0.04	7.1	1.9	79.0	97.7	14 400	6.0	11.0	83.0	38	27.2	1100.0	391.0	-	-	0
Mayotte	374	193.6	46	52	2	16.9	3.93	518	41.6	7.9	5.62	62.4	5.9	61.4	68(1)	2 600	-	-	-	30(1)	38.0	-	51.7	-	-	0
Montserrat	100	9.3	23	66	11	28.6	1.04	93	17.6	7.2	0.00	7.4	1.8	78.7	97.0	3 400	5.4	13.6	81.0	48	6.0	1.9	-	1075	1.0	0
N. Caledonia	18 575	216.5	29	65	6	27.5	1.30	12	18.5	5.7	0.00	7.7	2.3	74.0	91.0	15 000	5.0	30.0	65.0	37	19.0	1500.0	240.2	531	0.5	0
No. Marianas	477	80.4	20	79	2	29.3	2.61	169	19.5	2.3	8.92	7.1	1.3	75.9	98.0	12 500	5.0	20.0	75(1)	53	7.8	-	261.2	9760	5.6	0
Polynesia	3660	270.5	27	67	6	27.5	1.52	74	16.9	4.6	2.89	8.4	2.0	75.9	98.0	17 500	6.0	28.0	76.0	26	11.8	459.2	194.1	1479	0.8	0
Reunion	2500	776.9	30	64	6	26.7	1.38	311	19.3	5.5	0.00	7.8	2.5	73.9	90.0	6 200	8.0	19.0	73.0	40	36.0	1100.0	386.2	400	0.6	0
Netherland Antilles	960	219.9	24	67	9	32.5	0.82	229	15.0	6.4	-0.40	10.0	2.0	75.8	96.7	11 400	1.0	15.0	84.0	40	15.6	945.8	368.3	3237(3)	2.9(3)	0
St Helena	410	7.5	19	71	10	35.4	0.59	18	12.3	6.4	0.00	19.0	1.5	77.8	97.0	2 500	5.0	40.0	55(1)	47	14.0	4.7	293.3	-	-	0
St Pierre/Miquelon	242	7.0	24	65	11	33.7	0.21	29	13.8	6.7	-4.99	7.5	2.0	78.5	99.0	7 000	20.0	30.0	50(1)	47	9.8	41.1	685.7	-	-	0
Turks/Caicos	430	20.5	33	64	4	27.4	2.90	48	22.2	4.3	11.09	15.7	3.1	74.5	98.0	11 500	15.0	10.0	75(1)	50	10.0	4.7	278.0	14634	8.0	0
US Virgins	349	108.7	23	66	11	36.5	-0.07	311	14.2	6.3	-8.64	8.0	2.2	78.9	96(1)	17 200	1.0	19.0	80.0	45	9.3	967.3	638.5	11693	7.3	0
Antigua	440	68.7	28	68	4	29.7	0.57	156	17.3	5.4	-6.11	19.5	2.3	71.9	89.0	11 000	3.9	19.2	76.8	43	11.0	93.0	553.1	4204	3.9	1
Bahrain	620	688.3	28	69	3	29.2	1.51	1 110	18.1	4.1	1.04	17.3	2.6	74.2	89.0	20 500	0.6	42.5	56.9	55	15.0	6800.0	269.9	1431	4.7	1
Bahamas	10 070	301.8	28	66	6	27.6	0.67	30	17.9	9.0	-2.18	25.2	2.0	65.5	95.6	18 800	3.0	7.0	90.0	52	10.2	1700.0	436.4	5948	6.4	1
Barbados	430	279.2	21	71	9	34.2	0.33	649	12.8	9.2	-0.31	12.5	1.7	72.6	99.7	17 300	6.0	16.0	78.0	46	10.7	761.7	479.9	2747	2.2	1
Cape Verde	4030	418.2	39	54	7	19.4	0.67	104	25.3	6.6	-11.90	47.8	3.5	70.5	76.7	6 200	12.0	23.0	66.0	30	21.0	41.4	171.4	328	0.3	1
Comoros	2170	671.2	43	54	3	18.6	2.91	309	37.5	8.4	0.00	62.0	5.1	62.0	56.5	600	40.0	4.0	56.0	22	20.0	16.7	19.7	18	0.0	1
Cyprus	9240	780.1	21	68	11	34.7	-0.54	84	12.6	7.6	0.43	7.2	1.8	77.7	97.6	21 600	3.8	20.0	76.2	47	3.5	3500.0	547.9	2875	3.0	1
Dominica	750	69.0	27	65	8	29.6	-0.27	92	15.7	6.8	-11.60	14.2	2.0	74.7	94.0	5 500	18.0	24.0	58.0	36	23.0	65.1	343.5	739	1.4	1
Fiji	18 270	893.4	31	65	4	24.3	1.40	49	22.7	5.7	-3.00	12.6	2.8	69.5	93.7	6 000	16.6	22.4	61.0	15	7.6	721.4	114.2	601	0.8	1
Grenada	340	89.3	34	63	3	21.3	0.19	263	22.3	7.2	-13.25	14.6	2.4	64.5	98.0	5 000	7.7	23.9	68.4	47	12.5	148.6	374.3	1162	1.8	1
Iceland	103 000	296.7	22	66	12	34.0	0.91	3	13.7	6.7	2.06	3.3	1.9	80.1	99.9	34 600	12.0	22.0	66.0	54	2.1	7800.0	642.7	1641	2.6	1
Kiribati	811	103.1	39	58	3	20.1	2.25	127	30.9	8.4	0.00	48.5	4.2	61.7	85(1)	800	30.0	7.0	63.0	30	2.0	11.1	43.6	40	0.1	1
Maldives	300	349.1	44	53	3	17.7	2.82	1 164	35.4	7.2	0.00	56.5	5.0	64.1	97.2	3 900	20.0	18.0	62.0	25	5.0	125.6	82.2	1152	1.6	1
Malta	320	398.5	18	69	14	38.4	0.42	1 245	10.2	8.0	2.06	3.9	1.5	78.9	92.8	18 800	3.0	23.0	74.0	40	7.0	1900.0	522.7	2148	3.0	1
Marshall Is	181	59.1	28	59	3	19.9	2.27	327	33.5	4.9	-5.91	29.5	3.9	70.0	93.7	1 600	14.0	16.0	70.0	49	30.9	-	76.1	102	0.1	1

(continued)

Appendix Table 4.1 (Continued)

Island	Area (km²)	Pop. ('000)	Age distribution % (0–14)	(15–64)	(65+)	Median Age	Pop. Growth	Pop. Density	CBR	CDR	NMR	IMR	TFR	LE	LIT %	GDP/ Pop. (U.S.$)	% GDP Agr.	Ind.	Ser.	LFPR	% UN	Elect. Millions	# Phones (000)	Spend/ Pop. (US $) (2)	Visitors/ Pop. (2)	Status (4)
Mauritius	1850	1 200.0	24	69	7	30.5	0.84	649	15.6	6.8	−0.41	15.0	1.9	72.4	85.6	13 300	6.1	29.9	64.0	48	10.5	1 800.0	290.2	788	0.6	1
Micronesia	702	108.1	37	60	3	18.9	−0.08	154	25.1	4.9	−21.01	30.2	3.3	69.8	89.0	2 000	50.0	4.0	46.0	35(1)	16.0	178.6	93.4	157	0.2	1
Nauru	21	13.0	38	61	2	20.2	1.83	619	25.1	6.8	0.00	10.0	3.2	62.7	87(1)	5 000	–	–	–	–	90.0	21.4	146.2	–	–	1
Palau	458	20.3	26	69	5	31.4	1.39	44	18.4	6.9	2.36	14.8	2.5	70.1	92.0	9 000	–	–	–	48	2.3	–	330.0	3 350	3.4	1
St Kitts	269	38.9	28	64	8	27.6	0.38	145	18.1	8.5	−5.90	14.5	2.3	72.2	97.0	8 800	3.5	25.8	70.7	47	4.5	103.9	604.1	1 568	2.4	1
St Lucia	610	166.3	30	65	5	24.8	1.28	273	20.1	5.1	−2.19	13.5	2.2	73.6	90.1	5 400	7.0	20.0	73.0	26	20.0	261.4	187.0	1 696	2.0	1
St Vincent	340	117.5	27	66	7	26.4	0.27	346	16.3	6.0	−7.61	14.8	1.9	71.8	96.0	2 900	10.0	26.0	64.0	57	15.0	88.4	232.3	723	0.9	1
Samoa	2850	177.3	27	66	6	24.6	−0.23	62	15.9	6.5	−11.73	27.7	3.0	70.7	99.7	5 600	14.0	23.0	63.0	51	–	107.9	66.6	299	0.5	1
Sao Tome	1001	187.4	48	49	4	16.1	3.16	187	40.8	6.7	−2.51	43.1	5.7	67.0	79.3	1 200	16.7	14.8	68.4	23	–	13.9	37.4	53	0.1	1
Seychelles	455	81.2	26	67	6	27.7	0.38	178	16.2	6.3	−5.54	15.5	1.8	71.8	91.9	7 800	3.2	30.4	66.4	38	–	224.4	267.2	164	1.5	1
Solomons	27450	538.0	42	55	3	18.6	2.68	20	30.7	4.0	0.00	21.3	4.0	72.7	90(1)	1 700	42.0	11.0	47.0	30	–	51.2	12.3	12	0.0	1
Tonga	718	112.4	36	60	4	20.5	1.98	157	25.2	5.4	0.00	12.6	3.0	69.5	98.9	2 300	23.0	13.0	64.0	30	13.3	31.6	99.6	133	0.4	1
Trinidad	5 130	1 100.0	21	71	8	31.0	−0.74	214	12.8	9.4	−10.87	24.3	1.8	66.7	98.6	12 700	0.7	57.0	42.3	56	8.0	5 700.0	295.5	409	0.4	1
Tuvalu	26	11.6	31	64	5	24.5	1.47	446	21.9	7.2	0.00	20.0	3.0	68.0	88(1)	1 100	–	–	–	60	–	–	60.3	172	0.2	1
Vanuatu	14760	205.8	33	63	4	22.6	1.52	14	23.1	7.9	0.00	55.2	2.8	62.5	74.0	2 900	26.0	12.0	62.0	40(1)	–	38.1	31.6	345	0.3	1

Sources: All indicators except tourism from The World Factbook (CIA, 2005) and McElroy and Sanborn (2005); tourism data for 2003 or latest year from Compendium of Tourism Statistics 2005 (WTO, 2005).

Notes
1 Authors' estimate based on level of development and regional norms.
2 Calculated as number of stay-over tourists plus (one-day visitors × 0.14) divided by the resident population.
3 The two tourism indicators for Netherland Antilles exclude Saba and St Eustatius.
4 '1' denotes sovereign political status and '0' denotes affiliation.

5 In or out: sub-national island jurisdictions and the antechamber of para-diplomacy

Barry Bartmann

THE SETTING

When East Timor achieved sovereignty on 20 May 2002, the ceremony marked not only the end of an agonizing process of self-determination for the islanders of this small territory, but also arguably the final act of European decolonization itself. Yet was East Timor truly the last scraping of the bottom of the colonial barrel? There are various types of dependencies scattered across the oceans of the world, many of them islands, still subject to European metropoles. The quest for sovereignty, as the only acceptable path to self-determination, does not seem to be the burning issue in these few remaining territories. Many are content to maintain the security of metropolitan relationships into the distant future. Some, like Aruba, have actually considered and then rejected sovereignty as an appropriate future for the island. Most recently in Tokelau, with a population of 1500, a referendum on independence failed to win the two-thirds majority required as the islanders elected to retain the continued financial security of their relationship with New Zealand (Chapman, 2006). In some cases, as in Mayotte, a relationship with a distant metropole is seen as a safer and more secure association than the possible alternative of dependence on a larger central government nearby.

Yet the recent efforts of Nevis to secede from neighbouring St Kitts are a dramatic example of continuing centrifugal forces at play in archipelago states (Premdas, 1998, ch. 2; Dee, 2001, ch. 5). Similarly the very small federation of the Comoros has been plagued by secessionist movements from the time of its independence, first with Mayotte, still in the colonial womb, and more recently with both Moheli and Anjouan (Rushby, 2001). Even in the Åland Islands there has been a dramatic growth in recent years of a pro-independence movement in public opinion at large, while two political parties unequivocally support sovereignty (Anckar, 2002, pp. 221–224).

The issue of sovereignty, then, is not entirely off the table, even in those small sub-national island jurisdictions where domestic debate seems to be preoccupied with other issues. It retains a powerful appeal for many Nevisians, it is a pressing ambition for many Kanaks of New Caledonia, and it commands persistent minority support in other French territories such as Guadeloupe and French Polynesia. It is the basis of a government-commissioned report in Bermuda. It continues to shape the constitutional debate in the Faeroe Islands and it remains a long-term vision or contingency plan in other island jurisdictions such as Greenland or the Isle of Man. It is a nostalgic fantasy for many Newfoundlanders as an expression of their frustration and discontent in the Canadian federation. Even in tiny Tokelau, 60%

of the islanders voted in favour of independence in spite of the economic risks (Chapman, 2006).

For the most part, however, the remaining small island sub-national jurisdictions live contentedly in legally dependent relationships which typically allow considerable autonomy and latitude, even in relations with the outside world beyond their metropolitan centre. Indeed, the capacity to engage the outside world through varying patterns of communication and representation, a phenomenon now widely termed 'para-diplomacy', is one of the developments inviting a reassessment of these small islands' once conventional constitutional future towards sovereignty. The circumstances of these small island territories and the current options open to them are themselves striking evidence of a rapidly changing international system.

Long-standing distinctions, both legal and diplomatic, between established sovereign states and other international actors seem to be increasingly blurred by changing practices in international relations and particularly by the activity of non-sovereign and unrecognized jurisdictions in external representation. These alternative practices of international relations may be seen metaphorically as an *antechamber* to the formal, legal and recognized diplomacy of the grand hall itself. Some entities may be able to leave the antechamber for the great hall for specific purposes (such as membership of intergovernmental organizations), but not for others (such as the accreditation of legations). Others, indeed most others, are confined to the antechamber. Sub-national island jurisdictions are among the less recognized players in conventional international relations texts; but many of them are now engaged in unexpected external relations, acquiring means to enhance their regional and even global presence. To be sure, the increasingly assertive external engagement of sub-national jurisdictions is also evident among other international players: *de facto* states, often 'nations in waiting' (Bahcheli *et al.*, 2004), regional organizations edging towards approximations of confederacy, even cities and metropolitan areas seeking to create transnational regions of economic activity with some measure of jurisdictional or institutional identity transcending the state borders which divide them. In short, the remaining 'remnants of empire', as well as small jurisdictions linked with a non-colonial metropolitan centre, are participating in a rapidly changing global milieu characterized by multiple levels of legal, political and diplomatic status and capacity. As conventional distinctions of status and prerogatives seem to be blurred, particularly between internationally active dependent territories and sovereign states, the phenomenon of para-diplomacy appears as both an agent and a consequence of that change. It is not surprising, then, that most of the current discussion in the literature is focused on jurisdictions below the sovereign state.

Michael Keating sees the emergence of para-diplomacy as an understandable response to powerful currents of change within the international system: globalization and the rise of transnational regimes. Both "have eroded the distinction between domestic and foreign affairs and by the same token have transformed the division of responsibilities between state and subnational governments" (Keating, 1999, p. 1). Globalization has expanded economic space beyond the reach of national governments, thus pulling sub-national jurisdictions on to the larger stage of economic interaction. Both cultural and political consequences follow as states find it ever more difficult to exploit their traditional role as guardians of national identity with the economic space around them drifting in every direction and new currents of activity, linking both local and global players. Similarly, in such a setting, transnational regimes have emerged to meet the challenges of flux in all directions, with many such regimes speaking directly to the core interests and central issues of sub-national jurisdictions.

Keating reminds us, however, that the consequences of these changing dynamics within the international system do not necessarily fatally erode the importance of territorial competence and particularly of territorial identity. Indeed, Keating speaks of "the reinvention of territory" as a distinguishing feature of the contemporary international system (Keating, 1996, pp. 47–48; see also Bartmann, 1998, pp. 239–250). Moreover, territorial fault lines within states, particularly multinational states, may be accentuated and, if anything, a resurgent localism appears to be an unexpected response to globalization (Bartmann, 2000). This may be particularly true in small island jurisdictions, where territorial identity is both inescapable and ever intrusive and where "the geographies of the mind" (Knight, 1982, p. 517) are so pronounced. The affirmation of sub-national territorial identity and jurisdictional competence can only induce the elaboration of para-diplomatic relationships and thus reinforce the blurring of distinctions of status and privilege that were once at the core of international diplomatic practice.

Para-diplomacy can be best understood as a field of international interaction apart from the conventional channels of international diplomacy. Within this field are many players with different objectives and, most important, different levels of sanction. They include sub-national jurisdictions which may pursue agendas that are broadly functional or highly political, that is, identity-reinforcing and even state-building in their objectives. Some, following the work of Ivo Duchacek (1986), have narrowly defined *para*-diplomacy as essentially "political–functional contacts with foreign countries... which are bound to have some political dimension" (Lubin, 2003/04, p. 22). In contrast to this perspective, *proto*-diplomacy "describes those international outreach activities of a non-central government like... Québec that tries to graft some sort of a strong autonomist or even sovereigntist message onto its economic, social and cultural links with foreign countries" (Lubin, 2003/04, p. 22). These distinctions are typically very difficult to dissect. Yet identity affirmation may not be a stepping-stone to secession and the commitment to the latter can be muddied depending on the party in power or, more typically, on the vicissitudes of the governing coalition at the time. For our purposes in this article the term para-diplomacy refers to all those external activities by non-sovereign jurisdictions that stimulate and approximate the formal, legal and recognized diplomatic practices of sovereign states. Whatever the differences of purpose, all these sub-national players enjoy a latitude of international participation that was once far beyond their status, but which is now part of an expanding international network. But it is a network sanctioned by their metropolitan centres and consequently by the international system, itself still a system based on sovereign states.

It is a field which also includes a wide range of players without sanction, apart from a few patron states. These entities still attempt to participate in the same field as those which enjoy a recognized measure of legitimacy. For these territories, however, *de facto* states as opposed to sub-national jurisdictions, e.g. Northern Cyprus in contrast to the Faeroe Islands, the actual exercise of para-diplomacy is hugely different, although the cosmetics are similar. Engagement with sanction, however limited, will in the end determine the actual substantive relations of players in the field.

Para-diplomacy, then, is a field of international activity which simulates or approximates official and conventional international relations. All the cases discussed in this paper are within this 'antechamber'. But some can simulate the conventions of official diplomacy more effectively than others and typically do so with the acquiescence of their metropolitan centres and therefore of international society as a whole. In these cases long-standing conventions of international diplomacy are indeed stretched to accommodate entities that are not sovereign states, although the decision to make such accommodations is still vested in those sovereign states. Others also seek to simulate established conventions of diplomacy but their presence in the antechamber has much less resonance, for they can call upon no sanction, save that of a possible patron state or a handful of supporters among the ranks of the sovereign membership of international society. The fact that they are allowed to set up shop at all in accepting capitals is, of course, an acknowledgement of their presence; but, typically, this is countered by strict protocols of neglect and non-engagement.

For those jurisdictions without such sanction, there are still opportunities to participate in this antechamber, but the qualitative substance of that participation is very different: they remain quarantined in spite of their frantic activity. They are pariahs, near pariahs or simply ignored in even those basic channels of acknowledgement readily granted to sanctioned sub-national participants in the antechamber.

Para-diplomacy is the outreach of non-sovereign jurisdictions to actors beyond their own borders and the frontiers of their metropolitan relationships or claimant states. It may involve direct contact with sovereign states with which the metropolitan centre already enjoys diplomatic relations. It may include formal channels with other sub-national jurisdictions participating in areas of functional cooperation, perceived mutual economic advantage and cultural exchange. It may include associate membership or even full membership in intergovernmental organizations, particularly at the regional level (Corbin, 2001, pp. 136–159). Para-diplomatic missions may be simple and understated, a government mission of non-diplomatic status with an *ad hoc* and general mandate of representation and information gathering. This may be an office to promote tourism or trade initiatives. Similarly, non-sovereign jurisdictions may be the recipients of such para-diplomatic missions and even of consular offices. Para-diplomatic missions may even stretch the cosmetic features of the mission to simulate full diplomatic status, even though the actual accreditation falls well short of legal recognition, typical of the activity which Martin Lubin terms 'proto-diplomacy'.

Because most sub-national para-diplomatic missions are in functional areas of representation, they are frequently viewed as benign by the metropolitan centre. Nonetheless, benign or not, they do allow a non-sovereign jurisdiction to reach out beyond and around the metropolitan centre to engage in independent exchanges with the outside world. This can be particularly valuable if the sub-national jurisdiction can participate in intergovernmental organizations with its own delegation and under its own auspices and thus with direct access to sovereign governments around the world. Québec has long aspired to a separate delegation at UNESCO and recently the newly elected Canadian prime minister, Stephen Harper, indicated that his Conservative government is ready to concede this issue (Séguin, 2006, A5). UNESCO and other specialized agencies allow for associate membership, which grants participation in the agencies' deliberations but without a vote. If this is the formula adopted for Québec, then the province will join Aruba, the Netherlands Antilles, the British Virgin Islands, Tokelau, Cayman Islands and Macao as sub-national associate members in UNESCO (Corbin, 2001, p. 143). Yet the Cook Islands and Niue enjoy *full* membership of UNESCO, raising intriguing questions concerning their international status.

The legal rights of sovereign states have long been prized by entities seeking international recognition. It is one reason why so many advocates of national self-determination in the period of postwar decolonization could settle for nothing less than sovereignty as the full and final culmination of the self-determination process. Sovereignty provided a once dependent territory with a 'green card' with which to engage the international system fully and with legal equality on its own terms. It would be folly to underestimate the huge symbolic appeal of separate international legal personality for many dependent territories, however rational and persuasive the functional arguments for alternative forms of constitutional status might be. In no situation is the right to full international legal personality more cherished or coveted than in *de facto* states, where actual independence on the ground has meant little in their efforts to win international acceptance. The 30-year quarantine of the Turkish Republic of Northern Cyprus (TRNC) would argue powerfully for the substantive capacities of recognized international legal personality (Bartmann, 1999, pp. 260– 286). In the case of the TRNC, as in other unrecognized states, governments do engage in a necessarily low level of para-diplomacy; but this is still not sufficient to circumvent the punitive realities of their own pariah status.

AMBIGUITIES OF STATUS: THE BRITISH DOMINIONS AND THE EUROPEAN MICRO-STATES

If we consider the historical development of the twentieth-century state system, the apparent ambiguities of status and privilege concerning international representation are not unique to contemporary developments. With the establishment of the League of Nations in 1919, a shift to an inclusive and egalitarian ethos in international relations was clear and with it the problems of status and rights attending issues of membership. The international legal status of some founding members of the League was not unlike that of many of today's small island sub-national jurisdictions. League membership was seen to be an acknowledgement of international legal personality, 'fledgling' though it might be (Granatstein and Hillmer, 1991, p. 74), given the emphasis placed on the capacity of member states to fulfil their obligations under the Covenant, particularly Article 16, with its expectations of collective responsibility.

The historic narrative in this context is one of ambiguity and mixed signals. While accepting India, still a British colony, or Britain's dominions, as members of the League, the Admissions Committee refused the application of Liechtenstein, a long-standing European principality whose sovereignty and statehood the Committee acknowledged and whose application was enthusiastically sponsored by Switzerland (Gunter, 1974, pp. 496–501). Liechtenstein's rejection reflected assumptions about the nature of sovereignty and the attributes of statehood that were conventional at the time: in 1919 Liechtenstein initiated agreements with Switzerland which included Switzerland's representation of Liechtenstein's interests abroad when called upon to so act by the government in Vaduz. Most of these agreements did not take effect until after Liechtenstein's application had been rejected (Raton, 1970, pp. 76–77). Nevertheless, the Committee reasoned that because Liechtenstein had "chosen to depute to others some of the attributes of its sovereignty ... we are of the opinion that the Principality of Liechtenstein could not discharge all the international obligations which would be imposed on it by the Covenant" (League of Nations, 1920, p. 667). Yet other members, notably self-governing Dominions and colonies, did not possess the 'attributes of sovereignty' which Liechtenstein was alleged to have 'surrendered'. As Michael Gunter concluded: "the real reason for the rejection of Liechtenstein was her smallness, not her deputation of some sovereign attributes" (Gunter, 1974, p. 499). Moreover, as he further noted, Liechtenstein's rejection was "by inference" a rejection of "other ministates which might apply in the future" (Gunter, 1974, p. 499). Indeed, Luxembourg proved to be the single, notable exception (Hudson, 1935).

Iceland's constitutional status in the Danish Realm was not unlike that of the Dominions in the British Empire. Iceland did approach the League in 1918 through the French Foreign Ministry and it did so again in 1930, the 1000th anniversary of the Althing. But Icelanders showed little enthusiasm for League membership because, as Jónas Jónsson, Minister of Justice at the time, put it, "of smallness, poverty and a kind of shyness" (Gröndal, 1974, p. 25). Iceland's representations and interests in the world continued to be conducted by the Danes, although Iceland maintained an embassy in Copenhagen and posted Icelandic trade attachés to some embassies and consulates. With Germany's invasion and occupation of Denmark in 1940, Iceland established missions of its own in Washington, London and Moscow (Gröndal, 1974, p. 25). With independence in 1944 Iceland developed a full diplomatic service. For the other European micro-states, their international relations were confined to the margins of international diplomatic practice during this long interregnum. While they were sovereign states and ceremonially treated as such, in substance their external relations were para-diplomatic in nature and highly qualified; much the same as the external relations of non-sovereign jurisdictions today.

PARADIPLOMACY AS A STATE-BUILDING INSTRUMENT FOR *DE FACTO* STATES

The end of the decolonization process may be symbolically recognized in the final transfer of sovereignty to East Timor. But it was also marked by the international admission of 'leftovers' of the Westphalian system where events finally caught up with their long neglect. After St Kitts and Nevis, São Tomé and Príncipe, and the Seychelles, what residual arguments could be mounted against Liechtenstein, the most industrialized country per capita in the world, or San Marino, the oldest continuing sovereign state in Europe? In short, the eventual course of self-determination weakened whatever inhibitions constrained these states and the residual resistance within the international system itself, thus emboldening them to leave the antechamber and gatecrash the grand hall.

These 'state-building' functions of para-diplomacy are still powerful motives for some non-sovereign jurisdictions and players beyond the pale of normal international relations. For unrecognized, *de facto* states the search for legal recognition and the formal acknowledgement of their legal existence as self-governing nations are the core issues of their agenda. The TRNC is recognized by Turkey, of course, but it is a pariah state everywhere else, even in Europe, where its territory lies within the European

Union. The Cyprus issue is truly a bizarre combination of fiction and pretension. The territory of the TRNC is legally part of the space of the European Union but subject to an EU blockade. The TRNC is even shunned officially in the Islamic world, where there are prominent non-official constituencies of co-religionists and even muted empathy in official corridors. The TRNC has established, in addition to its embassy and consulates in Turkey, a network of representatives or missions in key capitals (see Table 5.1), but the nomenclature remains as ambiguous as the status of its personnel. Even in this understated presentation, these missions remain off the radar screen of official exchange.

In the TRNC case host countries insist these missions be registered as The Office of the Representative of the Turkish Cypriot Community and, of course, their personnel cannot claim diplomatic visas, an issue which presents recurring problems for the officers at these stations. For the missions in the Islamic capitals the rules of the European blockade are not in effect and consequently these missions are designated with a more official status as Trade and Tourism offices. But in Geneva, the mission exists physically and functionally as part of Turkey's permanent mission.

THE ANOMALY OF TAIWAN

There are certain entities which seek similar acknowledgement as the *de facto* states discussed above. These are governments-in-exile whose territory lies beyond their reach and, indeed, whose separation from that territory may span many generations as their lonely diplomats seek to keep the flicker of their national candle alive in distant capitals. At one time, when international divisions were more profound, these governments were common, particularly for the German-occupied territories during World War II. In the postwar years Western powers allowed the Baltic states of Estonia, Latvia and Lithuania to maintain their legations and did not recognize their legal incorporation into the Soviet Union, even as they acknowledged that these three republics were functioning as units subject to Soviet law and practice. In the contemporary international system the Chinese occupation of Tibet since 1949 continues to provoke anti-Chinese and pro-Tibetan demonstrations and activities around the world.

Yet, difficult as the question of Tibet is for China, Taiwan is the most pressing issue. The Republic of China on Taiwan may be superficially regarded as a

Table 5.1 Para-diplomatic missions of the Turkish Republic of Northern Cyprus

---

TRNC, Representatives Offices
London: Office of the Representative of the Turkish Cypriot Community
Baku: Trade and Tourism Office of the Turkish Cypriot Community
Brussels: Office of the Representative of the Turkish Cypriot Community
Washington: Office of the Representative of the Turkish Cypriot Community
New York: Office of the Representative of the Turkish Cypriot Community, UN Plaza
Islamabad: Trade and Tourism Office of the Turkish Cypriot Community
Abu Dhabi: Trade and Tourism Office of the Turkish Cypriot Community
Geneva: Office of the Representative of the Turkish Cypriot Community, Permanent Mission of Turkey

---

Source: www.trncgov.com/representativesoffices.htm.

government-in-exile. The Taipei government continues to maintain, after nearly 60 years, that it is the legitimate government of the whole of China. Of course, the island government maintains authority only over Taiwan itself and a handful of offshore islands. Nevertheless, 23 countries in the world recognize Taiwan (as the Republic of China) and allow it to have an embassy (along with Panama, which maintains a Taiwan Consulate-General). Fifteen countries (Belize, Burkina Faso, Dominion Republic, St Kitts-Nevis, Swaziland, El Salvador, The Gambia, Honduras, Marshall Islands, Nicaragua, Palau, Panama, Paraguay, São Tomé and Príncipe, Solomon Islands) have a resident diplomatic embassy in Taiwan. For 66 other countries, however, many with extensive and hugely important economic links to Taiwan, relations are of a purely para-diplomatic nature and – given China's own preoccupation on this issue – with a highly sensitive nomenclature to describe 'non-official' missions, although they may very well operate as *de facto* embassies. (Indeed, the most common nomenclature for the Taiwan office in their country is 'Taipei Economic and Cultural Office'.) For 57 of these countries there are para-diplomatic resident missions in Taipei, with such names as the Argentina Trade and Cultural Office, the Malaysia Friendship and Trading Centre, and American Institute in Taiwan. Similar cosmetic fudging has allowed for some Taiwanese participation in international bodies such as the Olympics and for direct personal representations between Taiwanese government leaders and their counterparts in other states. In short, Taiwan is at once a normal state, a government-in-exile and a *de facto* state engaging in both official and internationally recognized channels of diplomacy in some cases and cloaked para-diplomatic exchanges in others. Taiwan is an international anomaly both in and out of the antechamber (see www.mofa.gov.tw).

What is perhaps most striking here is that Taiwan, a major regional economic and military power, and one of the most stable democracies in Asia, is still very dependent on para-diplomacy in the antechamber of international relations. The official and recognized delegations which Taiwan receives as the Republic of China are confined to very small states, themselves on the margins of the international system. In contrast, Taiwan's para-diplomatic reach is dramatic in the status of its state partners and in the sheer numbers of its own para-diplomatic operations abroad. Similarly impressive is the number of major states (57) which maintain para-diplomatic missions on the island. In short, in spite of its economic clout and its strategic stature, Taiwan continues to engage the international system on two different levels; and it is the more informal, unofficial, para-diplomatic level which clearly provides for this controversial island's most critical relationships. Of course, this speaks to the depth of the taboo of Taiwanese separation and the paramount urgency of the territorial integrity principle for mainland China. Nevertheless, these circumstances also reflect the very elasticity of the para-diplomatic mission. The nomenclature chosen can convey simply a non-governmental relationship, so as to emphasize the distance between the emissary state and Taiwan. Note that some of the designations of foreign missions in Taipei are those of non-governmental bodies, such as the Swedish Trade Council or the Spanish Chamber of Commerce. Others, perhaps less sensitive to mainland sensibilities, even go so far as to include 'The Republic of China' in the registration of their offices in Taipei. Taiwan's own offices abroad indicate a fairly common standard, with an emphasis on trade, investment and cultural exchanges. In any case, both the para-diplomatic Taiwan missions abroad and the foreign para-diplomatic missions in Taipei carry on many substantive diplomatic duties. Taiwan's unique position in the international system enables it to follow established diplomatic protocols in some situations but to resort to para-diplomacy in most of its critical relationships with other states. Taiwan's major activity in an international organization is its membership in the World Trade Organization, where it maintains a regular permanent mission, although it comes under the awkward title of the Special Customs Territories of Taiwan, Penghu, Kinmen and Matsu.

THE PARADIPLOMATIC ACTIVITIES OF SUB-NATIONAL ISLAND JURISDICTIONS

The non-sovereign small island jurisdictions across the globe represent as broad a tapestry as any we have examined thus far. Some of them are still in essentially metropolitan relationships with European states: the non-sovereign islands in the Caribbean, for example, are British, French or Dutch territories, or very closely linked to the USA. Apart from the French-administered island territories in the South Pacific, and the lonely British island of Pitcairn, the small islands of this region are in varying associated relationships with Australia, New Zealand and the USA. There are many small islands which are essentially municipal, county or occasionally provincial jurisdictions of mainland states. And there are those European islands, the Danish and Finnish home rule territories and the ancient Crown dependencies of the Channel Islands and the Isle of Man, with a very distinctive constitutional status.

Para-diplomatic practices are being established and developed in several of these islands and, like the regions of the European Union, these activities vary in terms of the primacy given to political and identity issues and a more modest economic and functional agenda. It may seem surprising that the Crown dependencies, among the most historic of European jurisdictions and independent in so many respects, have not been drawn to separate representation beyond their shores. The British Home Office conducts whatever relations are necessary with Brussels or any other capital as issues arise. There has been no groundswell in these islands for a separate para-diplomatic network apart from these trusted good offices.

In some islands, however, there is a question of national island identity, which has encouraged an international projection of the island in the establishment of para-diplomatic offices. The Faeroe Islands are an example of the blend of identity and functional interests that make para-diplomatic representation attractive for many sub-national jurisdictions. The national question or the home rule question has dominated Faeroese politics throughout the postwar period. Following Maurice Duverger's model of "overlapping or equally competing cleavages" (Duverger, 1959, pp. 231–33), Faeroese political scientist Jogvan Mørkøre has argued that this question has been as divisive in Faeroese politics as the conventional social-economic state–market divisions on a familiar left–right continuum, thus producing a multiparty system with party formations based on ideological mixes across these two definitive issue-areas (Mørkøre, 1997, pp. 162–191).

Following the German invasion of Denmark in April 1940, the British occupied the islands and urged the islanders to fly their own flag at sea rather than the Danish red and white cross (Schei and Moberg, 1991, pp. 40–41). The years of British occupation were for "all intents and purposes, a period of Home Rule" (Schei and Moberg, 1991, pp. 40–41), which paved the way for a Danish-crafted referendum in

September 1946, offering a choice between independence and some form of self-government within the Danish Realm. Although the vote was exceedingly narrow (5650 for independence against 5500 for union), the Danish government initially accepted the results, as did the Faeroese Løgting. But the Danes soon rescinded their position, the Løgting was dissolved and new elections resulted in a government in favour of autonomy within the Union. The result was the Home Rule Act of 1948, in which the Faeroes were made "a self-governing community within the Danish Realm" enjoying a wide latitude of autonomy in domestic affairs, although foreign affairs and defence remained the prerogative of the Danish government in Copenhagen. The debate over independence did not abate, however, and in 1999 the Faeroese government, now led by a coalition committed to independence, laid out a detailed schema for an independent Faeroese state. One of the key chapters in this 'White Book' looked to the future international relations and security policy of an independent Faeroese state (see Table 5.2).

The Faeroes currently maintain three representative offices: London and Brussels with diplomatic status and Copenhagen without diplomatic status. The offices in London and Brussels "are located within the Danish embassies and the Faeroese diplomats are formally accredited to the respective host nations as Danish diplomats working with Faeroese affairs" (Isfeld, 2006). The Faeroese missions could be housed in another location, although they would still be regarded as part of the Danish Embassy. This arrangement is not unlike the position of the Canadian minister in the British Embassy in Washington in the years following World War I. And it is an arrangement in keeping with the Danish practice of providing means and channels for Faeroese representatives to speak directly to third parties on issues of importance to the Faeroes (Olafsson, 2000, pp. 127–129). Moreover, this para-diplomatic activity reflects further changes in the relationship between Torshavn and Copenhagen. On 29 July 2005, a new law involving the Islands' external relations came into effect. It allows

> the Faeroese government to enter into negotiations and conclude treaties with other states and international organizations without previous consent from Denmark regarding all areas that are under the Faeroese authorities... The Faeroes can accordingly negotiate and conclude *on its own* [emphasis added] a bilateral treaty with another state regarding trade, culture, fisheries or any other

Table 5.2 Expected diplomatic establishment of an independent Faeroes as set out in White Book of 1999

Reykjavik: Embassy
Oslo: Embassy, accredited to Moscow
Copenhagen: Embassy, accredited to Stockholm, consular office in Helsingfors
London: Embassy, accredited to Dublin
Washington: Embassy, accredited to Canada, Mexico and Central and South American states
Brussels: Embassy, accredited to all European states, except Norway, Russia, UK and Ireland: accredited to the European Union, OECD, WTO, NATO, OSCE
New York: Permanent Mission to the UN, accredited to Asian and African states

Source: Government of Faeroes (1999, pp. 75–77).

business where the legislation and execution in the Faeroes lies with the Faeroese authorities.

(Isfeld, personal communication, 20 January 2006)

This gives considerable substance to a Faeroese para-diplomatic network and is a clear demonstration of shared responsibilities between sovereign and sub-national governments, even in the sensitive areas of foreign policy typically seen as exclusively the prerogatives of the sovereign state (Olafsson, 2000, pp. 127–129).

There have been even more dramatic developments of late. In September 2007, the Faeroes opened a mission in Reykjavik as indicated in their 1999 White Book wish list. In December 2007, the Faeroes became an associate member of the Food and Agricultural Organisation (FAO) (www.tirnganes.fo). Following the January 2008 elections, a new three party coalition government was formed with the Social Democrats, the Independence Party and the Centre Party. Høgni Hoydal, the leader of the Independence Party, became Minister of Foreign Affairs (www.tinganes.fo). There are now plans to open three more Faeroese missions: in Geneva, Moscow and New York, bringing the total number of Faeroese offices of representation to seven (Jóannes Vitalis Hansen, Faeroese Civil Service, personal communication, June 2008).

There is a similar permissive latitude in the case of the other Danish home rule island territory, Greenland, although there has not been a comparable 50-year debate on the issue of home rule or independence. Greenland representatives have a similar power to negotiate directly on issues within the purview of the Home Rule Government (Larsen, 1992, pp. 219–220; Motzfeldt, 1997, pp. 193–194). Greenland maintains Representative Offices in Copenhagen and Brussels, the latter a direct monitoring base of EU developments that could directly affect the island (see www.Nanoq.gl/english.aspx). Both the Faeroes and Greenland host consulates from major European states. There are nine consulates in Torshavn: Finland, France, Germany, Iceland, Italy, Netherlands, Norway, Sweden and the UK. There are also nine consulates in Nuuk: Belgium, Canada, Finland, France, Germany, Iceland, Netherlands, Norway and Sweden. Moreover, both Greenland and the Faeroes sit as separate members of the Nordic Council of Ministers. (The three Baltic states have observer rights.) This participation in an important intergovernmental organization allows for relations with other member states and assures both territories of a genuine role in regional issues of importance to them.

The case of the Åland Islands is particularly interesting. Its status is unique since it is rooted in international law as the consequence of a decision of the League of Nations. Given the many particular jurisdictional guarantees which the Ålands can claim under the Autonomy Act with Finland (Myntti, 2002, pp. 107–124), the islanders had the right to determine whether or not they would join the European Union. In theory, Finland could have acceded to EU membership while the Ålands stayed out. Their autonomous status is also reflected in their separate membership in the Nordic Council, a privilege which they share with the Danish home rule territories. They are then in a position to reap the benefits of direct relations with their regional partners (Anckar and Bartmann, 2000).

However, their situation with the European Union is not as satisfying as initially expected. The Ålanders were able to extract some critical derogations from Brussels during the accession negotiations, particularly on the economically critical issue of continued duty-free shopping on Åland ferries (Scarpulla, 2002, pp. 138–141;

Jansson, 2002, pp. 201–212). Duty-free arrangements were abolished elsewhere in the European Union and this concession was certainly significant and contributed immensely to the 74% vote in favour of membership in the November 1994 referendum (Åland Legislative Assembly). However, since this initial success, islanders have become more disenchanted with the Union over a number of issues that are deemed important to their way of life and even their economic well-being. The first EU negative decision was the banning of traditional nets by island fishers, a decision that applied across the EU. This was followed by the abolition of spring duck hunting and most recently the banning of *snus*, a Swedish chewing tobacco, which is allowed only in Sweden, a special derogation to Stockholm and (until now) the Ålands. *Snus* chewing is a habit enjoyed by many Islanders, even though Finland accepted the ban on the mainland. Since Finland cannot change laws covering health in the Ålands, the parliament in Helsinki has no power to change the law on *snus*. The real problem here is one central to our discussion: a lack of direct representation. Although there is an Åland representative presence in the Finnish delegation in Brussels, the Åland Islands cannot represent themselves directly in Brussels on issues which are exclusive to them or primarily affect them. In an angry reaction over the *snus* controversy, Britt Lundberg, the Ålands head of EU affairs, has threatened to use the power to veto any Finnish international treaty. The threat implies that Åland will thwart Helsinki's commitment to revive the moribund European Constitution when Finland assumes the rotating presidency of the European Council later in 2006 (Rennie, 2006). While the Åland Islands maintains representatives in Stockholm, Helsinki and Brussels, it is a rather 'toothless' arrangement if Åland cannot make its own case directly. The European Court in Luxembourg will hear only from member states, clearly a provision that denies the regions a capacity which is the very logic of para-diplomatic representation.

Neither the Faeroes nor Greenland is subject to such EU edicts. The Faeroes did not join at the time of Danish accession and Greenland seceded from the EU in 1985, the only territory yet to do so, after achieving home rule government in 1979. The Danish permissive policy, to include Faeroese and Greenlandic representatives in negotiating arrangements which directly affect their interests (e.g. on the Nordic Council), is an optimal and positive template for small sub-national jurisdictions. It speaks to the very purpose expected of para-diplomatic activity among sub-national governments, an opportunity to reach out and address their particular interests while remaining inside a metropolitan relationship which offers many benefits to the citizenry of these territories.

The efficacy of regional institutions as channels for the international outreach and representation of sub-national or non-sovereign territories is particularly well established in the Commonwealth Caribbean. Caricom, the Caribbean Community, has 15 member states, which include the very small island of Montserrat. If, at one time, Montserrat contemplated independence, any prospects were dashed by the 1995 eruption of the Soufrière volcano, which destroyed the capital, Plymouth, and forced the emigration of 8000 islanders, two-thirds of the population. Some have returned, but the island's habitable space is now confined to a small section of the northwest. Soufrière erupts regularly and the island has been continually hit by hurricanes. In short, the status of Montserrat as a British overseas territory is unlikely to change. The same may be said of the other very small British islands in the Caribbean: Anguilla, the British Virgin Islands, the Cayman Islands and the Turks and Caicos

Islands. Along with Bermuda, where independence is being debated, these four small island territories are associate members of Caricom. Anguilla, Montserrat and the British Virgin Islands are also among the nine full members of the Organization of Eastern Caribbean States (OECS). Thanks to these two major regional bodies the smallest non-sovereign islands have an extensive 'diplomatic reach' which largely mitigates the need for and the appeal of sovereignty. Moreover, the OECS has its own diplomatic missions in Ottawa and Brussels, which allows Montserrat and the other very small island members a direct diplomatic channel to the outside world. Caricom maintains a permanent observer mission to the UN in New York, which is another channel of outreach for its non-sovereign members and associate members. These are generous and practical measures in keeping with a spirit of flexibility concerning status and privileges for non-state jurisdictions.

Bermuda stands apart from the other British overseas territories in the region since independence has been a matter of domestic debate for some years. In the referendum of 16 August 1995 the independence option was defeated, but largely because the parties could not agree on the appropriate vehicle for achieving independence. The Progressive Labour Party, which has long advocated independence, has subsequently won two national elections and in 2004 Premier Alexander Scott established the Bermuda Independence Commission (BIC) to revisit the issue. The Commission was chaired by Bishop Vernon G. Lambe and its report was published in August 2005. The Commission's work involved wide-ranging consultation with the British government, the US Department of State, Canada, the European Union, and various countries of the region (BIC, 2005).

At present the UK is responsible for Bermuda's external affairs both as the island's interlocutor with other states and its representative in major intergovernmental associations apart from Caricom. In the current arrangements, however, Bermuda does have input into issue-areas which directly affect the island. The Bermuda Independence Commission noted these provisions in its 2005 report:

> Britain, in negotiating a treaty on Bermuda's behalf, receives input from the Bermuda Government regarding matters affecting Bermuda and, in turn, the British Government keeps Bermuda appraised of the progress of the negotiations. At times Bermuda representatives are present as observers. The British Government has delegated some authority for certain treaty negotiations to Bermuda through the 1968 Entrustment. With greater frequency, Ministers of the Bermuda Government are, with prior approval, thus permitted to negotiate certain agreements, provided that they keep the British Government informed. One example is the Tax Convention that Bermuda was allowed to negotiate directly with the US.
>
> (BIC, 2005, p. 17)

These arrangements approximate those in place for the Danish home rule territories. On the other hand, Bermuda has not sought a high-profile network of para-diplomatic representation. Bermuda maintains tourist offices in Atlanta, Beverly Hills, Boston, London, New York and Toronto. Unlike other British small island overseas territories (Anguilla, British Virgin Islands, the Cayman Islands, Falklands, Montserrat, the Turks and Caicos, and St Helena), Bermuda does not have a Representative Office in London (see www.embassies.com). However, there are two consulates (Portugal and the USA) and 16 Honorary Consuls resident in Hamilton: Austria, Belgium, Canada, Denmark, Finland, France, Germany, Ireland, Italy, Jamaica, Luxembourg, Netherlands, Norway, Spain, Sweden and Switzerland (Bermuda Embassy and Consulate Listing, 2008).

Independence for Bermuda would mean virtually starting from scratch. With this in mind, the Bermuda Independence Commission envisaged two options for the establishment of a Foreign Ministry and diplomatic staff. It is interesting to compare these projections with those of the Faeroese White Book of 1999 discussed above. Option One (total projected annual costs: $1 336 000) would upgrade the Tourism Office in New York to a diplomatic mission, along with the establishment of an embassy in Washington and high commissions in Ottawa and London. Bermuda's relations with the European Union would be handled from either Bermuda or London. Bermuda would join the UN and its lead agencies and the Commonwealth (BIC, 2005, pp. 43–44). Option Two (total projected annual costs: $3 051 000) also expects that Bermuda would join the UN and its agencies, and the Commonwealth, with possible full membership of Caricom if this did not involve the Caribbean Single Market and Economy or the Caribbean Court of Justice (BIC, 2005, pp. 44–45). Independence could mean membership in other agreements such as the North American Free Trade Agreement, the Organization of American States, the World Trade Organization, the Free Trade Area of the Americas, the Inter-American Development Bank, and the European Union's Africa Caribbean Pacific (ACP) organization. Overseas missions would be established in Washington, Ottawa, New York, London and Brussels. The report suggests that, in the many countries where Bermuda would not have a mission, it would continue to rely on the UK to represent its citizens and interests and the reimbursement costs of these services are factored into the report's projected costs of independence. The report is confident that, in the end, the costs of independence "would not be outside the affordability of Bermuda" (BIC, 2005, p. 59).

Of course, costs and benefits cross a broad range of issues. In response to the report, the *Royal Gazette* noted that the issue of a British passport was 'glossed over', a privilege which presently gives Bermudians the right to live and work anywhere in the European Union (*Royal Gazette*, 2005). "And", the *Gazette* warns, "once it is lost, it would almost certainly be gone forever". But the *Gazette* also notes that: "For some black Bermudians, in particular, Independence represents a final act of freedom" (*Royal Gazette*, 2005). This echoes the clear symbolic priority in the report for the Progressive Labour government:

> Some Black Bermudians associate Bermuda's current colonial status as being only slightly removed from its history of slavery and segregation. An advantage for them is the logical and necessary step towards full emancipation. This may be a difficult concept for some in the White community to grasp; but, until they do, it is nigh impossible to have a meaningful debate on the subject...here is a significant sector of the Bermudian population who feel that full emancipation, full adulthood and full equality may only be achieved when the last vestiges of colonialism have been removed.
>
> (BIC, 2005, pp. 61–62)

Clearly, this debate would not be conducted in most of the small non-sovereign islands subject to metropolitan relationships. But in Bermuda it lies at the core of the question. A detached assessment of Bermuda's status would suggest that the island's current relationship with the UK is largely beneficial, even in terms of external links and overseas representation. Yet it is precisely in this area that the report concludes there would be clear gains with independence: "A distinct advantage to an independent Bermuda could be the value of international relationships and organizations and the expertise available to emerging nations" (BIC, 2005, p. 62). Clearly the case for para-diplomatic outreach within a continuing metropolitan relationship has not been conclusive in the Bermuda debate.

In the South Pacific there is a pattern of permissive arrangements both in terms of regional intergovernmental bodies and in the particular latitude granted by New Zealand with the status of free association. The Pacific Islands Forum represents the heads of government of all its 16 members. The Cook Islands and Niue, both states in free association with New Zealand, are full members (see www.forumsec.org.fj). Most remarkable for this discussion is the international legal personality of these territories. New Zealand officially describes the Cook Islands as "a self-governing state in free association with New Zealand" (Government of New Zealand, n.d., p. 7). "New Zealand cannot make laws for the Cook Islands...the Cook Islands Government has full executive powers...The Cook Islands remains a part of the Realm of New Zealand (albeit a separate part)...Cook Islanders retain New Zealand citizenship (and do not have additional Cook Islands citizenship" (Government of New Zealand, n.d., p. 7).

The separate international legal personality of the Cook Islands, given their New Zealand citizenship, truly illustrates the elasticity and innovation possible within the context of 'dependent relationships' (see Table 5.3).

Moreover, the Cook Islands has established separate diplomatic relations with over 20 states at embassy or high commission level. The Cook Islands High Commission in Wellington is also accredited as the Cook Islands High Commission to Australia, Papua New Guinea and Fiji. The Cook Islands Embassy in Brussels is also accredited to the European Union. There are in fact no fewer than 23 states (including Australia, New Zealand, the USA and the European Union) with full diplomatic relations accredited to the Cook Islands at the embassy or high commission level. There is also a supplementary consular network with honorary consuls for the Cook Islands in Honolulu, Los Angeles, Oslo, Sydney and a consulate-general in Auckland. There are honorary consuls in Avarua Town for the UK, France and Germany and a warden for the USA. The Cook Islands has

Table 5.3 Membership of the Cook Islands in international organizations

Asian Development Bank
Food and Agriculture Organization
World Health Organization
United Nations Educational, Scientific and Cultural Organization
Commonwealth (Associate member)
UN Economic Commission for Asia and the Pacific (Associate member)
Pacific Islands Forum
Secretariat of the Pacific Community

Source: Government of the Cook Islands (2005).

independently concluded treaties with a number of states, including China, the USA, the Republic of Korea and France (Government of the Cook Islands, 2005). This very small state is also an independent signatory to several multilateral conventions, including the Cotonou Agreement between the ACP states and the European Union.

A similar status is enjoyed by Niue, also a self-governing state in free association with New Zealand, but on a more modest scale. New Zealand has a high commission resident in Alofi, Niue, and, astonishingly, Niue maintains a high commission in Wellington and shares an ambassador and embassy with the Cook Islands in Brussels, although the two states are accredited separately (see www.embassypages.com).

Even in Tokelau New Zealand will only act on behalf of this tiny territory if instructed to do so by the government of Tokelau. This was precisely the arrangement for Swiss representation of Liechtenstein until the late postwar years, an arrangement which many jurists insisted at the time was one that unequivocally established the sovereignty of the principality (Farran, 1960).

The Cook Islands has not presented itself to the international community as a sovereign state, although it behaves in exactly that fashion in its international relations. Cook Islanders are New Zealand citizens and that citizenship is clearly of value in itself, given the large Cook Islands population in New Zealand. The islanders are able to enjoy *all* the prerogatives of sovereignty with the most permissive and generous arrangements for international relations available to any dependent territory in the world. Indeed, to return to our opening historical discussion, the Cook Islands today enjoys an official diplomatic reach beyond the smallest European states before 1990, even though the European micro-states were classified, at least formally, as sovereign entities at the time.

In short, these are arrangements far beyond what is understood to be the various practices of para-diplomacy. When a territory has the separate and independent legal capacity to enter into full diplomatic relations with other states, to send and receive missions at the embassy level, to negotiate bilateral treaties, to be a signatory to multilateral conventions, to participate independently in intergovernmental organizations, especially when those organizations' membership is confined to sovereign states, then what is possibly left to meet the full international legal personality of sovereignty?

Only UN membership remains absent for the Cook Islands, but this was never a litmus test unto itself. Until very recently some states did not apply for UN membership, even though their sovereignty was not in question: (Western) Samoa achieved independence in 1962 but did not join the UN until 1976.

CONCLUSIONS

The twenty-first-century international system is more universal and inclusive in that full international legal personality is shared by jurisdictions which would have been considered improbable and absurd as sovereign states even in 1960 at the beginning of the mass suffrage of colonial territories. Indeed, the apparent ambiguities of status and international prerogatives beyond decolonization have reinforced an ongoing trend to universalism and inclusiveness, a trend which is dramatically reflected in the expanding opportunities and practices in the antechamber of para-diplomacy.

Across this comparative and historical view of para-diplomatic practices there is a consistent pattern of muddied credentials for access to and status within the central international channels of diplomacy. Moreover, there are very different kinds of entities to be found in this antechamber and it is important to retain a clear sense of these distinctions when assessing the phenomenon of para-diplomacy in general. Some of these distinctions have been noted in the current literature on para-diplomatic practices among sub-national units in federations and regions in the European Union. There are jurisdictions which entertain 'national' or 'identity' agendas with pressing political objectives: Québec, Flanders, Catalonia, and to some extent even certain small island sub-national entities such as the Faeroes. Most others engage in para-diplomatic practices for relatively modest functional objectives, and these efforts are almost entirely focused on information: "they gather information concerning [EU] legislation; they exchange information in subnational networks; they mediate information to their respective home territories, and they provide information to [EU] decision makers" (Marks *et al.*, 2002, p. 2).

Are some of the entities more likely to develop or win para-diplomatic practices than others? Clearly those jurisdictions with a distinct identity agenda can be expected to pursue a para-diplomatic outreach aggressively. And small islands, because of their physical separateness and insularity, are obvious candidates for the same reasons that they have gained self-government and even constitutional separateness. However, all sanctioned para-diplomatic practices function within the context of a national or metropolitan relationship and with the consent of the central government. To be sure, agitation and political pressure for greater status recognition and external access from the jurisdiction itself may well result in the central government moving cautiously beyond its own initial comfort levels. But it is a sphere which is only accessible if the metropolitan or central government agrees. It is not some new and swampy terrain of international relations which sub-national governments can enter by stealth. It is not a case of a state being ambushed by its dependent units, suddenly, awkwardly and embarrassingly discovered in the antechamber by sheer chutzpah. No, there are guards at the door and credentials are checked; only those with a metropolitan stamp of approval are admitted. The Faeroes mission in London, the Montserrat delegation at Caricom and the Cook Islands Embassy in Brussels function within the legitimacy of external representation as acknowledged by their metropolitan centres and therefore by the international system itself.

Para-diplomacy is not a new and innovative sphere of international relations, much less one that undermines the finality of sovereign states' judgements on international status and access. Para-diplomacy is not a breach of conventional distinctions in diplomatic practice as much as a redefinition of the frontiers of domestic authority within sovereign states, conceding practices which central governments in some cases have come to accept and even promote for their dependent territories. Indeed, in those cases where para-diplomacy seems to be most advanced and conventional distinctions of status most blurred, the new parameters of international engagement and outreach are determined in the end where they have always been determined: in the capitals of the sovereign members of the international system.

References

Anckar, D. (2002) Åland as a micro-state: the independence scenario, in H. Jansson and J. Salminen (Eds), *The Second Åland Islands Question: Autonomy or Independence?*, pp. 213–242 (Mariehamn: Julius Sundbloms Minnesstifelse).

Anckar, D. and Bartmann, B. (2000) *Ett ramverk för ett självständigt Åland* (Mariehamn: Sällskapet Ålands framtid).

Bahcheli, T., Bartmann, B. and Srebrnik, H. F. (Eds) (2004) *De Facto States: The Quest for Sovereignty* (London: Routledge).

Bartmann, B. (1998) The future political foundation for territorial policy in a global context, in B. Lindström (Ed.), *Den Regionala Utmaningen: Territoriell politik I ett europeiskt Norden*, pp. 239–250 (Stockholm: NordREFO).

Bartmann, B. (1999) The quest for legitimacy: international status of the TRNC, in C. H. Dodd (Ed.), *Cyprus: The Need for New Perspectives*, pp. 260–286 (Huntingdon: The Eothen Press).

Bartmann, B. (2000) Patterns of localism in a changing global system, in G. Baldacchino and D. Milne (Eds), *Lessons from the Political Economy of Small Islands: The Resourcefulness of Jurisdiction*, pp. 38–55 (London: Macmillan).

BIC (2005) *Report of the Bermuda Independence Commission*, Government of Bermuda, August, at www.bermudaindependencecommission.bm

Bermuda Embassy and Consulate Listing (2008), *Bermuda 4U: A Comprehensive Guide to the Rock*, www.bermuda4u.com/Essential/bermuda-embassy.html.

Chapman, P. (2006) Tiny Tokelau decides that self-rule is too expensive, *Daily Telegraph*, 18 March.

Corbin, C. (2001) Direct participation of non-independent Caribbean countries in the United Nations: a method for self-determination, in A. G. Ramos and A. I. Rivera (Eds), *Islands at the Crossroads: Politics in the Non-Independent Caribbean*, pp. 136–159 (Kingston: Ian Randle Publishers).

Dee, W. (2001) *In Pursuit of Sovereignty: A Historical Documentation of Nevis' Secession Odyssey* (St Joseph, Barbados: Cranlake Publishing).

Duchacek, I. D. (1986) *The Territorial Dimension of Politics Within, Among and Across Nations* (London: Westview Press).

Duverger, M. (1959) *Political Parties* (New York: John Wiley).

Farran, C. D'Olivier (1960) The position of diminutive states in international law, in E. Brüel et al. (Eds), *Internationalrechtliche und Staatsrechtliche Abhandlungen–Fetschrift für Walter Schätzel zu Seinem Geburtstag*, pp. 131–147 (Dusselfdorf: Hermes).

Government of the Cook Islands (2005) *Cook Islands Diplomatic and Consular Corps*, at www.cookislands.de/index.php?page=1074121959&f=18j=1074121959

Government of the Faeroes (1999) *Hvitabok: The White Book* (Torshavn: Foroya Landsstyri).

Government of New Zealand (n. d.) *Cook Islands, Political, Economic and Social Relationship*, Country Paper: Pacific Division, March 2006, at www.mfat.govt.nz/foreign/regions/pacific/country/cookislandspaper.html

Granatstein, J. L. and Hillmer, N. (1991) *For Better or Worse: Canada and the United States to the 1990s* (Toronto: Copp, Clark, Pitman).

Gröndal, B. (1974) *Iceland: From Neutrality to NATO Membership* (Oslo: Universitetforloget).

Gunter, M. (1974) Liechtenstein and the League of Nations: a precedent for the United Nations, *American Journal of International Law*, LXVIII (July), pp. 496–501.

Hudson, M. O. (1935) The members of the League of Nations, *British Yearbook of International Law*, XVI, pp. 130–152.

Isfeld, S. (2006) Counsellor and Representative of the Faeroe Islands in London, in personal correspondence with the author, 22 January.

Jansson, C. (2002) Åland's prospects for development in the European Union, in H. Jansson and J. Salminen (Eds), *The Second Åland Islands Question: Autonomy or Independence?*, pp. 201–212 (Mariehamn: Julius Sundbloms Minnesstiftelse).

Keating, M. (1996) *Nations Against the State* (London: Macmillan).

Keating, M. (1999) Regions and international affairs: motives, opportunities and strategies, in F. Aldecoa and M. Keating (Eds), *Paradiplomacy in Action: The Foreign Relations of Subnational Governments*, pp. 1–16 (Portland, OR: Frank Cass).

Knight, D. B. (1982) Identity and territory: geographical perspectives on nationalism and regionalism, *Annals of the Association of American Geographers*, LXXII, pp. 514–531.

Larsen, F. B. (1992) The quiet life of a revolution: Greenlandic home rule, 1979–92, *Inuit Studies*, XVI(1–2), pp. 199–226.

League of Nations (1920) *Report of the Second Sub-Committee to the Fifth Committee, Records of the First Assembly, Plenary Meetings,* Geneva: Switzerland.

Lubin, M. (2003/04) Perforated sovereignties in the Americas: the Canada–US borders and the international outreach activities of Québec, *London Journal of Canadian Studies*, XIX, pp. 19–40.

Marks, G., Haesly, R. and Mbaye, H. A. D. (2002) What do subnational offices think they are doing in Brussels?, *Regional and Federal Studies*, XII(3), pp. 1–23.

Mørkøre, J. (1997) The Faeroese home rule model: theory and reality, in L. Lyck (Ed.), *Constitutional and Economic Space of the Small Nordic Jurisdictions*, pp. 162–191 (Stockholm: NordREFO).

Motzfeldt, J. (1997) Home rule in Greenland, in L. Lyck (Ed.), *Constitutional and Economic Space of the Small Nordic Jurisdictions*, pp. 192–195 (Stockholm: NordREFO).

Myntti, K. (2002) The Åland model: background and special characteristics, in H. Jansson and J. Salminen (Eds), *The Second Åland Islands Question: Autonomy or Independence*, pp. 107–124 (Mariehamn: Julius Sundbloms Minnesstiftelse).

Olafsson, Á. (2000) Constitutionalism and economics in the Faeroes, in G. Baldacchino and D. Milne (Eds), *Lessons from the Political Economy of Small Islands: The Resourcefulness of Jurisdiction*, pp. 121–140 (London: Macmillan).

Premdas, R. R. (1998) *Secession and Self-Determination in the Caribbean: Nevis and Tobago* (St Augustine: School of Continuing Studies, University of the West Indies).

Raton, P. (1970) *Liechtenstein: History and Institutions of the Principality* (Vaduz: Liechtenstein-Verlag).

Rennie, D. (2006) Tiny island that's ready to stop Europe in its tracks, *Daily Telegraph*, 15 February.

Royal Gazette (Bermuda) (2005) Independence position, 16 November, at www.theroyalgazette.com/

Rushby, K. (2001) Another day, another coup, *Guardian*, 1 October.

Scarpulla, C. (2002) The special status of Åland in Finland and the European Union, in H. Jansson and J. Salminen (Eds), *The Second Åland Islands Question: Autonomy or Independence?*, pp. 125–146 (Mariehamn: Julius Sundbloms Minnesstiftelse).

Schei, L. K. and Moberg, G. (1991) *The Faeroe Islands* (London: John Murray).

Séguin, R. (2006) Dawn of a new era?, *Globe and Mail* (Toronto), 9 March.

6 Island disaster para-diplomacy in the commonwealth

Ilan Kelman, Megan Davies, Tom Mitchell, Iain Orr and Bob Conrich

ISLAND GOVERNANCE AND DISASTERS

This chapter covers one particular aspect of the foreign relations of non-sovereign island jurisdictions (SNIJs), namely relations arising from disaster-related activities. Islands are among the territories most seriously affected by calamities, including the spectre of rising seas that may come with climate change. Yet non-sovereign islands are not so well equipped to speak and act effectively *for themselves* in the face of such threats. This may be true even within the governing structures in which these islands find themselves, but it is even more serious given the weaknesses that may exist in their capacity to speak to and act in the international community on disaster-related activities. This chapter explores this issue of 'disaster para-diplomacy' for non-sovereign island jurisdictions, drawing on the para-diplomacy work of Duchacek *et al.* (1988), Michelmann and Soldatos (1990), Soldatos (1993) and Lecours (2002), and adapting it to address the special circumstances of island disaster para-diplomacy where a SNIJ could interact with foreign governments and with international agencies.

For SNIJs, determining responsibility for pre-disaster actions, such as planning and mitigation, and post-disaster actions, such as response and recovery, is not always straightforward, even if legal responsibilities are clearly delineated. Where a SNIJ and its governing state's capital are far apart – geographically as well as in terms of communication, culture and/or cooperation – an event could affect the SNIJ without the national authorities realizing, or being willing to accept, the extent of the impact. Similarly, internationally or nationally mandated programmes related to disaster risk reduction (e.g. UNISDR, 2005, including national platforms for disaster-risk reduction) might be implemented inappropriately from the SNIJs' perspective because less attention is given to the SNIJs' needs compared with (typically much larger) national needs, as determined by and from the capital. Where perceived or real inadequacies arise in a state's disaster-related activities, a SNIJ has five principal options, some of them interconnected:

- Do nothing.
- Pursue full sovereignty or more autonomy from the state.
- Focus on improving the state's actions.
- Focus on improving the SNIJ's capabilities.
- Focus on dealing directly with international organizations and other governments.

That a SNIJ has any options at all is a function of its jurisdictional power. However, its power is granted in the context of an overarching political architecture that will typically circumscribe *how* and *when* it may use these political resources. This is particularly the case in the 'grey area' of para-diplomacy, where neither legal rules nor practice will tell us enough about what a sub-national island can do in representing itself to the outside world.

This chapter examines in some detail the fifth and last option in the above list: a sub-national island territory flexing its jurisdictional muscle in a direction that could be seen as threatening to or destabilizing of the balance of power with its governing state by engaging in inter-state relations which have typically been, and are often vigorously defended as, the exclusive preserve of sovereign states. The SNIJ does so in the context of disaster-related activities that may find the same governing state disposed to tolerate some flexibility and concede departures from the official rule book. But would these departures create precedents for other forays into international relations by the SNIJ, or other thus emboldened SNIJs?

This chapter's exploratory proposition is that there is some, but little current, evidence for island disaster para-diplomacy; yet scope exists for it to become more significant, so the matter should be addressed at the policy level. An overview of case studies is provided as illustrative of the legalities and realities which are evident when seeking island disaster para-diplomacy 'on the ground'. Case studies presented are from the Commonwealth because that geographic scope is *The Round Table*'s main interest. The lessons are then discussed, leading to advice regarding the relevance of island disaster para-diplomacy to the Commonwealth. Thus the chapter does not consider SNIJs such as Hawai'i, Hainan, Sakhalin, Sardinia, Sicily, Corsica, Crete, and the French and Dutch territories; nor does it cover para-diplomacy in other areas such as trade negotiations, offshore finance, sport (e.g. the Island Games) and tourism.

Disaster diplomacy and disaster para-diplomacy

Kelman and Koukis (2000, p. 214) ask: "Do natural disasters induce international cooperation amongst countries that have traditionally been 'enemies'?" Although the answer to this question has thus far been mainly negative (e.g. earthquakes in Greece and Turkey in 1999 (see Ker-Lindsay, 2000) or monitoring hurricanes which could hit both Cuba and the USA (Glantz, 2000)), these and other case studies, along with theoretical analyses on disaster diplomacy (see http://www.disasterdiplomacy.org), suggest that disaster-related activities can catalyse but rarely create international cooperation amongst hostile partners (e.g. Kelman, 2003; 2005b; 2006a; Holloway, 2000; Rajagopalan, 2005; Waarner, 2005).

If disaster-related activities could positively improve relations among states which would not normally be prone to such cooperation, then a similar change could occur in the relations that SNIJs may have, or may not have had previously, with state governments which are not their governing state, or with international agencies. Disaster-related activities could then prove to be the catalyst to launch a SNIJ into international relations.

ISLAND DISASTER PARA-DIPLOMACY EXAMINED

Legalities

Three legal regimes are examined regarding island disaster para-diplomacy: constitutions, disaster-related SNIJ legislation, and intergovernmental organizations. Illustrative examples from different regions of the world are provided as an overview.

Constitutions

A review of constitutions of Commonwealth states with SNIJs reveals limited mention of disaster-related activities (see Appendix 6.1). Where emergency powers are detailed, they tend to rest with either the head of state or the head of government or are split between the two roles, sometimes with provision to delegate authority in case the designated individuals are unable to assume these duties.

Four constitutions suggest connections between sub-national jurisdictions and disaster-related activities. South Africa's constitution's Schedule 4 states that 'disaster management' is a joint national–provincial responsibility, but no South African provinces are SNIJs. Clause 187E(4) of Papua New Guinea's constitution gives the National Executive Council the authority to suspend a provincial government or a local authority which cannot govern as the result of a disaster: in some ways pre-empting sub-national para-diplomacy because it gives the SNIJ less authority. Chapter XII, 114(2)(b) of the Solomon Islands' constitution states that parliament shall "consider the role of traditional chiefs in the provinces", which leaves a possibility for chief-based, disaster-related SNIJ roles. Chapter II, Section 19 of the St Kitts and Nevis constitution describes Nevis' responsibilities and powers regarding declarations of emergency. Nevis can declare or revoke states of emergency, but no mention is made of requesting international assistance.

The lack of mention in constitutions of SNIJs' disaster-related activities is not surprising, not only because constitutions are deemed to be documents covering an entire state, but also because an emergency is not normally a substantive area of jurisdiction for purposes of a constitutional division of powers. In practice, it would (at best) be a *shared* field in a federal arrangement, with the national government having the ever-present right to declare a national emergency (even if confined to only a part of the state), since it would presumably by then have become a matter of national interest and concern. Emergencies referred to here are *national* emergencies, even if and when affecting only part of the state. No state constitution expressly forbids a sub-national jurisdiction from undertaking disaster para-diplomacy. But, depending on the exact situation and judicial precedents, it would be possible to challenge before the courts any such action as violating the national government's responsibilities for national security, defence, foreign affairs or external borrowing (for example, regarding reconstruction loans).

In the case of the UK's island overseas territories the constitutions of Anguilla, Bermuda, the Cayman Islands, Montserrat, and the Turks and Caicos Islands (TCI) mention emergency procedures, but no other disaster-related activities. External affairs, however, is a power specifically reserved for each territory's governor (or equivalent), who is the British government's representative for each SNIJ (see also House of Commons, 2004). The constitutions therefore effectively preclude para-diplomacy from a legal perspective because any external affairs activities must be conducted with or through the governor (or equivalent), i.e. the British government. Nevertheless, as seen below, the matter is not that simple, since SNIJ action cannot be altogether excluded.

Legislation

Moving beyond constitutions to disaster-related SNIJ legislation in the Common-wealth, there is hardly any provision to call for international assistance. For example, paragraphs 12d, 21h and 22j of Tasmania's Emergency Services Act 1976 permit help to be requested from the Australian government or from another Australian state or territory, but other sources are not mentioned.

Both Canada's island, or mainly island, provinces – Newfoundland and Labrador (Emergency Measures Act 1990, amended 2004) and Prince Edward Island (Emergency Measures Act 1998) – have disaster-related legislation. Both SNIJs have signed the International Emergency Management Assistance Memor-andum of Understanding (MOU) (18 July 2000) along with New England's states, Québec, Nova Scotia and New Brunswick. The MOU permits emergency-related training and assistance to be provided across the US–Canada border without directly involving the national governments. This is because the Canadian constitution, as interpreted by the courts, has left open a role for provinces in external relations, provided they act within their areas of jurisdiction. Disaster-related, cross-border collaboration is relatively common at the sub-national level (e.g. Local Authorities Confronting Disasters and Emergencies, at www.ulai.org.il/lacde.htm) but has not yet translated into legislation explicitly addressing para-diplomacy.

Inter- or supra-governmental organizations

In dealing with inter- or supra-governmental organizations, other examples of island disaster para-diplomacy are evident.

The Delegation of the European Commission in Barbados and the Eastern Caribbean (www.delbrb.cec.eu.int) is accredited to three UK overseas territories (UKOTs) – Anguilla, British Virgin Islands (BVI) and Montserrat – and deals with those SNIJ governments directly on some disaster-related activities. Montserrat has received millions of euros for reconstruction following the start of volcanic eruptions there in 1995, one example being €2 543 000 for a 'Montserrat Resettlement Project' in 2005 (Selected Projects, 2005). Anguilla received 'some funds' to repair road damage after Hurricane Lenny hit the island in 1999 (European Development Fund, 2006). Additionally, after Hurricane Ivan in 2004, the Cayman Islands were promised relief money from the European Commission in Brussels (Cayman Islands Government Information Service, 2006). The respective governors of these islands are involved in these projects to some extent; but their specific role in each case is not always clear, suggesting that island disaster para-diplomacy is happening to some degree between the European Commission and the UKOTs.

In the Pacific the Delegation of the European Commission for the Pacific (www. delfji.cec.eu.int) deals with three Commonwealth SNIJs: Cook Islands, Niue and Pitcairn. On disaster-related activities, after Cyclone Heta hit Niue in 2004, €600 000 of previously committed funds was redirected to reconstruct the island's single hospital (Niue, 2006).

Again in the Caribbean, the Caribbean Disaster Emergency Response Agency (CDERA) is involved in disaster-related activities with its members through their national disaster management organizations. For example, the national organization of St Kitts and Nevis is the National Emergency Management Agency (NEMA). Despite lack of specific reference in the state's constitution, the Nevis Disaster Management Office (NDMO) exists. NEMA is mandated to control all international disaster matters and acts on behalf of both islands within CDERA. One of CDERA's roles is to provide an immediate and coordinated response to a disaster event once the affected state requests such support. In a disaster affecting a SNIJ only, such as Barbuda or Tobago, a request for CDERA assistance would have to be lodged through the SNIJ's governing state.

Four UK SNIJs are CDERA members: Anguilla, BVI, Montserrat and TCI. CDERA works through the national disaster management organizations, yielding examples of SNIJs dealing directly with a regional organization for disaster-related activities, although again with their respective governors' involvement to different degrees.

In the Pacific, two New Zealand SNIJs, Cook Islands and Niue, are members of the South Pacific Applied Geoscience Commission (SOPAC). Its Community Risk Program has the goal "to improve disaster risk management practices to build safer and more resilient communities" (www.sopac.org/tiki/tiki-index.php?page=Goal). As with CDERA, this interaction with SOPAC provides examples of Commonwealth SNIJs dealing with a regional organization for disaster-related activities.

Montserrat, the Cook Islands and Niue were each represented by delegations separate from each SNIJ's governing state's delegation at the UN World Conference on Disaster Reduction in Japan from 18 to 22 January 2005, run by the United Nations International Strategy for Disaster Reduction (UNISDR). As a follow-up to the World Conference on Disaster Reduction, as of March 2006, BVI and the Cayman Islands were the only sub-national jurisdictions to have provided UNISDR with a *National Report on the Implementation of the Hyogo Framework for Action* (see www.unisdr.org/eng/hfa/hf-implemt-states.htm).[1] Also, as of March 2006, Montserrat and BVI are the only sub-national jurisdictions listed by UNISDR as providing country-related disaster information (www.unisdr.org/eng/country-inform/introduction.html). Island disaster para-diplomacy is occurring through the UN system.

The Alliance of Small Island States (AOSIS) is another intergovernmental organization with SNIJ members: the Cook Islands and Niue. AOSIS "functions primarily as an *ad hoc* lobby and negotiating voice for small island developing states (SIDS) within the United Nations system" on global climate change issues (www.sidsnet.org/aosis). As these creeping environmental changes (e.g. Glantz, 1999; 2003) begin to affect SNIJs more, and perhaps to a greater extent than the SNIJs' governing states, SNIJs could take to the international stage to try to address these issues, thereby effecting disaster para-diplomacy. Sea-level rise and salinification of water resources are strong candidates for precipitating such efforts because they have the potential to threaten a SNIJ's very existence.

Examining these three different sets of legal regimes provides scattered evidence of island disaster para-diplomacy in the Commonwealth. Despite the relatively weak legal basis for SNIJs to engage in disaster para-diplomacy in the Commonwealth, there are various examples of sanctioned initiatives. They include having disaster-related agencies at SNIJ level partaking in regional or international disaster-related forums; disaster management coordination among sub-state actors of different states; and receiving international funds to mitigate disaster effects.

Realities

The absence of legal sanction, however, may not constitute so strong a barrier against action. In fact, SNIJs frequently provide examples where *de jure* principles are tweaked by *de facto* practices. The presence of some degree of sanctioned local autonomy, coupled with physical distance from the governing state, provides a vehicle for challenging, deliberately or inadvertently, the current regime of mainland–island relations. In addition to legal principles, the realities of a SNIJ's situation could influence whether or not disaster para-diplomacy occurs.

Tristan da Cunha, home to some 300 people, is the remotest inhabited island in the world and is a dependency of the UK overseas territory of St Helena. On 21 May 2001, hurricane-force winds caused extensive damage to Tristan's sole settlement. Despite damage worth at least several hundred thousand pounds (Brock, 2005; Brock and Glass, 2005; Glass, 2003), the UK government only donated £75 000 (*Banking News*, 2001). Meanwhile, an international appeal was sent out through expatriate Tristanians who, within a few months, raised £79 936.08 for a Disaster Fund (personal communication from Colin Topping, 27 November 2001, quoting a letter he received from Tristan da Cunha's Chief Islander). The remainder was covered by subsequent international donations as well by the Tristanians, including their volunteer labour for the repairs. The majority of materials were ordered and shipped from Cape Town, South Africa.

A situation existed where, according to the Tristanians, the UK government was not providing Tristan da Cunha with all the needed post-disaster support. Tristanians solicited funds from elsewhere, setting up a disaster fund for this purpose. They could also have approached non-UK state governments or international agencies for post-disaster supplies and for implementing mitigation. Tristanians, though, are highly loyal to the UK. One of the authors (Conrich) visited Tristan da Cunha in January 2002 and found a resigned acceptance of the limitations of the UK government's reconstruction and development assistance, with no impetus towards considering looking elsewhere. Another important factor contributing to this acceptance was the islanders' wish not to be considered beggars, and their own strong sense of self-reliance. To use para-diplomacy to find other sources of support also entailed opposing the UK government's representative on the island, an idea foreign to Tristanian culture. Yet the disaster fund allowed international donors (state and non-state) the opportunity to support the rehabilitation effort on Tristan directly, hence bypassing the UK government.

Hurricane Ivan struck the Cayman Islands in September 2004. Timothy Adam, the Chief Executive of Cable and Wireless (Cayman Islands), suggested that one of the islands, Grand Cayman, needed outside help: "Grand Cayman urgently needs military intervention to restore and to preserve law and order" (Adam, 2004a). Adam requested US military intervention because "the police are very limited in number and they are exhausted yet reports are that the British have refused to send in Royal Marines or Military Police to help". Nine days later Adam (2004b) noted that his original letter was not intended for publication and represented himself, not his company. However, he added:

> the local officials in the Cayman Islands are doing an outstanding job, considering the extent of the storm damage and the resources they have ... they're not sitting there helpless waiting for outside assistance, but frankly I believe they are less inclined to ask for help or expect any rapid assistance especially from Britain given their experiences over the past week.

American help did *not* arrive; but this example illustrates a SNIJ-based suggestion of external governmental assistance when the governing state did not fulfil requests for help.

Following the 26 December 2004 Indian Ocean tsunamis, the Andaman and Nicobar Islands, a SNIJ of India, suffered 1395 people killed, 1514 people injured, and 40 542 people displaced (Andaman and Nicobar Administration, 2005). India's government waived paperwork restrictions on tsunami-related foreign contributions for affected regions in India, including the Andaman and Nicobar islands (Government of India, 2004). Normally, any organization receiving foreign funds must register with India's government or obtain prior permission to accept funds. Tsunami-related donations were exempted. This decision acknowledged that, for efficient disaster response, money could go directly to the SNIJ's government. The Andaman and Nicobar Islands Administration has the capability to manage aspects of crises, which includes dealing with state governments other than its governing state and with international agencies to gain post-disaster aid.

The Caribbean Association of Electric Utilities and Energy Service Providers (CARILEC) has created a disaster fund into which members contribute. After an affected member utility requests assistance in restoring a damaged electricity grid, the fund pays for emergency teams from other member utilities to assist. One CARILEC member is BVI Electricity Corporation, whose sole shareholder is BVI's government. When this company requests post-disaster assistance from CARILEC, a form of para-diplomacy is occurring, involving a regional agency and a SNIJ government represented through a public utility.

The small islands of Tikopia and Anuta are located in the far eastern Solomon Islands. Officially part of Temotu province, the islands lack airstrips, jetties and reliable off-island communication. Governance is undertaken by the island chiefs who, as noted earlier for the Solomon Islands, have constitutional recognition. On 28 December 2002 the islands were hit by Category 5 Cyclone Zoë (Anderson-Berry *et al.*, 2003; Kelman, 2005a; Vettori and Stuart, 2004; Yates and Anderson-Berry, 2004). None of the inhabitants perished, but the devastation made their food, water and shelter situation dire.

The first formal aid supplies arrived by ship from Honiara, the Solomon Islands' capital, despite the distance of more than 1000 km plus logistical and political delays. However, the closest location to Tikopia and Anuta from which relief supplies could have been brought is in Vanuatu, with Luganville being just 400 km away from

Tikopia. This possibility was demonstrated by journalist Geoff Mackley, who flew relief supplies to Tikopia from Vanuatu by helicopter (*The Australian*, 2003).

In principle, thanks to the constitutional clause quoted earlier, the chiefs might have been able to request assistance by boat or helicopter from Vanuatu, albeit as a short-term measure. In practice, Tikopia and Anuta had only one radio each and both had been broken before Cyclone Zoë, being made operational only after a post-cyclone aid team had arrived (Anderson-Berry *et al.*, 2003). In addition, such action could have had diplomatic implications. First, Honiara could have lost face because Vanuatu would have helped Solomon Islanders (instead of, or before, the Solomon Islands government). Second, aid supplies crossing state lines normally have to be approved by the recipient state, so if that protocol were followed, Honiara would have had to actively accept help from Vanuatu. Third, with the residents of Tikopia and Anuta being ethnically more closely related to the people of Vanuatu than to those in the western part of the Solomon Islands, the Honiara government might have interpreted Vanuatu's assistance as fuelling conflict within the Solomon Islands.

Nevertheless, islanders in a post-disaster situation would presumably be more interested in obtaining relief supplies and rebuilding their communities as soon as possible wherever the help arrived from, rather than being intent on playing para-diplomacy games. This is important because the opportunities presented for para-diplomacy by disaster-related activities are at the same time circumscribed by pragmatism. A governing state may tolerate, absolve, or sanction para-diplomatic initiatives by any of its SNIJs in the interests of expediency, such as faster provision of supplies or facilitated evacuation. The SNIJ may do likewise for similar purposes, rather than as a strategic choice. Disasters are often short-sightedly seen as rare 'one-off' events, even though successful disaster risk reduction is a long-term endeavour and needs to be integrated into development and sustainability processes (Lewis, 1999; Mileti *et al.*, 1999; Wisner *et al.*, 2004). Where the short-term view prevails for a disaster event, expectations could be made regarding the relationship between the SNIJ and its governing state, even though such temporary approaches could harm disaster para-diplomacy in the long term, as shown for disaster diplomacy cases (Kelman, 2003; 2006a; Ker-Lindsay, 2000).

DISCUSSION

The evidence and cases drawn from Commonwealth SNIJs suggest that island disaster para-diplomacy has so far occurred infrequently in practice. In law no official documents or mechanisms were found which provided explicit permission for Commonwealth SNIJs to engage in para-diplomacy for specific, disaster-related activities, even though disaster risk reduction is best achieved at the local level with community involvement (e.g. Lewis, 1999; Twigg, 1999; Wisner *et al.*, 2004). Where the power to request external assistance for disaster-related activities, usually emergencies, is prescribed by law, such 'external assistance' normally refers to a higher jurisdiction *within* the governing state, such as a provincial or national government. The power to call for disaster-related international assistance generally rests with the governing state. Examples of SNIJs bypassing that legal authority were rarely evident, although opportunities were not lacking.

Where a SNIJ is geographically distant from its governing state – making disaster-related logistics from this source more difficult, more expensive and slower to obtain – is para-diplomacy more likely? After all, if a governing state does not provide sufficient disaster-related support, and sufficiently quickly, for a SNIJ, as in the cases of Tristan da Cunha (see above) and Montserrat (Clay, 1999; Davison, 2003; Mitchell, 2006; Pattullo, 2000), then the SNIJ might be forced to look elsewhere, even if logistic difficulties increase and even if the governing state considers such action to be illegal (which would need to be tested in court). In such a situation, an option to avoid bypassing the governing state would be using the media to embarrass the governing state into acting more appropriately. Rather than para-diplomacy, the media option was exercised for Tristan da Cunha following the 1961 volcanic eruption there which led to the island's evacuation (de Boer and Sanders, 2002).

Even where para-diplomacy might alleviate the situation, as in cases requiring evacuation where the nearest population centre to a SNIJ does not belong to its governing state, para-diplomacy is not necessarily enacted. Additionally, island para-diplomacy occurs for many non-disaster activities – including sport, culture, trade, and tourism (Baldacchino, 2004; 2006) – irrespective of any logistical constraints and, at times, legalities. Indeed, SNIJ para-diplomacy is far more present for non-disaster-related acts than for disaster-related ones.

Two other reasons might explain why Commonwealth SNIJs have not yet much exploited disaster para-diplomacy. First, many SNIJs have a limited interest in seeking sovereignty, as long as they continue to enjoy domestic law-making authority that cannot be challenged by the central government (Baldacchino, 2004; 2006). One advantage is the 'umbilical cord' to a larger entity, the governing state, which would then be officially responsible for the SNIJ during crises (Baldacchino, 2004; McElroy and Mahoney, 2000). Although this responsibility might not always be acted upon, or might not be acted upon with the required speed or to the required extent (as shown by some of the examples in this chapter), the connection to the governing state provides a psychological crutch which, in times of need, is hopefully transformed into a physical crutch, especially through disaster response and reconstruction resources. The crutch could fuel the view that external assistance is always at hand, hence local preparation is unnecessary: a 'handout mentality' identified for many islands (Tuiloma-Palesoo, 2004). Actively pursuing disaster para-diplomacy could push SNIJs towards greater autonomy, threatening the availability and disposition of the governing state to provide disaster-related support. However, to succeed, such initiatives would need to be entertained as part of long-term relationship building (that is, para-diplomacy proper), which should not be tied down to one specific disastrous event.

Second, similarly to many sovereign governments, SNIJs and their governing states do not always pay sufficient attention to disaster-related activities until the issue is forced upon them, often by a dramatic event. The volcanic threat to Montserrat was documented scientifically, and the information was communicated to both Montserratian and British authorities (e.g. Wadge and Isaacs, 1987; 1988) but little action was taken until the volcano erupted (Mitchell, 2006). As Kelman (2006b) describes, the threat of Indian Ocean tsunamis was well documented and efforts had been made for at least 30 years to garner support for warning systems, but other activities were deemed to be a higher priority until over 250 000 people were killed by tsunamis on 26 December 2004. An Indian Ocean tsunami warning system has since been started. Disaster para-diplomacy is not pursued by SNIJs partly because disaster-related activities are not a high priority for the SNIJ or for its governing state.

Overall, these reasons suggest that Keating's (1999) para-diplomacy motivators – economic, cultural and political – exclude disaster-related activities; however, a disaster event could nonetheless harbour political capital. A SNIJ's government or political grouping *could* exploit a disaster situation to promote its views about sovereignty. Successful disaster para-diplomacy, such as using external assistance for effective mitigation or reconstruction, could provide evidence of SNIJ government efficacy and thus garner support for sovereignty among the locals. In contrast, continued reliance on external assistance, particularly from or managed by the SNIJ's governing state, could illustrate the need and logic for persisting dependency, garnering support for those islanders who oppose outright sovereignty. The poor response following the 1970 cyclone in East Pakistan contributed towards a subsequent revolt that led to the creation of Bangladesh (Lewis, 1999). However, the initially inadequate response from the UK government to the volcanic eruptions on Montserrat did not promote a push for sovereignty there (Fergus, 2002).

In linking autonomy concerns with disaster para-diplomacy, balance of interests is a factor deserving of analysis. This compares the disaster-related interests of the SNIJ with those of its governing state. Balance of interests does not indicate directly whether increased autonomy would be promoted or inhibited by a SNIJ's disaster-related activities. It provides a baseline for dialogue on disaster-related activities between a SNIJ and its governing state by indicating each party's starting point for this topic. Acceptance of similarities and differences can assist in building trust and in tackling disaster-related issues properly, possibly influencing a SNIJ's direction towards or away from increased autonomy. Yet the autonomy-related decisions of a SNIJ or its governing state are not necessarily based on practicalities such as balance of interests, needs, or the population's desires. Nationalism or a governing state's wish to get rid of a 'liability' could be a key driver nudging a SNIJ towards sovereignty – what has been called "upside down decolonization" (Hoefte and Oostindie, 1989) – and a specific response (or non-response) regarding disaster-related activities *may* be part of a governing state's and/or a SNIJ's wider plan regarding the SNIJ's future.

CONCLUSION

This chapter supports the conclusion drawn by Kelman and Koukis (2000) that a disaster could significantly spur a diplomatic process which had another basis, but that a disaster *per se* is unlikely to generate new diplomacy. Disaster-related activities can catalyse, but do not create, or sustain cooperation.

There are, however, 'windows of need' which present opportunities for pragmatism in the context of disasters. Para-diplomacy has been an option in such situations; but rarely has this option been adopted and such powers usurped. Moreover, a disaster event might not be the best situation to entertain para-diplomacy, since the latter is essentially a sustained, cultivated and groomed long-term relationship with significant state and non-state actors, as disaster-related activities ought to be. Regrettably this is not always so with decisions made during and immediately following disaster events.

Given the impact of disasters on SNIJs and the strong link of disaster-related activities to development, sustainable livelihoods and environmental management (e.g. Lewis, 1999; Mileti *et al.*, 1999; Wisner *et al.*, 2004), there is no obvious reason for disaster-related activities to be outside the purview of para-diplomacy. Moreover, a disaster could present an opportunity to the politically resourceful. Both pro- and anti-sovereignty movements in a SNIJ could use disaster para-diplomacy or the lack thereof to support broader political goals, irrespective of legal coda.

Finally, the comparison by Sims (2000) of the Commonwealth with the International Court of Justice for the purpose of solving disputes is pertinent. With disaster-related activities increasingly becoming a human rights concern (e.g. Kent, 2001; Radix Network, at www.radixonline.org), could a Commonwealth SNIJ request adjudication on its governing state's allegedly inadequate disaster-related actions? Could the Commonwealth be asked to judge, or would it be ignored and bypassed, with these concerns taken elsewhere? Should the Commonwealth, as a global organization, promote itself as a first or last resort for such disputes? Some precautionary preparation and planning appear timely.

Note

1. As of March 2006 the Cayman Islands' report was from November 2005 and comprises 19 tables for action, of which 16 tables were blank. BVI's report (undated) was two pages long, listing disaster-related project titles, timeframes and contact points.

References

Adam, T. (2004a) Urgent US military intervention needed in Grand Cayman, *Cayman Net News Online*, at http://caymannetnews.com/2004/09/738/letter.shtml

Adam, T. (2004b) Cable & Wireless Chief Executive clarifies his personal position, *Cayman Net News Online*, at http://www.caymannetnews.com/2004/09/738/letter.shtml

Andaman and Nicobar Administration (2005) *Damages Due to Tsunami, Daily Report Dated 15th February*, Port Blair, Andaman Islands: Ministry of Home Affairs (NDM Division), Andaman and Nicobar Administration.

Anderson-Berry, L., Iroi, C. and Rangi, A. (2003) *Tropical Cyclone Zoë, Tikopia and Anuta, Solomon Islands, December 26–29, 2002* (Townsville: Centre for Disaster Studies, James Cook University).

The Australian (2003) Islanders' miracle survival, 4 January.

Baldacchino, G. (2004) Autonomous but not sovereign? A review of island sub-nationalism, *Canadian Review of Studies in Nationalism*, XXXI(1–2), pp. 77–91.

Baldacchino, G. (2006) Innovative development strategies from sub-national island jurisdictions? A global review of economic policy and governance practices, *World Development*, 34(5), pp. 852–867.

Banking News (2001) Tristan da Cunha – disaster relief fund, Press release, Crown Agents Financial Services, 25 June, at http://www.crownagents.com/news/news.asp?step=4& NewsID=199.

Brock, J. (2005) Tristan da Cunha: flags half-mast for tsunami victims, *Tristan Times*, 5 January.

Brock, J. and Glass, S. (2005) Tristan: poaching threatens Tristan da Cunha's hurricane recovery, *Tristan Times*, 12 June.

Cayman Islands Government Information Service (2006) Top FCO official pledges more Cayman support, Press release, Cayman Islands Government Information Service.

Clay, E. (1999) *An Evaluation of HMG's Response to the Montserrat Volcanic Emergency,* DFID Evaluation Report EV635 (London: DFID).

Davison, P. (2003) *Volcano in Paradise* (London: Methuen).

De Boer, J. Z. and Sanders, D. T. (2002) *Volcanoes in Human History* (Princeton, NJ: Princeton University Press).

Duchacek, I. D., Latouch, D. and Stevenson, G. (Eds) (1988) *Perforated Sovereignties and International Relations: Trans-Sovereign Contacts of Sub-national Governments* (Westport, CT: Greenwood Press).

European Development Fund (2006) Delegation of the European Commission in Barbados and Eastern Caribbean, at www.delbrb.cec.eu.int/en/eu_and_country/oct_anguilla_development.htm

Fergus, H. (2002) Constitutional modernisation in Montserrat and the Cayman Islands: taking the British seriously? Paper presented at the Montserrat Country Conference, 13–14 November, Montserrat.

Glantz, M. H. (Ed.) (1999) *Creeping Environmental Problems and Sustainable Development in the Aral Sea Basin* (Cambridge: Cambridge University Press).

Glantz, M. H. (2000) Climate-related disaster diplomacy: a US–Cuban case study, *Cambridge Review of International Affairs,* XIV(1), pp. 233–253.

Glantz, M. H. (2003) *Climate Affairs: A Primer* (Covelo, CA: Island Press).

Glass, J. (2003) Tristan: official hurricane report, *Tristan Times,* 17 November.

Government of India (2004) *Order* and *Press Release,* document II/21022/11(19)/2004-FCRA I (New Delhi: Government of India, Ministry of Home Affairs, Foreigners Division).

Hoefte, R. and Oostindie, G. (1989) Upside down decolonization, *Hemisphere,* 1(2), pp. 28–31.

Holloway, A. (2000) Drought emergency, yes…drought disaster, no: southern Africa 1991–93, *Cambridge Review of International Affairs,* XIV(1), pp. 254–276.

House of Commons (2004) Written Answers to Questions [8 November], Foreign and Commonwealth Affairs, United Kingdom Overseas Territories, *Hansard (House of Commons Daily Debates),* 426, Part No. 51, Column 515W.

Keating, M. (1999) Regions and international affairs: motives, opportunities and strategies, in F. Aldecoa and M. Keating (Eds), *Paradiplomacy in Action: The Foreign Relations of Subnational Governments,* pp. 1–16 (London: Frank Cass).

Kelman, I. (2003) Beyond disaster, beyond diplomacy, in M. Pelling (Ed.), *Natural Disasters and Development in a Globalizing World,* pp. 110–123 (London: Routledge).

Kelman, I. (2005a) Some outlying effects of Cyclone Zoë, in Tudor Rose Publications & International Strategy for Disaster Reduction (eds) *Know Risk,* p. 237 (Leicester and Geneva: Tudor Rose Publications and the International Strategy for Disaster Reduction).

Kelman, I. (2005b) Tsunami diplomacy: will the 26 December, 2004 tsunamis bring peace to the affected countries?, *Sociological Research Online,* 10(1), at http://www.socresonline.org.uk/10/1/kelman.html

Kelman, I. (2006a) Acting on disaster diplomacy, *Columbia Journal of International Affairs,* 59(2), pp. 215–240.

Kelman, I. (2006b) Warning for the 26 December 2004 tsunamis, *Disaster Prevention and Management,* 15(1), pp. 178–189.

Kelman, I. and Koukis, T. (Eds) (2000) Disaster diplomacy, Special section, *Cambridge Review of International Affairs,* XIV(1), pp. 214–294.

Kent, G. (2001) The human right to disaster mitigation and relief, *Environmental Hazards,* 3, pp. 137–138.

Ker-Lindsay, J. (2000) Greek–Turkish rapprochement: the impact of 'disaster diplomacy'?, *Cambridge Review of International Affairs,* XIV(1), pp. 215–232.

Lecours, A. (2002) Paradiplomacy: reflections on the foreign policy and international relations of regions, *International Negotiation,* 7, pp. 91–114.

Lewis, J. (1999) *Development in Disaster-prone Places: Studies of Vulnerability* (London: Intermediate Technology Publications).

McElroy, J. L. and Mahoney, M. (2000) The propensity for political dependence in small island microstates, *Insula: International Journal of Island Affairs*, 9(1), pp. 32–35.

Michelmann, H. J. and Soldatos, P. (1990) *Federalism and International Relations: The Role of Subnational Units* (Oxford: Clarendon).

Mileti, D. and 136 contributing authors (1999) *Disasters by Design: A Reassessment of Natural Hazards in the United States* (Washington, DC: Joseph Henry Press).

Mitchell, T. (2006) Building a disaster resilient future: lessons from participatory research on St Kitts and Montserrat, PhD thesis, Department of Geography, University College London.

Niue (2006) Online article from the Delegation of the European Commission for the Pacific, at http://www.delfji.cec.eu.int/en/achievements/niue.htm

Pattullo, P. (2000) *Fire from the Mountain: The Tragedy of Montserrat and the Betrayal of its People* (London: Constable and Robinson).

Rajagopalan, S. (2005) Post-tsunami international relations: a sea change?, *Chaitanya Brief*, 1(2), Chennai: Chaitanya Consult.

Selected Projects (2005) *Delegation of the European Commission in Barbados and the Eastern Caribbean e-Newsletter*, 11, pp. 17–18.

Sims, N. A. (2000) The Commonwealth and the International Court of Justice, *The Round Table*, 354, pp. 205–230.

Soldatos, P. (1993) Cascading subnational paradiplomacy in an interdependent and transnational world, in D. M. Brown and E. H. Fry (Eds), *States and Provinces in the International Economy*, pp. 45–64 (Berkeley, CA: Institute of Governmental Studies).

Tuiloma-Palesoo, D. (2004) Handout mentality, *Small Islands Voice Global Forum*, 16 November, at http://www.sivglobal.org/?read=82.

Twigg, J. (1999) The Age of Accountability? Future community involvement in disaster reduction, *Australian Journal of Emergency Management*, 14(4), pp. 51–58.

UNISDR (2005) *Hyogo Framework for Action 2005–2015: Building the Resilience of Nations and Communities to Disasters* (Geneva: UNISDR).

Vettori, L. and Stuart, C. (2004) Cyclone in the Pacific, *Oxfam News* (Australia), Autumn, pp. 10–11.

Waarner, M. (2005) Shaken, not stirred: Iranian foreign policy and domestic disaster, Master's thesis, University of Amsterdam.

Wadge, G. and Isaacs, M. C. (1987) *Volcanic Hazards from the Soufrière Hills Volcano, Montserrat West Indies: A Report to the Government of Montserrat and the Pan Caribbean Disaster Preparedness and Prevention Project* (Reading: Department of Geography, University of Reading).

Wadge, G. and Isaacs, M. C. (1988) Mapping the volcanic hazards from Soufrière Hills Volcano, Montserrat, West Indies using an image processor, *Journal of the Geological Society of London*, 145, pp. 541–555.

Wisner, B., Blaikie, P., Cannon, T. and Davis, I. (2004) *At Risk: Natural Hazards, People's Vulnerability and Disasters* (London: Routledge).

Yates, L. and Anderson-Berry, L. (2004) The societal and environmental impacts of Cyclone Zoë and the effectiveness of the tropical cyclone warning systems in Tikopia and Anuta, Solomon Islands, December 26–29, 2002, *Australian Journal of Emergency Management*, 19(1), pp. 16–20.

Appendix 6.1

Disaster-related Activities in the Constitutions of Commonwealth States with SNIJs

The UK and its SNIJs Guernsey, Jersey and the Isle of Man do not have written constitutions. Constitutional matters are interpreted based on common law and constitutionally related legal documents such as the *Magna Carta*. The UK's island overseas territories have constitutions, the disaster-related activities of which are mentioned in the paper's text.

Constitutions with minimal mention of disaster-related activities:

- India's constitution's Article 83 permits the sitting of parliament to be extended beyond five years if a Proclamation of Emergency is in operation.
- New Zealand's constitution does not mention disaster-related activities, nor do the Cook Islands' and Niue's constitutions. Paragraph 6(5)(iv) of Tokelau's constitution states that, when the general parliament is not in session, a council will be formed to run government, of which one duty is to "respond to national emergencies".
- Tanzania's constitution's First Schedule notes that 'emergency powers' are a Union Matter, i.e. for the state, not for any sub-national jurisdictions, including Zanzibar.
- Tonga's constitution's paragraph 19(a)(ii) permits government expenditure without the prior vote of the Legislative Assembly "In cases of war or rebellion or dangerous epidemic or a similar emergency", although the Legislative Assembly must be informed immediately.

Constitutions which detail powers to declare, and act during, a state of emergency with no further discussion of disaster-related activities:

- Antigua and Barbuda
- Bahamas
- Fiji
- Kiribati
- Malaysia
- Malta
- Maldives
- Mauritius
- Mozambique
- St Kitts and Nevis
- St Vincent and the Grenadines
- Samoa
- Seychelles
- Solomon Islands
- Trinidad and Tobago
- Vanuatu

Constitutions which detail powers to declare, and act during, a state of emergency with further mention of disaster-related activities:

- Papua New Guinea's constitution's Paragraph 202 states "The functions of the Defence Force are ... (c) to provide assistance to civilian authorities – (i) in a civil disaster; or (ii) in the restoration of public order and security on being called out in accordance with Section 204 (call-out in aid to the civil power)".
- South Africa's constitution's Schedule 4 states that "functional areas of concurrent national and provincial legislative competence' include 'disaster management", but none of the provinces are SNIJs.
- Tuvalu's constitution includes a subsidiary section in which the prime minister is assigned responsibility for disaster preparedness.

7 Isolation as disability and resource: considering sub-national island status in the constitution of the 'New Tasmania'

Elaine Stratford

INTRODUCTION

> In an era where size becomes synonymous with might, the cultural, historical, and material importance of islands to world history has been generally ignored... British colonial activity in island spaces became mystified through the literary construction of isolated islands... awaiting... 'development'... [and it inscribed] an insoluble contradiction... that islands are simultaneously isolated yet deeply susceptible to migration and settlement... We have to question who benefits from the persistent myth of island isolation.
>
> (Deloughrey, 2004, p. 300)

Nikolas Rose suggests that government has been made possible only by "defining boundaries, rendering them visible, assembling information about that which is included and devising techniques to mobilize the forces [such as identities] and entities [such as nations] thus revealed" (Rose, 2003, p. 33). But these visible boundaries, assemblages and techniques are unstable, and this instability gives rise to new forms of economic space and spatializations of governmental thought. Three lines of inquiry are suggested. The first requires understanding the territorialization of governmental thought, the act of "marking out a territory in thought and inscribing it in the real" (Rose, 2003, p. 34). The second warrants an appreciation of the spatializing of the gaze of those who govern, using inscription devices such as maps, charts and diagrams (Richardson, 2005). These devices serve to produce conviction in others in order to stabilize the space to be governed as 'the real'. The third suggests the need to understand the impetus to model the space of government as isotropic – to render everywhere the same. These "concrete realizations of imaginary space stand in, in thought, for that which they realize... take on a life of their own, and are invested with powers which appear to allow the mastery of the phenomena they imagine or model" (Rose, 2003, p. 38). Among other things, what emerge are colonies, federations, states and their sub-national jurisdictions, citizens identifiable by their attachment to place, and the intergovernmental relations through which they negotiate their relative positions.

Intergovernmental relations in federal states may be typified by cooperative contest between those who govern the states nationally and those who govern their constituent sub-national jurisdictions. Equally, internal relations between sub-national governments and their citizens can be testing, especially where shifts in the global marketplace affect local attachment to place. Understanding how such relations influence our being in place means comprehending the consequence of various strategies and tactics of government that shape conduct and constitute regimes of truth (Dean, 1999).

Among other things, an island is a "sharply precise physical entity which accentuates clear and holistic notions of location and identity" (Baldacchino, 2004a, p. 272). Islands are also profoundly spatialized in governmental thought, and it is a distinct challenge to protect them from globalizing tendencies to render everywhere the same (Péron, 2004). Addressing such challenges has characterized much island scholarship. In the process, studies of the nation-state are favoured over those of sub-national jurisdictions (Anckar, 2002; Armstrong and Read, 2003; Baldacchino, 2004a; 2004b; Bertram and Watters, 1985; Cau, 1999; Hache, 1998). Yet, just as governments of island states may leverage insularity as a jurisdictional resource in international negotiations about development, so the sub-national island jurisdiction whose 'parent' is a mainland or continental territory may deploy its status as a key mechanism of distinction from mainland 'siblings', and strive to minimize certain asymmetries of federalism.

From the 1820s to the 1890s the idea of the federation of Australia was forged by colonial leaders seeking a 'common wealth of increase' within the constraint of British foreign policy and the imperial government's cautious position on the dominion following its North American losses (Brown, 2004). The jurisdiction was created by the Commonwealth of Australia Constitution Act 1901, and now comprises six provinces called 'states' – New South Wales, Victoria, South Australia, Western Australia, Queensland and Tasmania – and two territories – the Australian Capital Territory (ACT) and the Northern Territory. All but the last two have full statehood, the Northern Territory's more limited status being largely determined on the basis of population size and the ACT's because of its 'capital' function (just like the District of Columbia in the USA). In such an arrangement sub-national distinctiveness – expressed through the performance of place and identity – becomes imperative. The reasons for this need may be explained as follows. Federations such as Australia are constituted for diverse reasons, not least among them the ability to account for the presence of core and peripheral economic zones. In certain jurisdictions these zones have prompted the formation of "asymmetrical federal designs: certain regions receive more autonomy than others; or the autonomy that is granted to one type of region may be different from the autonomy that is granted to another type" (Swenden and Beaufays, 2005, no page number). In the case of Australia, however, zones of central and peripheral influence fostered the constitution of a symmetrical federation, in which enshrined uniformities are resisted and practices of distinction are cultivated among the sub-national jurisdictions that comprise the whole.

Such practices of distinction become apparent in various ways. Two such practices are intergovernmental fiscal negotiations to secure preferential treatment because of idiosyncratic circumstances, such as Tasmanians being able to claim remote island status and use isolation as a 'disability'; and efforts to attract offshore investment, such as when Tasmanians capitalize on the development appeal that adheres to island status as a 'resource' – isolation included (Baldacchino, 2004b).

In light of the foregoing I intend to examine the emergence of the 'New Tasmania' as an open and accessible island imaginary of global international desire, which some suggest is at risk of reduction to an 'everywhere'. The term 'New Tasmania' encapsulates a thrust by State Government to ensure that Tasmania benefits from economic globalization by marketing its natural advantages (as an island) without degrading those same advantages. The New Tasmania is meant to attract 'the big end of town' in ecotourist and sustainable tourism resorts, and in new coastal residential subdivisions, but this is the subject of considerable dissent. In view of this opposition, and given what is at stake for sub-national island peoples struggling to come to terms with the demands of modernity, it is instructive to ask how Tasmanians are using isolated and island status as resources to negotiate the direction of development – especially tourism and property development. What does the creation of the New Tasmania mean in the context of globalization's simultaneously homogenizing and destabilizing embrace? In addressing these questions, I first examine how isolation has been constituted as a disability in intergovernmental relations. I then explore how isolation is (re)deployed to Tasmania's apparent advantage in Australian federal fiscal equalization strategies featuring the Bass Strait as the maritime extension of the national highway that carries to the island's shore tourists and those seeking a more permanent sea change. I therefore elaborate on certain debates that characterize the controversial emergence of the New Tasmania to emphasize the use of isolation as a special resource among those who question the shape, directions and values of this newly spatialized place as a locus of globalized tourism and property development. Through these efforts the larger task at hand is to contribute to the growing literature on sub-national island jurisdictions as particular categories of place in which questions of governance play out, and to further pursue research on islands, sustainable development and globalization (Armstrong and Stratford, 2004; Stratford, 2003; 2006; Stratford, *et al.*, 2003).

OBSERVATIONS ON AUSTRALIAN FEDERAL FISCAL EQUALIZATION

Each sub-national jurisdiction in Australia has its own constitution, laws and economic activities. Each is also highly dependent on the Australian Government (Chapman, 1982; Kline, 2002; Walker, 1999). In a sense this is dependency by agreement, whereby central funds are distributed to the states using the principles of fiscal equalization (Australian Government, Commonwealth Grants Commission, 2005). It is based on the foundational assumption that "each State should be able to provide the same standard of services to its population, if it operates at the same level of efficiency and makes the same effort to raise revenues from its own sources" (Searle, 2002, p. 1).

There are various problems with ensuring horizontal political and economic balance among strong and weak states; and challenges exist in securing vertical fiscal balance between the Commonwealth and the states. Mathews (no date) notes that most of the costly expenditure functions have been retained by the states, with taxation being the privilege of the Commonwealth alongside the distribution of general revenue grants (GRGs) and special purpose payments (SPPs).[1] He also maintains that "imbalance has always been less marked in Australia...personal incomes per head in the smallest and poorest State, Tasmania, have never been more than about 20% below those of the most populous and richest States of New South Wales and Victoria" (Mathews, 1977, p. 4).

A relatively early response to intergovernmental fiscal imbalance[2] was the establishment in 1933 of the Commonwealth Grants Commission (CGC).[3] Its decisions about financial matters are based on need, and its operation has been remarkably effective, given what is at stake in terms of competition among territories and populations. However, discontent about apparent inequities in the system ran especially high in the 1980s and 1990s, and in June 1999 the parties signed an Intergovernmental Agreement on Principles for the Reform of Commonwealth–State Financial Relations (IGA) during the introduction of the Goods and Services Tax (GST) and abolition of various Commonwealth and state taxes. Under the IGA, "the Commonwealth returns...revenue collected from the GST...to the States, but no longer pays them revenue replacement payments or gives them untied financial assistance grants...[with the guarantee that they]...will be no worse off than under...former...arrangements" (Searle, 2002, p. 9). Nevertheless, Eslake's (2004) analysis of the state's economic outlook suggests that Tasmania has been receiving diminishing levels of commonwealth funds over a number of years.

So-called 'disabilities' are an important consideration for the CGC in its deliberations on fiscal equalization. These are "influences beyond a State's control that require it to spend more (or less) to provide the same service as other States, or mean that it cannot raise as much revenue as (or can raise more than) other States from the same tax rates" (Searle, 2002, p. 21). Isolation is one such disability for which states gain special consideration in negotiations over fiscal equalization because, in general terms, it is thought to impede development. "Isolation disabilities relate to unavoidable costs incurred by some States because of the distances of those States from other State capitals and sources of supply. Isolation-related costs are considered to affect most State functions" (Australian Government, Commonwealth Grants Commission, 2002, p. 1). They include labour and freight costs; airfares and travel allowances; travel-related subsidies; professional infrastructure; and commercial isolation.

The CGC assesses isolation-related expenditure for each state and compares that expenditure with the Australian average to derive an 'isolation factor'. The most remote and least developed, the Northern Territory, completely dominates the national scene, taking up just under 88% of the isolation factor by itself. However, when the latter is removed from the picture as 'anomalous' (justified because it is the least developed jurisdiction, has a low population threshold, and underdeveloped social and economic infrastructure), Tasmania accounts for just under 48% (Australian Government, Commonwealth Grants Commission, 2002; 2003).

PLAYING THE ISOLATION CARD

Baldacchino's (2006) observation that sub-national jurisdictions possess the capacity for both shared and self-rule; have autonomy and strong identity; and exhibit high levels of administrative, political, bureaucratic and cultural powers appears generally supported in the Australian federation. Separated from mainland Australia by the 250 km stretch of Bass Strait, Tasmania is the smallest and most peripheral state in the federation, and is its only island member at that jurisdictional level. According to the Australian Bureau of Statistics (2005), the total area of the state – including its 334-plus offshore islands – is 68 102 km^2 or 0.9% of the total area of Australia.

Total imports were valued at AU\$669 million, while exports were valued at \$2317 million in 2003–04 (Australian Bureau of Statistics, 2005). Crucial to that outcome were agriculture and horticulture, mining, aquaculture and fisheries, and forestry, as well as the manufacturing that derives from those primary industries. For the same period expenditure by some 739 800 adult visitors to Tasmania was $1073.5 million. It is useful to note at this point – in order to revisit below – that highly volatile debates often erupt around the direction of development in Tasmania. Tourism and property developments in particular are debated among the populace and raise questions about what it means to be Tasmanian and live on the island.

Isolation provides significant dividends to Tasmania via Commonwealth funding calculated to offset the disadvantages of peripherality more generally. Nevertheless, successive Tasmanian governments have avoided the term in marketing the state to national and international investors in tourism and property development, except where it is evocative of the 'island paradise'. To do so might be to emphasize the term's apparent disadvantages. Indeed, in Tourism Tasmania's (2004) *Tourism Development Kit* for prospective developers, the term does not appear, except implicitly as a burden to investment overcome:

> For most of its history, Australia's smallest and most distinctive State was a secret shared by a select group of holidaymakers captivated by its unspoilt nature, charming heritage and island lifestyle. But Tasmania is a secret no longer [and now its] island appeal is complemented by excellent sea and air access ... With $400 million worth of tourism development already underway or planned ... Tasmania [is] one of the world's hottest holiday destinations.
> (Tasmanian Government, Tourism Tasmania, 2004)

In short, the use of isolation in federal fiscal negotiations and marketing for tourism and property development suggests a clear understanding by government of the term's utility in the changing and competitive conditions of the market, and of the need to punctuate the island state's sameness and difference, its proximity and distance, *within* the Australian federation. This insight is worth exploring further, first by reference to the Bass Strait and then by considering recent conflicts over property development.

The bass strait factor

In Australia the condition of each sub-national jurisdiction is regularly standardized, such that federation is constantly stabilized and the principles of fiscal equalization are upheld. This observation extends to a most distinguishing feature of Tasmania – the Bass Strait, which separates it from the mainland and marks it both as island and as isolated.[4] Hence the State Government's introduction of the Tasmanian Freight Equalization Scheme[5] and the Bass Strait Passenger Vehicle Equalization Scheme.

Implemented in September 1996, the Bass Strait Passenger Vehicle Equalization Scheme is a rebate system to "reduce the cost disadvantage associated with transporting passenger vehicles across Bass Strait, thereby increasing passenger travel between Tasmania and the mainland, on what is essentially Tasmania's sea highway" (Addison, 2005, no page number). It is:

> calculated on the basis of charging a net fare for an eligible passenger vehicle plus driver travelling in standard share accommodation, that is comparable to the

notional cost of driving an equivalent distance on a highway...based upon the
sea distance of 427 kilometres between the ports of Devonport [in Tasmania] and
Melbourne [in Victoria] multiplied by an estimated running cost for an average
family saloon...The rebate is an 'up front' subsidy...provided to the driver [*as a
subsidy to the payable fare*]...[and funding] for the scheme is demand-driven.

(Carlson, 1998, no page number)

During the period between 1996 and 2002 the TT Line, a Tasmanian Government
business enterprise, received nearly 100% of Commonwealth Government subsidies
to payable fares. It also commissioned a second ferry to be built, the *Spirit of
Tasmania II*, implying that it owned and benefited from previous payments to *Spirit I*
(Australian Government, Bureau of Transport and Regional Economics, 2004). Of
the 1 070 334 adult passengers counted over the period, 652 234 (60%) were visitors
and, of those, 52% were in Tasmania for holidays – thought to be a positive sign for
tourism and the state's economy. Buoyed by these developments, the Tasmanian
Government determined in 2004 to purchase a *Spirit of Tasmania III* to work
between the island and Australia's largest and most popular tourist destination, the
city of Sydney.

However, in March 2005 it was revealed that passenger and freight movements on
the *Spirit III* had been grossly overestimated. The Tasmanian Department of Treasury
and Finance has since calculated that accumulated losses on the Sydney service may
amount to $90 million in the period to 2011–12 (Tasmania Government,
Department of Treasury and Finance, 2005). Were the service to cease, somewhere
between 5000 and 10 000 visitors (representing $10–$20 million per annum) could
be lost to the island. Yet its retention requires the Tasmanian Government to provide
a subsidy of $145 million to its TT Line over the period to 2012, a figure of $2500 per
visitor, "far in excess of the average benefit tourists bring through their spending in
Tasmania" (Tasmania Government, Department of Treasury and Finance, 2005, no
page number).

It is noteworthy that the preferred advice of the Tasmanian Department of
Treasury and Finance to sell *Spirit III* was rejected in favour of a subsidy programme.
In defending the decision to keep the service in the Tasmanian House of Assembly on
15 March 2005, Premier Paul Lennon stated:

If we don't take on challenges, we'll stand still...We have something special here
in Tasmania...We have a quality lifestyle and quality environment and we can
share that with other Australians. *Spirit III* is a key part of that strategy...[and
the] vision and determination to break into a new tourism market that led to [its
purchase] remains valid...to retain *Spirit III* is an investment in our future – and
in the future of generations to come.

(Lennon, 2005, no page)[6]

This statement is a clear articulation of the New Tasmania, and it appears to invoke
the conquest of isolation, summon up an image of Tasmania as a haven from the
madness of places 'off-island', and pay tribute to the intergenerational benefits of
engaging in the global market.

Yet for others in Tasmania isolation *must* be preserved if island life is to be
protected from those mad other worlds. How, then, is isolation also deployed as a

resource by which to combat that notion of the spatialization of governmental thought that emphasizes the perils of isomorphism, and shown in the New Tasmania?

Resisting development in the New Tasmania style

In February 2003 the then Premier Jim Bacon addressed delegates at the Second Global Summit on Peace through Tourism in Geneva. He remarked on the fact that:

> We are islands of tremendous resourcefulness and innovation, creatively connected to a diverse and spectacular landscape... As a state of islands we are especially connected to other islands of the globe. We have an affinity with all who, like us, have experienced a painful past, and we are building a new connection with those blessed with a creative culture that nurtures our future.
>
> (Bacon, 2003, p. 1)

Bacon's discursive construction of Tasmania as coherent, significant and international performs much spatialized governmental work: the New Tasmania is a safe, open, progressive and cosmopolitan location. It is an appropriate partner for any prospective other wishing to engage in the sophisticated transactions of globalization, deeply appealing as a destination, and to be understood as a 'spectacular' domain for investment. Such views stand in stark contrast to long-standing mainland caricatures of the state as an inward-looking mendicant or as permanently engaged in the plunder of the place. The latter was emphasized by Tasmanian author Richard Flanagan, who questioned the eulogizing of the Premier after his death in mid-2004 by suggesting:

> Tasmania remains the poorest state in the Commonwealth... its unique environment is being destroyed... its celebrated coast and world heritage areas are under attack from inappropriate tourist developments... its democracy has been left debased... Bacon's legacy was to hand Tasmania's economy and... direction over to... big businesses with too much influence, too much power and too little concern for ordinary Tasmanians.
>
> (Flanagan, 2004, no page number)

These observations exemplify a highly charged, alternative and resistant spatialization of governmental thought about Tasmania as a place for ordinary people. Such debates go to the heart of what it means to try and comprehend the consequence of various strategies and tactics of government that shape conduct and constitute regimes of truth about that being in place (Dean, 1999). On the one hand, for those who advocate the New Tasmania, the promise of development investment is incontrovertible, and its benefits should be capitalized upon. On the other, for those who question the values of the New Tasmania, the opposite holds: the risk of recreating Tasmania as part of the globalized 'everywhere the same' is too great to countenance.

Similar tensions are raised again in 'State of flux', a feature on Tasmania in the January 2005 issue of the broadsheet *Australian Financial Review Magazine*. It refers to a proposal by a mainland developer, Lang Walker Corporation, to construct a $400 million suburb of 800 residences around canals, jetties and marinas in an internationally significant migratory bird conservation zone and village community known as Ralphs Bay (Neales, 2005). That sea-change development draws attention to two wider problems. First, similar plans by that corporation on the mainland have been criticized as unsustainable on social, economic and environmental grounds (*New South Wales Legislative Council Hansard*, 2004), and protesters concerned about the possible Tasmanian development suggested that the corporation came to see the island as an easy target – its state and some local governments, and some citizens eager for investment dollars to offset economic peripherality. Second, Australia's housing boom has inflated the Tasmanian property market and some Tasmanians have been pushed out of the market altogether (Tasmanian Council of Social Services (TasCOSS), 2005). As elaborated below, others are gravely concerned about what may happen to island life if coastal land continues to be privatized and alienated.

Located on the eastern shore of the Derwent River in the capital city of Hobart, Ralphs Bay has been the subject of major protests about development in Tasmania between 2003 and the present, after which Lang Walker Corporation temporarily withdrew its proposal.[7] During the period profoundly sovereigntist and highly spatialized sentiments have been articulated by key protesters against the corporation, sentiments that re-inscribe Tasmania's island status and certain values of social equity that have underpinned the national imaginary since federation:

> the beach is our birthright as citizens of this island continent. At the ocean's edge we are all equal whatever our station in life, wherever we have come from. The laconic, easy going aspects of our national character have been shaped in part by the love of sand, sunshine and saltwater. We take it for granted that our coastline belongs to no one and it belongs to every one of us...It is our true common wealth.
>
> (O'Connor, 2004, no page number)

Neales refers to Tasmania's position in the 1990s, when it was "haemorrhaging economically, socially and demographically" (2005, p. 28), and describes how, after 1998, it began aggressively to pursue international investment dollars, with the result that "80% of Tasmanians now feel confident about the future. A place where there is a sense of excitement. Where we are no longer the butt of jokes, but are now the leaders" (Lennon, in Neales, 2005, p. 28).

Such optimism does not preclude the possibility that the New Tasmania is much like the old, described by Tasmanian and island scholar Peter Hay as follows: "if this government's New Tasmania is...about record investments in forestry, mineral extraction, urban coastal development and attracting new industry at any cost, then actually it is an old Tasmania of the sixties and seventies, and not a New Tasmania at all" (Hay, in Neales, 2005, p. 32a). During those decades Tasmanian governments and the Hydro Electric Commission, among others, were engaged in what has become known as hydro-industrialization – massive infrastructure projects involving the construction of dams in pristine wilderness areas. Walker (1999) suggests that such activities are symptomatic of 'statist developmentalism', the persistence, in policy, of which is aided by particular features in Australian government, not least among them "the political relationship of granter and grantee [which] has the effect of distorting project evaluation away from economic and ecological rationality towards political [rationality]" (Walker, 1999, p. 38). For Walker, statist developmentalism in Tasmania has been especially parasitic.

In this light it is ironic that Tasmania is seen as special for its remarkable natural heritage, and for a population already characterized by an "unusually high proportion of writers, artists and artisans" (Neales, 2005, p. 32b). She quotes one such figure, the Tasmanian writer and publisher Lindsay Tuffin, who suggests that Premier Bacon:

> [misunderstood] why locals love their island state... [and thought that] an unspoken 'pact'... has been smashed by government... [a pact that explains]... why many highly skilled professionals – 'the creative class' – stayed in Tasmania, with its lower wages and higher living costs... you put up with Tasmania's dark gothic underbelly and less pay and fewer jobs, because you had access to these wonderful spots. [But the boom means that]... ordinary Tasmanians have been locked out... by this other big business vision of Tasmania of the Bacon – Lennon government.
>
> (Tuffin, in Neales, 2005, pp. 32a – b)

For Tuffin, like Flanagan before him, Tasmanians and their uniquely *placed* ways of life are at stake. To open Tasmania for business in the manner planned, to elide the isolation factor, is to risk all.

Neales' article generated at least two further responses from the different perspectives of the development divide. One appeared in a major national financial broadsheet and was by the Chief Executive Officer of the Tourism Council of Tasmania, Daniel Leesong. His is a defence of the New Tasmania and the value of tourism developments to the state, and it questions the elitist nostalgia of those who would hold Tasmania back (Leesong, 2005). The other was a feature in Tasmania's *Island* magazine by 'ex-pat' Tasmanian writer, Natasha Cica. Hers, in contrast, was a lamentation on 'Turbo Tassie', an island exposed to the over-drive of globalization whose various factions had been struggling over such issues for generations (Cica, 2005, p. 10). As one of those who left the island because of the practices of 'Old Tasmania', she observed that:

> Tasmania's political battles are not just internecine, they're intimate, and frequently incestuous... Reasons for this have included Tasmania's unusually small number of distinct family bloodlines and *the island's peculiar and extreme geographical isolation from real centres of population, political and economic power.* This paradoxical and parochial tolerance is the upside of... a sentimental tribalism born of living at the edge of the Western world, and near the bottom of its heap... [T]hings seem to be changing, now, even as some stay the same [and] Tasmania's now part of the wider world as never before [but]... I don't like a lot of the look, smell and taste of New Tasmania because it's making Tasmania look, smell and taste more like everywhere else.
>
> (Cica, 2005, pp. 11 – 14, emphasis added)

FINAL REMARKS

Earlier I observed that intergovernmental relations in federal states can sometimes be typified by cooperative contest between and among national and sub-national jurisdictions, as each and all strive for a commonwealth of increase. At the same time internal relations between sub-national governments and their citizens can be difficult, and this can be particularly pronounced where the dynamics of the global marketplace affect local attachments to place. I also suggested that understanding how such relations influence our being in place also requires comprehending the outcomes of particular forms of conduct and regimes of truth, and the spatialization of governmental thought – especially that which privileges isomorphism.

In examining such matters I asked: how are Tasmanians using the isolated and island status of the jurisdiction as resources to negotiate the direction of development – and of tourism and property development above all? What does the creation of the New Tasmania mean in the context of globalization's homogenizing tendencies? What lessons might be afforded to the study of sub-national island jurisdictions from this case? Some final observations related to these questions are now possible.

First, islands are important analytic categories in the study of governance and the spatialization of governmental thought. Sub-national island jurisdictions are also important and generally neglected categories in this task. There may be much to learn about globalization and its effects on island life by studying the resources that island peoples bring to bear in negotiating their real-and-imagined futures among themselves, with 'siblings' and 'parents', and with others beyond the sovereign state.

Second, in Australia the use of intergovernmental agreements on the distribution of Commonwealth funds to sub-national jurisdictions is based in part on so-called physical asymmetries and disabilities. Among these disabilities, the idea of isolation provides significant dividends to Tasmania, just as smallness and peripherality do to the ultra-peripheral regions of, for example, the European Union. In this calculus the Bass Strait – a powerful icon of the state's separation and island status – is a significant mechanism for the flow of funds and tourists. Isolation is also used in paradoxical fashion in marketing the state to national and international investors: explicitly as a burden now overcome in terms of transport infrastructure and fiscal equalization payments; and as metonymous for the best that islands have to offer. Yet there are those in Tasmania – not least among them significant members of the endogenous 'creative class' – who suggest that to open the New Tasmania to business and to share (and perhaps even sell) its isolated splendour is to expose to great risk the Tasmanian way of life. Identifying this differential deployment of 'islandness' and isolation pinpoints significant contradictions in the rhetorics of governance in Tasmania that provide lessons about the spatialization of governmental thought and the ways in which globalization is understood, accommodated and resisted.

Acknowledgements

This paper has benefited greatly from discussions with Godfrey Baldacchino, University of Prince Edward Island in Canada, David Milne in Malta, and Richard Herr, Stewart Williams and Andrew Harwood at the University of Tasmania. Research informing the paper was supported by an Australian Research Council Discovery Grant (DP0342802) funded between 2003 and 2005.

Notes

1. The Commonwealth provides SPPs to influence "State expenditure priorities to satisfy national objectives...[and to] achieve performance equalisation" (Searle, 2002, p. 15).

Untied GRGs comprise the "single largest avenue through which financial capacity is transferred" (Searle, 2002, p. 17). The commonwealth also transfers around AU$1265 million each year to municipal governments via State Grants Commissions.

2. Fiscal imbalance among states varies from around 75% (Tasmania) to 114% (New South Wales) of the per capita Australian average. Variance arises from differentials in payroll tax, land revenue, stamp duty on conveyances and mining revenue.

3. The CGC is a small, independent advisory body established in 1933; it has no constitutional status and is an integral element of Australia's federal structure. Members are appointed by the commonwealth, after discussion with the states which have an informal right of veto over the three or four nominees. Its first task is to decide what range of state-type services and areas of revenue-raising should be considered in the equalization assessments; and that is the subject of much jockeying (Searle, 2002, pp. 18–20).

4. Western Australia is 'islanded' from the southeastern hub of population and economic activity by desert, as is the Northern Territory. Other characteristics of statehood have variously affected other sub-national jurisdictions (Brown, 2004; Kline, 2002; Mathews, no date).

5. The TFES gives assistance to those shipping eligible non-bulk goods by sea. Different criteria of eligibility exist for ex-Tasmania and ex-mainland goods, and for people in special categories recognized in federal fiscal equalization considerations apparent through isolation. Consideration is given to those competing for prize money in sporting events, to professional entertainers, and to Tasmanian horse breeders. I do not elaborate further on the TFES in this chapter.

6. On 5 June 2006, following successive months of declining patronage, the Premier, Paul Lennon, announced the sale of the *Spirit III*. The Chairman of the TT Line, Denis Roger, noted that the purchase price of $111 million paid by European company Corsica Ferries was $6 million greater than the original paid in Tasmania (*Courier Mail*, 2006; *The Age*, 2006).

7. On 2 September 2005, Walker Corporation announced that it would not proceed with the development at Ralphs Bay, and it was widely suggested that the withdrawal was partly prompted by concerns about its unpopularity and possible effects on the looming State election. Following Labor's return to power in March 2006, on 6 July, the development's possibility re-emerged when the Premier tabled a bill to give the proposal status as a project of State significance. The bill was passed, and the Corporation invited to table an integrated impact assessment in due course. As of late May 2008, it had yet to do so. In the same month, Premier Lennon resigned from politics and was replaced by his Deputy, David Barttett. See also Stratford (in press).

References

Addison, A. (2005) *Sea Programs. Bass Strait Passenger Vehicle Equalisation Scheme* (Canberra: Australian Government. Department of Transport and Regional Services, Maritime Branch, Maritime and Land Transport Division), available at http://www.dotars.gov.au/transport/programs/maritime/bass/index.aspx, accessed 14 November.

The Age (2006) Sydney to Devonport ferry sold to Europe, The Age Company Ltd, available at: http://www.theage.com.au/news/National/Sydney-to-Devonport-ferry-sold-to-Europe/2006/07/04/1151778925884. html#, accessed 2 September 2006.

Anckar, D. (2002) Why are small island states democracies?, *The Round Table*, 365, pp. 375–390.

Armstrong, D. and Stratford, E. (2004) Partnerships for local sustainability and local governance in a Tasmanian settlement, *Local Environment*, 8(6), pp. 541–560.

Armstrong, H. W. and Read, R. (2003) The determinants of economic growth of small States, *The Round Table*, 368, pp. 99–124.

Australian Bureau of Statistics (2005) *Tasmania at a Glance. ABS Catalogue No. 1305.6* (Canberra: Australian Bureau of Statistics).

Australian Government. Bureau of Transport and Regional Economics (2004) *Bass Strait Passenger Vehicle Equalisation Scheme. BTRE Monitoring Report No. 7 2002–03* (Canberra: Australian Government. Department of Transport and Regional Services. BTRE).

Australian Government. Commonwealth Grants Commission (2002) *Discussion Paper CGC 2002/43. Isolation* (Canberra: Commonwealth Grants Commission).

Australian Government. Commonwealth Grants Commission (2003) *Discussion Paper CGC 2003/5. Treatment of Economic Development Assistance* (Canberra: Commonwealth Grants Commission).

Australian Government. Commonwealth Grants Commission (2005) *Report on State Revenue Sharing Relativities* (Commonwealth Grants Commission, Canberra).

Bacon, The Hon. J. (2003) Building a culture of peace through tourism – a global perspective, paper presented at the *Second Global Summit on Peace through Tourism*, Geneva, 6 February.

Baldacchino, G. (2004a) The coming of age of island studies, *Tijdschrift voor Economische en Sociale Geografie*, 95(3), pp. 272–283.

Baldacchino, G. (2004b) Autonomous but not sovereign: a review of island sub-nationalism, *Canadian Review of Studies in Nationalism*, 31(1–2), pp. 77–89.

Baldacchino, G. (2006) Innovative development strategies from non-sovereign island jurisdictions? A global review of economic policy and governance practices, *World Development*, 34(5), pp. 852–867.

Bertram, I. G. and Watters, R. F. (1985) The MIRAB economy in South Pacific microstates, *Pacific Viewpoint*, 26(3), pp. 497–519.

Brown, A. J. (2004) One continent, two federalisms: rediscovering the original meanings of Australian federal ideas, *Australian Journal of Political Science*, 39(3), pp. 485–504.

Carlson, A. (1998) *Maritime Programs – Bass Strait Passenger Vehicle Equalisation Scheme. Monitoring Report No. 1* (Canberra: Australian Government. Department of Transport and Regional Services. Sea, Air and Safety Branch), available at: www.dotars.gov.au/transprog/maritime/bspves_mon1.aspx, accessed 14 November.

Cau, L. (1999) Islands within islands: inner isolation in Sardinia and Ireland, in E. Biagini and B. Hoyle (Eds), *Insularity and Development: International Perspectives on Islands*, pp. 322–357 (London: Pinter).

Chapman, R. J. K. (1982) Regionalism, national development and governmental institutional arrangements: regions as moderating institutions, *Occasional Paper No. 24*, Centre for Research on Federal Financial Relations (Canberra: The Australian National University).

Cica, N. (2005) Turbo Tassie, *Island*, 101, pp. 6–17.

Courier Mail (2006) Ferry set to float away, 29 August, available at: http://www.news.com.au/couriermail/story/0,23739,20280657-953,00.html#, accessed 2 September 2006.

Dean, M. (1999) *Governmentality: Power and Rule in Modern Society* (London: Sage Publications).

Deloughrey, E. (2004) Island ecologies and Caribbean literatures, *Tijdschrift voor Economische en Sociale Geografie*, 95(3), pp. 298–310.

Eslake, S. (2004) Tasmania's economic recovery: is it the 'Real McCoy'?, paper presented to a symposium at the *Tasmanian Economic Forum*, 10 December, Hobart.

Flanagan, R. (2004) The selling-out of Tasmania, *The Age*, Melbourne, 22 July.

Hache, J.-D. (1998) Towards a political approach to the island question, in G. Baldacchino and R. Greenwood (Eds), *Competing Strategies of Socio-Economic Development for Small Islands*, pp. 31–68 (Charlottetown, Prince Edward Island: Institute for Island Studies, University of Prince Edward Island).

Kline, J. M. (2002) Australian federalism confronts globalisation: a new challenge at the centenary, *Australian Journal of Public Administration*, 61(3), pp. 27–37.

Leesong, D. (2005) Tasmania forges ahead on creative wave, *The Australian Financial Review*, 10 February, p. 59.

Lennon, The Hon. P. (2005) *Ministerial Statement. Future of the TT-Line, in particular, Spirit of Tasmania III and the Service between Sydney and Devonport*, Tasmanian Parliament, House of Assembly, Hobart, 15 March.

Mathews, R. (1977) Philosophical, political and economic conflicts in Australian federalism, paper presented to the Institute of Public Administration of Canada, Victoria, British Columbia.

Mathews, R. (no date) Fiscal equalisation in Australia: the methodology of the Grants Commission, Occasional Paper of the Centre for Research on Federal Financial Relations, Australian National University.

Neales, S. (2005) State of flux, *Australian Financial Review Magazine*, 28 January, pp. 28–32.

New South Wales Legislative Council Hansard (2004) Save Orange Grove Bill, Second Reading, 9 September, p. 10582.

O'Connor, C. (2004) 'We shall fight them on the mudflats if it comes to it'. Ralphs Bay is critical for all Tasmanians, *The Tasmanian Conservationist*, No. 295, available at: http://www.tct.org.au/n34c.htm, accessed 10 November.

Péron, F. (2004) The contemporary lure of the island, *Tijdschrift voor Economische en Sociale Geografie*, 95(3), pp. 326–339.

Richardson, B. W. (2005) *Longitude and Empire: How Captain Cook's Voyages Changed the World* (Vancouver: University of British Columbia Press).

Rose, N. (2003) Governing, in *Powers of Freedom: Reframing Political Thought*, pp. 15–60 (Cambridge: Cambridge University Press).

Searle, R. (2002) *Federal Fiscal Relations in Australia – 2001* (Torino: International Centre for Economic Research).

Stratford, E. (2003) Editorial – Flows and boundaries: small island discourses and the challenge of sustainability, community and local environments, *Local Environment*, 8(5), pp. 495–499.

Stratford, E. (2006) Technologies of agency and performance: Tasmania Together and the constitution of harmonious island identity, *Geoforum*, 37, pp. 273–286.

Stratford, E. (in press) Belonging as a resource: the case of Ralphs Bay Tasmania and the local politics of place, *Environment and Planning A*.

Stratford, E., Armstrong, D. and Jaskolski, M. (2003) Relational spaces and the geopolitics of community participation in two Tasmanian local governments: a case for agonistic pluralism?, *Transactions of the Institute of British Geographers*, NS28, 4, pp. 461–472.

Swenden, W. and Beaufays, J. (2005) Socio-cultural identities and asymmetrical federalism, paper presented at the International Conference on Federalism, European Parliament, Brussels, 3–5 March.

Tasmanian Council of Social Services (TasCOSS) (2005) Summary guide to the TasCOSS budget priorities statement 2005–06, available at: www.tascoss.org.au/uploads/BPS_2005-06_Summary.pdf, accessed 16 November.

Tasmania Government. Department of Treasury and Finance (2005) *Budget Information. Future of Spirit of Tasmania III and the Sydney–Devonport Service* (Hobart: Tasmanian Government).

Tasmanian Government. Tourism Tasmania (2004) *Tourism Development Kit: Product Analysis, Market Insights, Opportunities* (Hobart: Tourism Tasmania).

Walker, K. J. (1999) Statist development in Australia, in K. Crowley and K. J. Walker (Eds), *Australian Environmental Policy 2: Studies in Decline and Devolution*, pp. 22–44 (Sydney: University of New South Wales Press).

8 Unitary state, devolution, autonomy, secession: state building and nation building in Bougainville, Papua New Guinea

Yash Ghai and Anthony J. Regan

SCENE SETTING

There are often difficulties in accommodating the interests of minority nationalities within nation-states. The proliferation of states created by decolonization has magnified such problems. Colonial borders often included groups with emerging identities, and the problems of fostering national cohesion within borders encompassing such diversity has sometimes been especially intense.

Various forms of federalist and similar arrangements for the territorial distribution of power have been employed in efforts to accommodate the concerns of ethnic and other identity groups (Watts, 1999; Ghai, 2000; 2002a). Implementation and operation of such arrangements can be far from easy in postcolonial states, where capacity and resources are often limited. Pressures for asymmetrical arrangements for nationalist minorities can magnify such problems, as they tend to be seen as "an incentive for spiralling devolution, fuelling secession, catalysing the eventual implosion of the state" (Baldacchino, 2006).

Island sub-national jurisdictions offer an instructive distinct category for examining the ways in which tensions between nation-states and sub-national units are managed (Baldacchino, 2006). Indeed, as Baldacchino points out, islands represent "quintessential platforms for nation states...[as] finite island geography smoothens the nurturing of a sense of identity that is contiguous with territory" (Baldacchino, 2006), a perception that would raise expectations of pressure for nation-state status on the part of non-sovereign island territories.

In fact, over the past 20 years that has *not* been happening – most sub-national island autonomies have not been seeking nation-state status. McElroy and Mahoney (1999) suggest that in large part this is because there are substantial economic advantages to small non-sovereign island units remaining part of a larger state. Many island autonomies have developed innovative economic policy and governance practices that enable them to escape the economic vulnerability that would tend to go together with either full sovereignty or the absence of autonomy (Baldacchino, 2004). The economic practices involve powers over key aspects of finance; natural resources; access (through transport); free movement of persons; and tourism policy. The creative political practices involve high levels of jurisdictional prerogative; articulation of national identity; defence and promotion of minority rights; and para-diplomacy. Through use of such devices, asserts Baldacchino, island autonomies can develop high standards of living and levels of self-rule, the outcome being that "there hardly appears to be any sentiment for independence among non-sovereign island territories today...[and while] there are a number of peoples waiting in the proverbial wings to declare their statehood...only one of these is an island" (Baldacchino, 2004, p. 78)

That exception is Bougainville, a reluctant part of the southwest Pacific state of Papua New Guinea (PNG). If other secessionist situations, such as the Indonesian examples of Papua and Aceh, and the Philippines case of Mindanao, are also classified as non-sovereign island territories, then the detail of Baldacchino's classification can be contested, but not his basic point about the tendency of many such territories to explore innovative alternatives to secession. The question then arises as to why Bougainville and other island secessionist cases are not also exploring such alternative strategies. One factor that may be of significance is that, unlike many of the island autonomies considered by Baldacchino, Bougainville and the other divergent cases just mentioned do not involve autonomy arising from a colonial relationship (as, for example, with the former colonial territories of New Zealand and the USA or the continuing Pacific island colonial territories of France). It is in the special circumstances of making choices about the management of continuing or modifying such relationships that the autonomy arrangements and the innovative strategies have developed.

In the Bougainville case nationalism was first asserted in the years leading to PNG's 1975 independence from Australia (Griffin, 1972; 1973; Mamak and Bedford, 1974). The emergence of several 'micro-nationalist' movements (May, 1982), including one in Bougainville, was among the complex factors that had to be taken into account in making choices for PNG's independence constitution. PNG had a weak state and fragile administration and no national identity to help foster national cohesion. Its constitution would have to deal with both state building and nation building. But how was this to be done?

This chapter examines the tensions between various approaches used since PNG's independence in efforts to respond to minority nationalist pressures, the initial choice being between a unitary state and a devolved state with substantial self-government for territorially based communities. The particular focus is Bougainville, the one part of PNG where sub-national identity has not been accommodated by devolution. Rather, there have been two secession attempts, one in 1975 and the other from 1988 to 1989 as part of a bitter and bloody civil war. The latter conflict was settled in 2001 only by PNG agreeing to both asymmetrical autonomy and keeping open the possibility of independence through a constitutionally guaranteed but deferred referendum on the issue. The autonomy arrangements have been in their early stages of implementation since 2006.

The analysis addresses the vexed question of whether asymmetrical autonomy, in particular, inevitably creates pressure for progress towards independence. It also considers the extent to which the economic policy and governance practices identified by Baldacchino have been available to and used by Bougainville.

PNG AND BOUGAINVILLE

Bougainville is an island autonomy within a nation-state comprising half of one of the world's largest islands, and thousands of other islands of various sizes. The PNG 'mainland' consists of the eastern half of New Guinea and, to the east, includes the three large islands of New Britain, New Ireland and Bougainville, each with numerous associated small islands. With well over 800 distinct languages, PNG is a country of unparalleled linguistic and cultural diversity. Bougainville's roughly 200 000 people (about 4% of PNG's population of more than five million) reflect that same diversity, speaking 25 distinct languages and many more sub-languages and dialects (Tryon, 2005).

PNG is a creation of the late colonial era. The UK and Germany took control of the southern (Papua) and northern (German New Guinea) parts, respectively, in 1884. Australia assumed control of Papua in 1906, and ousted Germany from New Guinea at the beginning of World War I, later taking a League of Nations mandate over the former German territory, including Bougainville. Papua and New Guinea were administered jointly only from 1946 until PNG's independence in September 1975. Governing through a highly centralized, bureaucratic system (Tordoff and Watts, 1974; CPC, 1974; Conyers, 1976), Australia had limited objectives (largely concerned with its own security and extraction of some resources). Large parts of the territory remained almost untouched by either colonial administration or the market until the late colonial period, Christian missions bringing more change to the lives of perhaps most communities than either state or market. Pre-colonial social structures persisted, most people living in groups of no more than a few hundred. Internal communications were poor, there was little mobility of people or goods, and little political or economic integration. Thus, little sense of a common identity developed among PNG's disparate communities.

Bougainville is a group of islands about 1000 kilometres east of the mainland PNG capital of Port Moresby, close to the western islands of the neighbouring country of Solomon Islands, with whose inhabitants the islanders share appearance, language groups and culture. The two main islands are Bougainville and the much smaller Buka, separated by a narrow sea passage. Cultural and linguistic differences and uneven development during and after the colonial era have been among factors contributing to differing identities and economic interests among Bougainvilleans. In particular, many groups in Buka and on the east coast of Bougainville adjacent to the colonial administrative centre and plantations have had much greater access than others to education, employment and opportunities for economic advancement, a source of inequality that contributes to tensions and divisions (Ogan, 1996; Nash, 2001; Regan, 2005b; Tanis, 2005). On the other hand, a sense of identity separate from the rest of PNG emerged during the twentieth century, the primary marker being the distinctive very dark skin colour of most Bougainvilleans (Griffin, 1972; 1973; Mamak and Bedford, 1974; Nash and Ogan, 1990; Oliver, 1991).

Identity was politicized by grievances about colonial neglect, compounded by the imposition by the Australian colonial administration of the operationalization by Bougainville Copper Ltd (BCL) of one of the world's largest copper and gold mines at Panguna in central Bougainville (Bedford and Mamak, 1977; Connell, 1991; Oliver, 1991; Regan, 1998a; 2003; Denoon, 2000). Bougainvilleans perceived the mine as being established for the economic benefit of the rest of PNG, with Bougainville carrying the social and environmental costs, but receiving little mine revenue. BCL's total earnings in its 17 years of operation (April 1972 to May 1989) were US$4.6 billion, which generated $1.9 billion in revenue, of which just 5.63% went to Bougainville: 4.27% (mostly mineral royalties) to Bougainville's provincial government (see below) and 1.36% to Bougainvillean owners of land leased for mining purposes (rents, compensation and a small share of royalty payments) (Connell, 1991; Quodling, 1991, p. 55; Regan, 2003, p. 139).

From the late 1960s, with PNG's independence from Australia approaching, there was growing talk in Bougainville of possible independence from PNG (Griffin, 1972; 1973; Ghai and Regan, 2000, pp. 244–247). Educated leaders mainly used talk of independence in efforts to mobilize support for more modest goals of autonomy and increased mining revenue. Yet, in the process, many Bougainvilleans increasingly saw independence as a solution to a wide range of social problems, and as a real possibility.

A UNITARY OR A DEVOLVED STATE?

In the lead-up to an independence resulting more from Australian responses to emerging international pressure than from internal demands, people in some areas of PNG sought a significant degree of autonomy from the unknown emerging state through local organizations and institutions (Conyers, 1976; Ballard, 1981; May, 1982). Nowhere was the demand for local autonomy stronger than in Bougainville.

At the same time there was strong support for the opposing view that PNG's diversity would best be kept unified through a continuation of the unitary arrangements of the colonial state. This approach was preferred by the departing colonial regime and key leaders of PNG's first indigenous government, in power after the last election to the colonial legislature (1972), and with self-governing status from 1973.

In the independence constitution-making process (1972–75), two contrary paradigms emerged, each claiming to be best suited to the needs of building national identity and unity.[1] The main support for the local autonomy approach came from the Constitutional Planning Committee (CPC), a committee of the colonial legislature under the leadership of a young member of the legislature from Bougainville, John Momis. The CPC developed proposals for the independence constitution presented in a long and detailed report in mid-1974 (CPC, 1974). It saw local autonomy as both accommodating ethnic identity (thereby contributing to national unity) and improving the efficiency and responsiveness of the hitherto inefficient centralized colonial state by encouraging popular participation (Wolfers *et al.*, 1982, p. 286; Ghai and Regan, 1992, pp. 8–52; Ballard, 1981). The CPC was in part responding to pressure from Bougainville (Griffin *et al.*, 1979; Ballard, 1981; Ghai and Regan, 1992), where from 1973 the national government reluctantly conceded limited autonomy by recognizing a Bougainville Interim Provincial Government.

No one seriously pushed for federalism, however, largely because there were no strong ethnic or territorial groupings – other than Bougainville – demanding territorial autonomy. Yet the CPC's conceptualization of devolution entrenched in the constitution came close to a form of quasi-federalism.[2]

After initial ambivalence the government, under Chief Minister Michael Somare, ultimately opposed the CPC proposals (on the grounds of unity, efficiency and economic rationality) and in July 1975 persuaded the colonial legislature (sitting as a constituent assembly) to reject them (Conyers, 1976; Ballard, 1981; Ghai and Regan, 1992). This precipitated a major crisis in Bougainville. The choice between a unitary or a devolved state thus emerged as the most contentious constitutional issue.

DEVOLUTION, 1976–2001[3]

On the rejection of constitutionally protected devolution Bougainville declared its separate independence from PNG on 1 September 1975, days before PNG's Independence Day. Failure to secure international recognition and concern about dangers of violence encouraged Bougainville leaders to negotiate, with John Momis (who resigned from the national legislature in support of Bougainville secession) playing a moderating role (Ballard, 1981; Griffin and Togolo, 1997; Momis, 2005, pp. 312–314). A central government under its first prime minister, Michael Somare, who knew John Momis well, was both conscious of the risk of other areas in the fragile new nation following Bougainville's example and concerned about possible loss of revenue from the mine. It was thus also under pressure to resolve its differences with Bougainville. Six months of negotiations concluded with an August 1976 agreement on constitutionally entrenched autonomy arrangements for Bougainville. A major question, however, was whether autonomy should be asymmetrical – with many powers and resources reserved to Bougainville – or symmetrical, with arrangements negotiated by Bougainville being extended to PNG's other 18 provinces.

Even in the lead-up to independence there had been concern that special arrangements for Bougainville would be divisive for PNG, and the concessions towards autonomy secured by Bougainville had been generalized to other provinces (Conyers, 1976; Ballard, 1981; Ghai and Regan, 1992). However, in 1976 the negotiations were truly bilateral, and Bougainville argued for special arrangements. PNG's negotiators were initially open to the proposal and as a result conceded significantly greater provincial powers than would otherwise have been the case. But, as final details were negotiated, fears of special arrangements being divisive again dominated, and PNG reserved the right to extend the concessions to all the provinces. Bougainville agreed reluctantly, mainly because of awareness that amendments to the national constitution would require a high degree of support in parliament, where representation was still seen in provincial terms.

In the end the constitutional amendment provided for an almost completely uniform system of devolution. The main exception involved distribution of mining royalties that in practice applied only in Bougainville (at least until other major mines began to operate elsewhere in PNG from 1984) (Axline, 1986; Ghai and Regan, 1992, pp. 234–259). This ensured a unique degree of fiscal independence for the North Solomons Provincial Government (NSPG) – a name chosen to emphasize Bougainville's links to communities in the neighbouring country of Solomon Islands.

The devolution arrangements were even more quasi-federal than the original CPC proposals on which they drew. The legal provisions were contained in the constitution, in the form of principles, with an organic law (the Organic Law on Provincial Government) setting out details. Organic laws are as difficult to amend or repeal as the constitution, and so devolution enjoyed considerable legal protection.

The Organic Law distributed legislative powers through two lists (Ghai and Regan, 1992, pp. 33–38, 135–194): a short one of 'primarily' provincial subjects and a long one of concurrent powers. In the former, provincial laws prevailed over national laws, which could be made only if a province had not made an exhaustive law on a subject in this list. For concurrent subjects, national law prevailed over provincial law, but national laws could be made only on a matter 'of national interest' and 'to the extent that the matter is of national interest'. Another principle qualified the scope of national laws on concurrent subjects. Since, at the start of devolution, there were national laws on most such subjects, a provincial government desiring to make a law in a field occupied by national law could request repeal of national government law in relation to the province to the extent necessary to permit provincial law to be made on matters of provincial interest. The presumption was that the national government would oblige, unless there was a pressing national interest in having central legislation on the subject. Subjects not listed stayed with the national government. Thus the system, while maintaining the ultimate authority of one or the other level of government in respect of every subject, was intended to provide considerable flexibility.

Provincial government structures (Ghai and Regan, 1992, pp. 77–134) were required to meet basic criteria set out in the Organic Law – notably an elected legislature – but some latitude in choice of structures was provided for in provincial constitutions made through consultative processes. The effective working of the complex provisions for fiscal arrangements (guaranteed grants and some exclusively provincial taxes), the allocation of legislative authority and the division of administrative powers and staff were all intended to depend on cooperation between governments. Such cooperation was to be secured through basic principles and procedures (such as the obligation of a government at one level to give notice to government/s at the other level of its legislative proposals, and a general obligation for consultation), and through intergovernmental institutions. The Premiers' Council was the main institution. Bringing together the prime minister and senior ministers with premiers of provinces, its primary function was to discuss fiscal policies and transfers, legislative powers of provinces, intergovernmental cooperation and the resolution of disputes. To avoid excessive legalism, disputes had to be resolved through negotiations or mediation, if possible, before they could be taken to a court.

This description comes close to a model of cooperative federalism or devolution. Within broad principles it provided a framework for continuing negotiations, especially on the gradual transfer of powers from the centre under the two legislative lists, and on the allocation of resources. It put a premium on trust and good faith; but also on capacity to handle complex institutions and negotiations.

Implementation started well, with considerable support from the national government. Popular consultation to prepare provincial constitutions heightened a consciousness of a common identity and future. The pace was set by Bougainville, whose leaders brought great energy and planning to developing the NSPG. Tensions between the national government and provinces keen on autonomy (including Bougainville) seemed to be getting resolved. By 1979 all 19 provincial governments had been established (Ghai and Regan, 1992, pp. 49–75). Devolution seemed to have transformed, constructively, the PNG political scene. State building and nation building appeared indeed to go hand in hand.

But this rosy picture did not last, the most critical reason being that the intended fluidity of political power gave way to the reality of consolidation of the central state apparatus (Ghai, 1997; Ghai and Regan, 1992; 2001). The dominant position of the state in relation to the PNG economy meant that political and bureaucratic access to the state was the main means of accumulation of wealth. The central state remained the primary site of power, attracting most leading politicians. But at the same time national politicians resented the competition for powers and resources from provincial leaders. Moreover, few provincial governments operated effectively and they thus failed to mobilize strong popular support (Ghai and Regan, 2000). Nor were provincial governments able to cooperate effectively through the intergovern-mental mechanisms to apply pressure to the national government to transfer increasing powers and resources. More importantly, capacity for policy and administration was weak at all levels of government (in large part because of the failure of the Australian colonial administration to develop an educated elite). Provincial governments made little use of the legislative powers available to them. Resources of most provincial governments decreased rather than increased.

By the early 1980s relations between the national government and provincial governments were often strained. The national government paid little more than lip service to aspects of the machinery that it could not ignore. Arrangements for suspension of provincial governments were amended in 1983, removing important procedural safeguards against abuse. Those powers were subsequently used extensively against provincial governments and often for purely political reasons.

The NSPG was one of few exceptions to the gloomy picture (Ghai and Regan, 1992; Griffin and Togolo, 1997), with its strong base in community support mobilized by the identity politics of the 1970s and its comparatively strong revenue base. In the 1970s the central priorities of Bougainville's elite leadership had been to achieve autonomy and a share of mining revenue. The 1976 decentralization arrangements and the economic opportunities available to them ensured that members of the elite were accommodated. Hence the NSPG could manage relations with the national government within the framework of the constitutional arrange-ments, admittedly with some tensions. For the most part it was fully occupied with maintaining basic services, managing its capital expenditure programme and gradually building capacity from the very weak local base left by the centralized colonial administration. Until the early to mid-1980s it was unable to put much effort into developing its own policies (Ghai and Regan, 2000).

In terms of the kinds of innovative strategies used by island autonomies to bolster their positions *vis-à-vis* the central government, the creative political capacities identified by Baldacchino (2006) were not readily available to Bougainville. It did not already have established high levels of jurisdictional prerogative, and was instead gradually working to develop these. It was still in the early stages of articulation of national identity. The defence and promotion of minority rights was not a strategy readily available in PNG, where all language and culture groups are small minorities. Para-diplomacy had not been developed. Much the same was true of the five economic strategies highlighted by Baldacchino (Baldacchino, 2006), in large part because the powers of the NSPG under the constitutional devolution arrangements were quite limited. It did not have control of key aspects of finance, such as banking and insurance, and had limited tax powers. It had virtually no control over land and natural resources policy. It did not control access through power over transport. It had almost no control over movement of persons, and so could not control the influx of large numbers of persons from elsewhere in PNG, attracted by economic opportunities in Bougainville, often squatting on customary land. The many outsiders were seen by Bougainvilleans as both undermining their traditional authority and culture, and a major contributing factor to growing law and order problems. Mining and agriculture being the major economic sectors, tourism was not a major concern in Bougainville. Overall, the NSPG had limited power to respond to the ongoing tensions associated with the unresolved grievances of ordinary people over the impacts of the mine and the influx of outsiders, something that was a contributing factor to the violent conflict that developed in 1988–89 (Regan, 1998a, 1998b; Premdas, 1998; Ghai and Regan, 2000; Kauona, 2001; Tanis, 2005).

CONFLICT AND PEACE PROCESS, 1988–2001

Neither the NSPG nor the national government expected that such tensions would contribute to a civil war in Bougainville from late 1988.[4] The conflict was precipitated by inter-generational disputes within communities owning land where the mine was located over distribution of mine revenues payable to landowners. Frustration on the part of younger landowners with links to disgruntled Bougainvillean mine workers led to destruction of mine property. Mainly intended to create pressure for increased benefits, this action instead led to generalized violent responses by PNG forces. This violence acted as a catalyst for a broader rebellion led by a key figure among the younger mine lease landowners, Francis Ona. Had the NSPG wielded power over land and mining, and possessed some ability to limit squatting on customary land by outsiders, the situation would probably have developed quite differently. But, as the rebellion gathered force in 1979, the NSPG, led by Joseph Kabui, the young premier from the mine lease area with close relationships with many of the leaders of the rebellion, was in a difficult position, suspected by both the national government and the rebels.

Political support for secession was mobilized around both the long-held Bougainvillean grievances concerning the mine and Bougainvillean identity. However, the secessionist leadership, having made a unilateral declaration of independence soon after the withdrawal of PNG forces from Bougainville in March 1990, largely lost control of the situation soon after that, as internal Bougainville conflict undermined what would have otherwise been fairly broad support for secession. It was both civil war among Bougainvilleans and the fight between the pro-secessionist Bougainvillean faction and the national government that resulted in heavy loss of life and property, the breakdown of essential services, economic stagnation, missed educational opportunities for a whole generation, and the destruction of most of the impressive capacity of the provincial administration developed since the mid-1970s. The NSPG was suspended by the national government from mid-1990.

It would take too long to recite the causes and course of the complex conflict and its ending through a remarkable peace process beginning in mid-1997.[5] Rather, we have to jump to late 1998, when, active fighting having ceased, rival Bougainville factions began talks on reconciliation and resolving their differences. One faction was led by Joseph Kabui, who in the early 1990s had become the deputy to the rebel leader, Francis Ona. It advocated secession. The other faction, a coalition of groups supporting stronger autonomy within PNG, was led by John Momis, back in the national parliament ever since 1977. There was a third faction under Ona that refused to join the peace process, claiming that independence had already been achieved in 1990, but this group had limited popular support.

The compromise reached in advance of negotiations with PNG beginning in June 1999 involved those supporting independence dropping their demands for early independence and instead agreeing to deal with that issue through a referendum among Bougainvilleans on the question, but deferred to allow time for divided

Bougainvilleans to reconcile (Regan, 2002c). On the basis that those favouring integration would agree to back the holding of the referendum, the secessionists agreed to support the high autonomy for Bougainville preferred by the integrationists, a level of autonomy greatly in advance of the 1976 arrangements.

This latter demand alone was a strong call, for by now PNG had effectively dismantled the 1976 devolution scheme, with provinces having much reduced (and uniform) autonomy (May, 1997; 1999). From 1995 elected provincial governments had been replaced by bodies made up of members of the national legislature from the provinces, together with heads of local-level government, all holding provincial office *ex officio*. In large part the reform was possible because the provincial government in Bougainville, the area of strongest support for devolution, was suspended, and Bougainville embroiled in civil war (Ghai and Regan, 2000).

But the Bougainvilleans were in a strong negotiating position throughout the two years of talks that produced the Bougainville Peace Agreement of August 2001. The secessionists had held the upper hand militarily when the fighting ended in 1997, and retained arms and the capacity for disruption. Further, while the dissident Ona faction had limited support, its refusal to join the process limited the scope for compromise on the part of the Bougainville side to the negotiations, and added to the pressure on the PNG side. The nine years of conflict had involved a high cost for PNG in terms of impacts on the economy, damage to morale in the police and the army, and undermining the country's international human rights reputation. PNG was also under considerable international pressure to settle the conflict for purposes of regional stability. Moreover, it realized that the strong sense of grievance in Bougainville concerning the conflict required substantial concessions to be made if the conflict was to be resolved. It was also anxious to disarm the factions and remove weapons.

Agreement was reached on enhanced autonomy only by PNG conceding that the issue of independence would be kept alive and revisited through a referendum for Bougainvilleans on Bougainville's independence deferred for a minimum of 10 years and a maximum of 15 years after establishing the autonomous government for Bougainville. Both referendum and autonomy would be constitutionally guaranteed, provided arms held by the Bougainville factions were disposed of.

This time, the clear intention was that the new autonomy arrangements would apply only to Bougainville, which now therefore has a special status in the country: an asymmetry that may in turn spawn its own problems. But, for the time being, sufficient consensus was developed in the national cabinet and parliament for the extensive amendments to the national constitution to incorporate the 2001 Peace Agreement to be enacted early in 2002. In other ways too, considerable progress has been made towards its implementation.

ASYMMETRICAL AUTONOMY AND THE POSSIBILITY OF INDEPENDENCE, 2001 TO THE PRESENT

As with the 1976 arrangements, large parts of the 2001 Peace Agreement have been implemented through amendments to the national constitution and an Organic Law on Peace-building in Bougainville – Autonomous Bougainville Government and Bougainville Referendum. These provisions cannot be amended by the PNG parliament without agreement by the Bougainville legislature.

As for the nature of the enhanced autonomy now available to Bougainville, we can highlight here just a few aspects that enable comparisons with features of the 1976 arrangements summarized earlier. Only a small list of legislative powers in relation to Bougainville is reserved to the national government. Further, in the exercise of some of its powers (such as defence, foreign affairs and law and order), PNG is obliged to consult with Bougainville and to encourage its participation when Bougainville interests might be involved. In foreign affairs, for example, PNG may authorize Bougainville to enter into treaties with other states, and to have independent participation in international cultural or sporting activities. A long list of powers is made available to Bougainville, on an exclusive basis, which includes most subject areas likely to be covered by law, including power to establish a judiciary (subject to the ultimate appellate powers of the PNG Supreme Court), a public service and a police force. Bougainville has the right to initiate the process of transfer of powers from the national government by giving 12 months' notice, following which the two governments are required to cooperate to enable Bougainville to develop the capacity needed to exercise the power.

The financial arrangements do not, however, guarantee as much to Bougainville as did the 1976 arrangements, reflecting both the fiscal crisis facing the PNG government since the mid-1990s and the absence of mine revenues in Bougainville (the Panguna mine not having operated since 1989). On the other hand, autonomy is far higher in terms of both choice of Bougainville government structures and intergovernmental relations.

Concerning government structures, Bougainville now has its own constitution, drafted and adopted on behalf of its people by broadly representative bodies – a Bougainville Constitutional Commission and a Bougainville Constituent Assembly – and endorsed by PNG in December 2004. As authorized by the 2001 Peace Agreement and the PNG constitutional provisions implementing it, the Bougainville Constitution contains Bougainvilleans' choice of names for their government (Autonomous Bougainville Government – ABG) and for Bougainville (the Autonomous Region of Bougainville), both choices emphasizing a unique status, distinct from the provinces elsewhere in PNG. It also establishes an elected legislature, including three seats each reserved for women and former combatants. The ABG executive is headed by a directly elected president. Provision is made for a range of processes directed towards encouraging both accountability and close relations between the new government and the holders of customary authority in Bougainville society, and for a range of new institutions, most to be established in the future, when funding resources become available.

As for intergovernmental relations, a joint supervisory body with equal representation of both governments is responsible for overseeing the implementation of the autonomy arrangements and for being the first formal stage of a dispute settlement process. In contrast to the subordination of provinces to the centre under the previous system, powers to suspend provincial governments or withdraw powers from them do not apply to Bougainville, a major move towards a coordinate status.

It was possible to sell autonomy to Bougainville precisely because the 2001 agreement kept alive the option of secession through the provision for a deferred referendum. The reluctant acceptance by the national government of the referendum provisions was facilitated by the manner in which provision on the subject was hedged in the agreement. The referendum can be held only after specified conditions are met (weapons disposal achieved and good governance established and maintained). The Bougainville government can decide after all not to have a referendum, after consultation with the national government and by decision made in accordance with a process set out in the Bougainville Constitution (although the special majorities and consultative procedures laid down in that constitution make it unlikely that such a decision will ever be made). But, most importantly, the outcome of the referendum will at best be advisory, for to be effective it has to be ratified by the national parliament. It is evident that these rules and restrictions could themselves be a cause of friction in the future; but for the time being they have secured peace.

The non-binding outcome of the referendum was contrary to the strong position of the Bougainvilleans for the first 18 months of the negotiations on political agreement. It was an issue on which they eventually compromised, under international pressure, in order to persuade the national government to agree to a constitutionally guaranteed referendum. They did so in the belief that, if they could unify Bougainvilleans and achieve a very high vote for independence, then, provided that the international community remained interested and involved, the PNG government would find it difficult to ignore the result. For its part the national government agreed not just because of international pressure, but also because it could argue that a non-binding referendum did not undermine its sovereignty, and it would have 10 to 15 years to demonstrate to Bougainvilleans that it would be in their interests to vote against independence.

Although implementation of autonomy has occurred more slowly than expected, progress to date has been reasonable, but not without some strains on relations. Elections for the ABG were held in mid-2005. The capacity of the ABG's administrative arm is weak, making the process of taking over the many powers and functions available to the ABG very slow. In terms of funding, the inherent logic of the combination of autonomy and a deferred referendum on independence suggests that the national government will make available the significant levels of funding needed to persuade Bougainvilleans to vote in favour of staying within PNG when the referendum is held (much as France has been doing in relation to New Caledonia). So far, however, funding for the ABG from the national government in the first full year of autonomy has not been much more than the minimum. There are signs of the beginnings of frustration in the ABG, and increasing talk of allowing mining activity to resume as a way of ensuring that Bougainville has its own resources both to operate autonomy effectively and to provide the capacity needed for independence following the referendum. On the PNG side there are the beginnings of concern that the ABG is being too confrontational in some of its dealings with the national government, and unreasonably pushing the limits of some aspects of autonomy, notably its competence to participate in international meetings in the region.

ASSESSMENT AND REFLECTIONS

Asymmetry begets complexity, but it also has a wider political significance. With the 2001 agreement Bougainville gains the prize that eluded it in 1976. Will it turn out to be a pyrrhic victory? Asymmetry seldom remains a bilateral matter between the asymmetrical unit and the centre. Others resent it for a variety of reasons.

Asymmetrical arrangements have become a common feature of federal and autonomy arrangements in ethnically based societies. They facilitate the devolution of powers according to the circumstances of different regions and communities, but they tend to set the pace for others. They can also lead to complex arrangements, especially as the central government has to manage diverse relationships with different parts of the country.[6] There was relatively little opposition to a special status for Bougainville this time round, with widespread recognition that special arrangements were needed in the interests of reconciliation and peace building.

Can this accommodation be sustained? If one goes by the experience of some other countries, one would have to accept that Bougainville asymmetry will most probably create tensions. Sometimes these tensions are managed by extending 'asymmetrical' relations to others – asymmetry is eliminated by enhanced autonomy for all (as happened in PNG in 1976). Pressure is already being applied by the East New Britain provincial government, which has a reasonable administrative record, seeking increased autonomy by drawing on the 2001 agreement (though taking care, so far, to indicate acceptance that peace building requires special arrangements for Bougainville). Would increasing pressures of this kind further loosen the structures of the state, making it harder for the centre, both at political and administrative levels, to manage centre–provincial relations?

What has devolution represented for PNG, and what will the enhanced autonomy do for Bougainville? Earlier we noted two impulses behind the original devolution proposals: accommodation of ethnic identity and participation intended to increase efficiency and responsiveness. Ethnicity has played a limited role elsewhere in PNG since independence (see, however, Larmour, 1990, 1992). This is perhaps because the very existence of numerous communities and identities dilutes the force of ethnicity; the ethnic base is often too slender to mobilize. It also means that the province is too large a unit for any one group to capture and dominate to make it the basis of ethnic identity. Perhaps cultural differences were not so substantial as to matter, at least politically. When we examine the purposes to which provinces put their powers under the 1976 arrangements, culture does not figure highly. In fact most provinces were not effective in mobilizing political support for provincial institutions, making it easy for the central government to repeal the 1976 arrangements in 1995.

Perhaps the lesson is that, while internal administrative boundaries can stimulate territorial identity, prior strong political or cultural consciousness is necessary for effective devolution. The role of provincial government could have been to foster provincial consciousness as part of nation building and, in the early days, particularly as people engaged in provincial constitution making, provincial identity seemed to be emerging (Ghai and Regan, 1992). But it seems not to have been sustained largely because the interests of some leading provincial personalities turned to national politics and most provincial governments were singularly inept at delivering material goods or political participation.

Is Bougainville, much given to the rhetoric of cultural identity, and where the conflict and the peace process have heightened a sense of distinct experience and identity, exceptional? Its 'islandness' and physical separation from the rest of the country, the distinctive appearance of its people and their proximity to Solomon Islands all emphasized Bougainvilleans' sense of uniqueness. But the conflicts with the rest of the country were not fundamentally ethnic. In 1976 they had more to do with the allocation of resources, particularly mining revenue. In 1989 mining revenue was still a major factor in an extraordinarily complex situation which worsened into armed conflict in part because of internal Bougainville differences, as well as of dissent from central government policies (some of the strongest champions of devolution, in the form of provincial government, were Bougainvilleans). But the dynamics of the conflict enhanced a distinction between 'us' (Bougainvilleans) and 'them' (other Papua New Guineans). Autonomy is now seen as providing an opportunity for Bougainvilleans to further develop their own identity (Bougainville Peace Agreement, 2001, para. 4). It is yet to be seen if the experience will be significantly different from that under the 1976 Agreement. While the terms of both the 2001 Peace Agreement and the new Bougainville Constitution suggest that the Bougainvilleans are much more ambitious the second time round, it is ironic that, without mine revenues, the resources available to develop autonomy will be much less.

What light does this PNG history throw on the claim that devolution/federalism is the first step to secession (often the strongest argument against autonomy)? At first glance, Bougainville's experiences seem to substantiate the claim. It could be argued that, having obtained limited autonomy in 1976 (by the 'threat' of the loss of mining revenue), it used that autonomy to raise the stakes, and then in 1989 by force of arms demanded secession, settling temporarily for enhanced autonomy only by winning the option of independence. We believe that this is a misreading. After the 1976 autonomy Bougainville leaders established an effective government in accordance with national laws, and played a full role in national politics. The 1989 troubles in large part had a common source to those of the mid-1970s – the inequitable distribution of the income from the copper mine – but this time it was initially not a province-wide protest. Rather, it originated in internal disputes among mine-lease landowner communities over distribution of mine revenues. It was the violent responses of the PNG forces that wrongly assumed a broad-based rebellion, which enabled a broader Bougainvillean mobilization round ethnic identity. But that rebellion was opposed by some other Bougainvilleans, even in its early stages (Togolo, 2005), and deeper divisions emerged when the secessionist rebels were unable to control the situation after the PNG forces withdrew from Bougainville in March 1990.

The local democratic forces to which autonomy had given rise were as much the victims of the anger and violence of the rebels as of the central authorities. The 1976 devolution arrangements had strengthened Bougainville's links to the rest of the country, for they eliminated some genuine grievances and established a democratic order internally connected to the national system. There is little doubt that, without the 1976 autonomy, the rebellion of 1989 would have garnered more support in Bougainville. Hence autonomy limited support for secession rather than promoted it. In presenting its case for greater autonomy in the 1999–2001 negotiations, the potential of autonomy to strengthen national unity by producing a better balance between national and provincial interests was highlighted by some Bougainvillean negotiators.

The key to the settlement was the promise not so much of independence but the willingness of PNG to consider it – in effect, the postponement of this critical issue. The 2001 agreement represents a departure (albeit reluctant on the part of the national government) from obsession with state sovereignty. It not only diffused the sovereignty issue by hinting at the coordinate status of Bougainville with PNG, but also fudged that issue by postponing resolution of the ambiguity. Diffusing, fragmenting and fudging sovereignty will probably also be critical to the settlement of many internal disputes as the 2001 agreement is implemented. Sovereignty also becomes contingent, depending on circumstances beyond the control of the central state; in some situations it has to be earned. We have examples of this same phenomenon from New Caledonia,[7] where a peace agreement makes provision for a combination of autonomy and a deferred referendum on independence. Serious negotiations over Bougainville started only when it was agreed (even though, initially, only hypothetically on the part of the national government) that independence could in some sense be part of the agenda.

There are, however, risks for PNG in arrangements that keep open the possibility of independence for Bougainville. On the one hand, they create pressure on PNG to allocate high levels of resources to Bougainville (to encourage a majority pre-integration vote in the referendum vote). On the other hand, PNG faces severe fiscal problems that make it difficult to treat Bougainville as a special case. Some national government elements expect that a strong pro-independence vote is likely anyway, and so oppose allocating additional funding that they see as likely to build Bougainville capacity for independence. If Bougainvilleans' high expectations of autonomy are not met, frustration can be expected to grow.

There is no doubt that the high level of autonomy now available to Bougainville would enable it to explore the innovative development strategies that many other island autonomies have been deploying (Baldacchino, 2004). Even para-diplomacy is now much more readily open, with the ABG having some foreign affairs-related powers available. But the main examples of island autonomies that have made effective use of such strategies are autonomies arising from a colonial relationship, in which the capacities have developed gradually in a situation where the colonial authority (present or former) has interests in building capacity of and providing resources to the autonomous unit. These experiences may have little relevance to Bougainville, where capacity is low and will be difficult to build, and there are indications of limited interest at the national level in providing high levels of resources. If Bougainvillean expectations about autonomy are not met, then frustration about the operation of autonomy may contribute to growing nationalism and a tendency to assume that a referendum vote for independence is the only option. If so, it may be not so much autonomy that leads to increased pressure for secession but difficulties in managing the agreed arrangements for a combination of autonomy with a deferred referendum on independence.

Acknowledgements

Yash Ghai thanks the University of Hong Kong for the Distinguished Researcher Award that has supported his research on autonomy systems. Much of the analysis in this chapter derives from Ghai's participation in the preparation of the independence constitution of Papua New Guinea (1973–75) and in negotiations between the national government and Bougainville on their relationship in 1975–76, and from the participation of both Ghai and Regan in the implementation of the devolution package adopted in 1976, and in the 1999–2001 negotiations for the Bougainville Peace Agreement, plus reflections on these experiences.

Notes

1. For discussion of the process, see Griffin *et al.* (1979, pp. 217–229); Wolfers (1982); Ghai (1985; 1988a; 1997); Somare (2001); Momis (2001); Narokobi (2001); and Regan *et al.* (2001, pp. 345–365).
2. In Papua New Guinea the term decentralization rather than devolution was used. In this chapter we use the term devolution, as it more accurately describes the system that was favoured by the constitutional commission and as it is generally understood.
3. For detailed analysis of the origins and operation of the 1976 devolution arrangements, see Conyers (1976); Barnett (1979); Ballard (1981); Regan (1985a; 1985b); Axline (1986); Ghai and Regan (1992; 2001); May and Regan (1997); and May (1999).
4. For discussion of the origins and course of the conflict, see Filer (1990); May and Spriggs (1990); Ogan (1992); Spriggs and Denoon (1992); Wesley-Smith (1992); Regan (1998a, 2001a, 2003, 2005a); Denoon (2000); Ghai and Regan (2000); Kauona (2001); Regan and Griffin (2005); May (2005).
5. For discussion of the complex origins and unfolding of the peace process, see Regan (1997); Dinnen *et al.* (1997); Dorney (1998); O'Callaghan (1999); Wehner and Denoon (2001); Rolfe (2001); Adams (2001); Regan (2001a, 2001b, 2002a, 2002b, 2002c, 2003); Carl and Garasu (2002); Boege and Garasu (2004); and May (2005).
6. Agranoff (1994); Boase (1994); Browne-John (1994); Ghai (2002b, pp. 157–162); Milne (1994); and Stevens (1997).
7. See Chappell (1999); Maclellan (1999, 2005); Garde (2001); Angleviel (2003); Faberon (2003); Faberon and Postic (2004); Christnacht (2004); and Rumley (2006).

References

Adams, R. (Ed.) (2001) *Gudpela Nius Bilong Pis. Peace on Bougainville: Truce Monitoring Group* (Wellington: Victoria University Press).

Agranoff, J. (1994) Asymmetrical and symmetrical federalisms in Spain: an examination of intergovernmental policy, in B. de Villiers (Ed.), *Evaluating Federal Systems* (Cape Town: Juta).

Angleviel, F. (2003) The bet on intelligence: politics in New Caledonia, 1988–2002, *State, Society and Governance in Melanesia: Discussion Paper* (Canberra: SSGM, Australian National University).

Axline, W. (1986) *Decentralisation and Development Policy: Provincial Government and the Planning Process in Papua New Guinea*, IASER Monograph No. 26 (Waigani: PNG Institute of Applied Social and Economic Research).

Baldacchino, G. (2004) Autonomous but not sovereign? A review of island sub-nationalism, *Canadian Review of Studies in Nationalism*, 31(1–2), pp. 77–91.

Baldacchino, G. (2006) Innovative development strategies from non-sovereign island jurisdictions? A global review of economic policy and governance practices, *World Development*, 34(5), pp. 852–867.

Ballard, J. (1981) Policy making as trauma, in Ballard (Ed.), *Policy Making in a New State: Papua New Guinea, 1972–1977*, pp. 95–132 (St Lucia: University of Queensland Press).

Barnett, T. (1979) Politics and planning rhetoric in Papua New Guinea, *Economic Development and Cultural Change*, 27(4), pp. 769–784.

Bedford, R. and Mamak, A. (1977) *Compensation for Development: The Bougainville Case*, Bougainville Special Publication No. 2 (Christchurch: Department of Geography, University of Canterbury).

Boase, J. (1994) Faces of asymmetry: German and Canadian federalism, in B. de Villiers (Ed.), *Evaluating Federal Systems* (Cape Town: Juta).

Boege, V. and Garasu, L. (2004) Papua New Guinea: a success story of postconflict peacebuilding in Bougainville, in A. Heijman, N. Simmonds and H. van de Veen (Eds), *Searching for Peace in Asia Pacific: An Overview of Conflict Prevention and Peace-building Activities*, pp. 564–579 (Boulder, CO: Lynne Rienner).

Bougainville Peace Agreement (2001) *Bougainville Peace Agreement, 30 August 2001*, Papua New Guinea National Gazette, G 146, 16 November (Port Moresby: Papua New Guinea Government Printer).

Browne-John, L. (1994) Asymmetrical federalism: keeping Canada together?, in B. de Villiers (Ed.), *Evaluating Federal Systems*, pp. 16–29 (Cape Town: Juta).

Carl, A. and Garasu, L. (Eds) (2002) *Weaving Consensus: The Papua New Guinea–Bougainville Peace Process* (London: Conciliation Resources (*Accord*, Issue 12)).

Chappell, D. (1999) The Noumea Accord: decolonization without independence in New Caledonia?, *Pacific Affairs*, 72(3), pp. 373–391.

Christnacht, A. (2004) *La Nouvelle-Calédonie* (Paris: Documentation Française).

Connell, J. (1991) Compensation and conflict: the Bougainville copper mine, Papua New Guinea, in J. Connell and R. Howitt (Eds), *Mining and Indigenous Peoples in Australasia*, pp. 55–76 (Sydney: Sydney University Press).

Conyers, D. (1976) *The Provincial Government Debate: Central Control Versus Local Participation in Papua New Guinea*, IASER Monograph No. 2 (Waigani: PNG Institute of Applied Social and Economic Research).

CPC (1974) *Final Report of the Constitutional Planning Committee*, Parts 1 and 2 (Port Moresby: PNG Government).

Denoon, D. (2000) *Getting Under the Skin: The Bougainville Copper Agreement and the Creation of the Panguna Mine* (Melbourne: Melbourne University Press).

Dinnen, S., May, R. and Regan, A. (Eds) (1997) *Challenging the State: The Sandline Affair in Papua New Guinea* (Canberra: Asia–Pacific Press, National Centre for Development Studies, Australian National University).

Dorney, S. (1998) *The Sandline Affair: Politics and Mercenaries and the Bougainville Crisis* (Sydney: ABC Books).

Faberon, J. (2003) La Nouvelle-Calédonie et la révision constitutionelle de mars 2003 sur l'organisation décentralisée de la république, *Revue juridique, politique et économique de Nouvelle-Calédonie*, 1, pp. 3–7.

Faberon, J. and Postic, J. (2004) *L'Accord de Noumea, la loi organique et autres documents juridiques et politiques de la Nouvelle-Calédonie* (Noumea: Île de Lumière).

Filer, C. (1990) The Bougainville rebellion, the mining industry and the process of social disintegration in Papua New Guinea, in R. May and M. Spriggs (Eds), *The Bougainville Crisis*, pp. 112–140 (Bathurst: Crawford House Press).

Garde, F. (2001) *Les Institutions de la Nouvelle Caledonie* (Paris: L'Harmattan).

Ghai, Y. (1985) Land regimes and paradigms of development: reflections on Melanesian constitutions, *International Journal of the Sociology of Law*, 13(2), pp. 393–405.

Ghai, Y. (1988a) Constitution making and decolonisation, in Y. Ghai (Ed.), *Law, Government and Politics in the Pacific Island States*, pp. 1–53 (Suva: Institute of Pacific Studies, University of the South Pacific).

Ghai, Y. (1988b) Political consequences of constitutions, in Y. Ghai (Ed.), *Law, Government and Politics in the Pacific Island States*, pp. 350–372 (Suva: Institute of Pacific Studies, University of the South Pacific).

Ghai Y. (1997) Securing a liberal democratic order through a constitution: the case of Papua New Guinea, *Development and Change*, 28(2), pp. 303–330.

Ghai, Y. (2000) Ethnicity and autonomy: a framework for analysis, in Ghai (Ed.), *Autonomy and Ethnicity: Negotiating Competing Claims in Multi-ethnic States*, pp. 242–265 (Cambridge: Cambridge University Press).

Ghai, Y. (2002a) Global prospects of autonomies, in H. Jansson and J. Salminen (Eds), *The Second Åland Islands Question: Autonomy or Independence?*, pp. 29–54 (Mariehamn: Julius Sundblom Memorial Foundation).

Ghai, Y. (2002b) Constitutional asymmetries: communal representation, federalism and cultural autonomy, in A. Reynolds (Ed.), *The Architecture of Democracy: Constitutional Design, Conflict Management and Democracy*, pp. 157–162 (Oxford: Oxford University Press).

Ghai, Y. and Regan, A. (1992) *Law, Politics and Administration of Decentralisation in Papua New Guinea* (Port Moresby: PNG NRI).

Ghai, Y. and Regan, A. (2000) Bougainville and the dialectics of ethnicity, autonomy and separation, in Y. Ghai (Ed.), *Autonomy and Ethnicity: Negotiating Competing Claims in Multi-Ethnic States*, pp. 242–265 (Cambridge: Cambridge University Press).

Ghai, Y. and Regan, A. (2001) Decentralisation: 1976–1995, in A. Regan, O. Jessup and E. Kwa (Eds), *Twenty Years of the Papua New Guinea Constitution*, pp. 161–180 (Sydney: Law Book Co.).

Griffin, J. (1972) Bougainville: secession or just sentiment?, *Current Affairs Bulletin*, 48(9), pp. 259–280.

Griffin, J. (1973) Buka and Arawa: some black thoughts on a white history of Bougainville, *Meanjin Quarterly*, 32(4), pp. 452–456.

Griffin, J. and Togolo, M. (1997) North Solomons Province, in R. May and A. Regan (Eds), *Political Decentralisation in a New State: The Experience of Provincial Government in Papua New Guinea*, pp. 354–382 (Bathurst: Crawford House Publishing).

Griffin, J., Nelson, H. and Firth, S. (1979) *Papua New Guinea: A Political History* (Melbourne: Heinemann Educational).

Kauona, S. (2001) Freedom from fear, in R. Adams (Ed.), *Gudpela Nius Bilong Pis. Peace on Bougainville: Truce Monitoring Group*, pp. 84–94 (Wellington: Victoria University Press).

Larmour, P. (1990) Ethnicity and decentralisation in Melanesia: a review of the 1980s, *Pacific Viewpoint*, 31(2), pp. 10–27.

Larmour, P. (1992) The politics of race and ethnicity: theoretical perspectives on Papua New Guinea, *Pacific Studies*, 15(2), pp. 87–108.

McElroy, J. and Mahoney, M. (1999) The propensity for political dependence in island microstates, *Insula: International Journal of Island Affairs*, 9(1), pp. 32–35.

Maclellan, N. (1999) The Noumea Accord and decolonisation in New Caledonia, *Journal of Pacific History*, 34(3), pp. 245–252.

Maclellan, N. (2005) From Elois to Europe: interactions with the ballot box in New Caledonia, *Journal of Commonwealth and Comparative Politics*, 43(3), pp. 394–418.

Mamak, A. and Bedford, R. (1974) *Bougainvillean Nationalism: Aspects of Unity and Discord*, Bougainville Special Publication No. 1 (Christchurch: Department of Geography, University of Canterbury).

May, R. (Ed.) (1982) *Micronationalist Movements in Papua New Guinea*, Political and Social Change Monograph No. 1 (Canberra: Australian National University).

May, R. (1997) Postscript: the Organic Law on Provincial Governments and Local-Level Governments, in R. May and A. Regan (Eds), *Political Decentralisation in a New State: The Experience of Provincial Government in Papua New Guinea*, pp. 386–395 (Bathurst: Crawford House Publishing).

May, R. (1999) Decentralization in Papua New Guinea: two steps forward, one step back, in M. Turner (Ed.), *Central–Local Relations in Asia Pacific: Convergence or Divergence?*, pp. 123–148 (London: Macmillan).

May, R. (2005) The Bougainville conflict and its resolution, in J. Henderson and G. Watson (Eds), *Securing a Peaceful Pacific*, pp. 459–469 (Christchurch: University of Canterbury Press).

May, R. and Regan, A. (Eds) (1997) *Political Decentralisation in a New State: The Experience of Provincial Government in Papua New Guinea* (Bathurst: Crawford House Publishing).

May, R. and Spriggs, M. (Eds) (1990) *The Bougainville Crisis* (Bathurst: Crawford House Press).

Milne, D. (1994) Exposed to the glare: constitutional camouflage and the fate of Canada's federation, in E. Seidle (Ed.), *Seeking a New Canadian Partnership: Asymmetrical and Confederal Options* (Ottawa: Institute for Research on Public Policy).

Momis, J. (2001) The constitutional planning committee and the constitution, in A. Regan, O. Jessup and E. Kwa (Eds), *Twenty Years of the Papua New Guinea Constitution*, pp. 19–24 (Sydney: Law Book Co.).

Momis, J. (2005) Shaping leadership through Bougainville indigenous values and Catholic seminary training: a personal journey, in A. Regan and H. Griffin (Eds), *Bougainville before the Conflict*, pp. 300–316 (Canberra: Pandanus Press).

Narokobi, B. (2001) The constitutional planning committee, nationalism and vision, in A. Regan, O. Jessup and E. Kwa (Eds), *Twenty Years of the Papua New Guinea Constitution*, pp. 25–32 (Sydney: Law Book Co.).

Nash, J. (2001) Paternalism, progress, paranoia: patrol reports and colonial history in south Bougainville, in N. McPherson (Ed.), *In Colonial Papua New Guinea: Anthropological Perspectives*, pp. 111–124 (Pittsburgh, PA: University of Pittsburgh Press).

Nash, J. and Ogan, E. (1990) The red and the black: Bougainville perceptions of other Papua New Guineans, *Pacific Studies*, 13(2), pp. 1–17.

O'Callaghan, M. (1999) *Enemies Within. Papua New Guinea, Australia and the Sandline Crisis: The Inside Story* (Sydney: Doubleday).

Ogan, E. (1992) The cultural background to the Bougainville crisis, *Journal de la Société des Océanistes*, 92–93, pp. 61–67.

Ogan, E. (1996) Copra came before copper: the Nasioi of Bougainville and plantation colonialism 1902–1964, *Pacific Studies*, 19(1), pp. 31–51.

Oliver, D. (1991) *Black Islanders: A Personal Perspective of Bougainville 1937–1991* (Melbourne: Hyland House).

Quodling, P. (1991) *Bougainville: The Mine and the People* (St Leonards, NSW: Centre for Independent Studies).

Premdas, R. (1998) Secession and decentralization: the Bougainville case, *Canadian Review of Studies in Nationalism*, 25(1), pp. 23–36.

Regan, A. (1985a) Papua New Guinea (b): implementing provincial government, in P. Larmour and R. Qalo (Eds), *Decentralisation in the South Pacific – Local, Provincial and State Government in Twenty Countries*, pp. 119–154 (Suva: University of the South Pacific).

Regan, A. (1985b) Papua New Guinea (c): national–provincial relations, in P. Larmour and R. Qalo (Eds), *Decentralisation in the South Pacific – Local, Provincial and State Government in Twenty Countries*, pp. 155–171 (Suva: University of the South Pacific).

Regan, A. (1997) Preparation for war and progress towards peace: Bougainville dimensions of the Sandline affair, in S. Dinnen, R. May and A. Regan (Eds), *Challenging the State: The Papua New Guinea Sandline Affair*, pp. 82–93 (Canberra: NCDS, Australian National University).

Regan, A. (1998a) Causes and course of the Bougainville conflict, *Journal of Pacific History*, 33(3), pp. 269–285.

Regan A. (1998b) Case study: Bougainville, in P. Harris and B. Reilly (Eds), *Democracy and Deep-rooted Conflict: Options for Negotiators*, pp. 171–178 (Stockholm: International Institute for Democracy and Electoral Assistance).

Regan, A. (2001a) Why a neutral peace monitoring force? The Bougainville conflict and the peace process, in M. Wehner and D. Denoon (Eds), *Without a Gun: Australia's Experience of Monitoring Peace in Bougainville, 1997–2001*, pp. 1–18 (Canberra: Pandanus Books).

Regan, A. (2001b) Establishing the truce monitoring group and the peace monitoring group, in M. Wehner and D. Denoon (Eds), *Without a Gun: Australia's Experience of Monitoring Peace in Bougainville, 1997–2001*, pp. 19–40 (Canberra: Pandanus Books).

Regan, A. (2002a) The Bougainville political settlement and the prospects for sustainable peace, *Pacific Economic Bulletin*, 17(1), pp. 114–129.

Regan, A. (2002b) Bougainville: beyond survival, *Cultural Survival Quarterly*, 26(3), pp. 20–24.

Regan, A. (2002c) Resolving two dimensions of conflict and division: the dynamics of consent, consensus and compromise, in A. Carl and L. Garasu (Eds), *Accord: Weaving Consensus – The Papua New Guinea–Bougainville Peace Process*, 12, pp. 36–43 (London: Conciliation Resources).

Regan, A. (2003) The Bougainville conflict: political and economic agendas, in K. Ballentein and J. Sherman (Eds), *The Political Economy of Armed Conflict: Beyond Greed & Grievance*, pp. 133–166 (Boulder, CO: Lynne Rienner).

Regan, A. (2005a) Clever people solving difficult problems: perspectives on weakness of the state and nation in Papua New Guinea, *Development Studies Bulletin*, 67(April), pp. 6–12.

Regan, A. (2005b) Identities among Bougainvilleans, in A. Regan and H. M. Griffin (Eds), *Bougainville before the Conflict* (Canberra: Pandanus Press).

Regan, A. and Griffin, H.M. (Eds), Bougainville before the conflict (Canberra: Pandanus Press).

Regan, A., Jessup, O. and Kwa, E. (2001) Transcript of panel discussion – panel of constitution-maker, in Regan *et al.* (Eds), *Twenty Years of the Papua New Guinea Constitution*, pp. 345–365 (Sydney: Law Book Co.).

Rolfe, J. (2001) Peacekeeping the Pacific way in Bougainville, *International Peacekeeping*, 12(4), pp. 599–608.

Rumley, D. (2006) The French geopolitical project in New Caledonia, in D. Rumley, V. Forbes and C. Griffin (Eds), *Australia's Arc of Instability: The Political and Cultural Dynamics of Regional Security*, pp. 229–246 (Dordrecht: Springer).

Somare, M. (2001) Reflections on constitution-making, in A. Regan, O. Jessup and E. Kwa (Eds), *Twenty Years of the Papua New Guinea Constitution*, pp. 15–18 (Sydney: Law Book Co.).

Spriggs, M. and Denoon, D. (Eds) (1992) *The Bougainville Crisis: 1991 Update* (Canberra: Australian National University in association with Crawford House Press).

Stevens, R. (1997) Asymmetrical federalism: the federal principle and the survival of small republics, *Publius: Journal of Federalism*, 7(4) (special issue on 'Federalism and Identity', ed. Ivo D. Duchacek), pp. 117–203.

Tanis, J. (2005) Nagovisi villages as a window on Bougainville in 1988, in A. Regan and H. M. Griffin (Eds), *Bougainville before the Conflict*, pp. 447–472 (Canberra: Pandanus Press).

Togolo, M. (2005) Torau response to change, in A. Regan and H. M. Griffin (Eds), *Bougainville before the Conflict*, pp. 274–290 (Canberra: Pandanus Press).

Tordoff, W. and Watts, R. (1974) Report on central–provincial government relations, mimeo, Port Moresby.

Tryon, D. (2005) The languages of Bougainville, in A. Regan and H. M. Griffin (Eds), *Bougainville before the Conflict*, pp. 31–46 (Canberra: Pandanus Press).

Watts, R. (1999) *Comparing Federal Systems* (Montreal and Kingston: McGill-Queen's University Press).

Wehner, M. and Denoon, D. (2001) *Without a Gun: Australia's Experience of Monitoring Peace in Bougainville, 1997–2001* (Canberra: Pandanus Books).

Wesley-Smith, T. (1992) Development and crisis in Bougainville: a bibliographic essay, *Contemporary Pacific*, 4(2), pp. 408–432.

Wolfers, E. (1982) Aspects of political culture and institution building in Melanesia: the Constitutional Planning Committee in Papua New Guinea and the Special Committee on Provincial Government in Solomon Islands, *Pacific Studies*, 6(1), pp. 85–108.

Wolfers, E., Conyers, D., Larmour, P. and Ghai, Y. (1982) *Manual on Decentralisation* (London: Commonwealth Secretariat).

9 Dependence and autonomy in sub-national island jurisdictions: the case of the kingdom of the Netherlands

Gert Oostindie

INTRODUCTION: THE COSTS AND BENEFITS OF CARIBBEAN DECOLONIZATION

Two centuries after the Haitian revolution the decolonization of the Caribbean still seems incomplete; nor is this situation likely to change in the near future. Of the four major European colonizers, only Spain has been forced to retreat from the region. With Puerto Rico (3.8 million people) and the US Virgin Islands (110 000), the USA has the largest share of the population in the non-sovereign Caribbean, followed by France with its *départements d'outre-mer* (DOM, roughly 1 million), The Netherlands with the Netherlands Antilles (180 000) and Aruba (90 000), and the UK with its overseas territories (155 000). In all, some 15% of the 37 million people living in the Caribbean today reside in non-sovereign territories.

Any analysis of political and development issues in the Caribbean must take stock of the fact that the region in itself is small, and that most Caribbean territories are too. Small islands need not necessarily suffer from their scale – some analysts point at advantages such as flexibility which come with smallness. Yet the odds are against small states when it comes to political clout. They are "mostly acted upon by much more powerful states and institutions...For all that, it is vulnerabilities rather than opportunities...that come through as the most striking manifestations of the consequences of smallness in global politics" (Payne, 2004, p. 634).

Another dimension of crucial importance in the Caribbean context is constitutional status. Sovereignty is a mixed economic blessing for micro-states generally. Even if sovereign micro-states may prove to be remarkably viable, non-sovereign territories world-wide definitely score better by economic standards (Armstrong *et al.*, 1998; Armstrong and Read, 2000). The Caribbean does not present an exception to this rule, as recently documented in a thorough analysis of both Caribbean and Pacific island economies, including their demographic characteristics (McElroy and Sanborn, 2005), and of the Caribbean only (McElroy and de Albuquerque, 1995). In the Caribbean, which contains an extremely heterogeneous collection of both real and virtual islands,[1] there is an evident positive correlation between non-sovereignty and standards of living (as measured by conventional economic variables), and to some degree between non-sovereignty and good governance, including guarantees of human rights and liberties (Oostindie and Klinkers, 2003, *passim*).

This observation certainly applies if the three major countries of the Caribbean are included in the equation. Cuba (11.3 million), Haiti (8.3 million) and the Dominican Republic (8.6 million) together account for three-quarters of the total Caribbean population. These three states, giants by Caribbean standards yet still small by international criteria, boast a history of sovereignty dating back one (Cuba) to two (Haiti) centuries. At the close of the twentieth century Haiti was the poorest country in the Caribbean. In a list of 28 entities, the Dominican Republic was in twenty-third position, and Cuba twenty-fifth, in GNP per capita (Bulmer-Thomas, 2001; Oostindie and Klinkers, 2003, pp. 154–155). Caribbean evidence thus suggests that sovereignty is a drawback for economic development, not only for the young micro-states of the region, but even for the largest states with a history of independence dating back one to two centuries.

When the 'big three' are excluded from the equation, one is left with four formal colonial subdivisions within the Caribbean region. Most of the former British West Indian colonies attained their sovereignty between 1962 (Jamaica) and 1983 (St Kitts and Nevis). Puerto Rico and the US Virgin Islands have remained attached to the USA. The French colonies were fully integrated into the French state in 1946 as *départements d'outre-mer* (DOM). The former Dutch colony of Suriname became an independent republic in 1975, whereas the six Dutch islands in the Caribbean are still part of the Kingdom of the Netherlands.

Glossing over the intermediate states of Cuba, the Dominican Republic and Haiti, we may observe that all the remaining Caribbean territories are small or even tiny by international standards. Puerto Rico has a population of 3.9 million, Jamaica 2.7 million, Trinidad and Tobago 1.1 million. All others are below the one million mark. At the extreme end we find independent nations such as St Lucia with 166 000 people, St Vincent and the Grenadines with 118 000, and St Kitts and Nevis with only 47 000 people. With the exception of Puerto Rico, the non-sovereign islands all belong to the category of the smallest Caribbean territories.

What is the situation of the postwar sovereign states compared to those that opted to retain some sort of constitutional and 'neocolonial' attachment to their metropolis? It is difficult to offer any hard evidence of a direct causality, but it is obvious that most of the non-sovereign entities are better off in terms of *per capita* incomes, assuming, that is, that no significant contrasts in overall distribution of income exist (Bulmer-Thomas, 2001; Oostindie and Klinkers, 2003, pp. 154–155). Out of the 10 richest entities in the Caribbean in the late twentieth century, nine are non-sovereign. Out of these 10, only the Bahamas is an independent state. Even when the big three are excluded, the 10 poorest countries include only one non-sovereign island, the tiny UK overseas territory of Montserrat, beleaguered by quite unique environmental hazards.

A particularly painful contrast is provided by the three Guyanas. The former British colony of Guyana and the former Dutch colony of Suriname are among the three poorest states of the Caribbean, whereas the French department of Guyane is among the richest. Another indication of the costs of independence is suggested by the divergent development within the former Dutch Caribbean. Suriname has experienced a continuous deterioration since independence, whereas the Dutch islands, with some significant contrasts between them, have maintained their position within the category of the privileged.

For present purposes we need not discuss at any length the variables explaining the better economic performance and higher standards of living of non-sovereign islands. Certainly, direct metropolitan monetary transfers are not the only or necessarily the most important factor. Being embedded in a larger and generally stable constitutional entity serves to strengthen these dependent territories' institutional environment, with ensuing positive effects for local business and governments and enhanced credibility for international finance. Then there is the major advantage of duty-free or preferential access to metropolitan markets. And, of course, the virtual guarantee that in extreme cases – particularly when natural disasters such as hurricanes wreak havoc – there will be immediate and relatively generous metropolitan disaster relief.

What of the functioning of democracy and particularly guarantees of human rights and liberties? The first and perhaps most important conclusion to be drawn is that the record of the Commonwealth Caribbean has been remarkably positive, in spite of enormous economic problems compounded by the ever more evident threats provided by international crime. This is a major accomplishment. Yet the small number of countries which have suffered serious disruptions in their postwar democratic development – Guyana, Grenada and Suriname; some would argue that Jamaica under Michael Manley's early socialist experiment should be added to this list – are all young independent states. Independent and non-sovereign states alike have experienced serious problems with the quality of governance, but no suspension of democratic institutions was ever enforced or seriously considered among the latter. In these dependent territories standards of governance are defined and if necessary enforced, by the metropolis.

The same metropolis also guarantees the territorial integrity of the non-sovereign unit. This may seem to be a hypothetical benefit, inasmuch as intra-regional warfare seems a phenomenon of the distant past in the Caribbean. Yet there have been some such threats in the postwar Caribbean, for example incidental Venezuelan claims against Trinidad and Tobago and the Netherlands Antilles, Guatemalan claims against Belize, and Guyanese–Surinamese skirmishes. So this potential benefit of being under the protection of a larger and more powerful external state cannot be dismissed and is indeed appreciated (e.g. Oostindie and Verton, 1998, pp. 54–55).

There is another major benefit to non-sovereignty. Migration to the USA and Canada has become a crucial strategy of survival for millions of people from the sovereign Caribbean. Potential migrants have to endure difficult, lengthy, often humiliating, and not always successful procedures to gain admittance, the right of abode, and eventually citizenship. None of this applies to the citizens of the non-sovereign Caribbean when they seek to migrate to their metropolis. (One significant but temporary exception to this was the restrictive British Dependent Territories Citizenship, from 1981 to 2002.) Even if *per capita* incomes are high in these territories by sovereign Caribbean standards, they clearly fall short of metropolitan standards of living. This, in addition to other pull factors such as educational opportunities, or the broadening of one's horizon, has persuaded large numbers in the non-sovereign Caribbean to move to their respective metropolis. They do not encounter major legal obstacles because they have metropolitan citizenship and thus the right of abode in the metropolis.

Thus, in at least three dimensions – *per capita* income, the protection of the citizenry against external or internal threats (particularly the functioning of a representative democracy and guarantees of civil rights and liberties) and with regard to migration – there are evident benefits to non-sovereignty. Yet there are also some disadvantages. Metropolitan protectionism and the frequently massive accompanying financial transfers may have boosted *per capita* income, but they have also served to create uncompetitive consumer economies and, particularly for Puerto Rico and the French DOMs, 'aid addiction'. Likewise, the easy migration outlet may have reduced population pressure in these densely inhabited islands, but at the same time may have caused a brain drain and an almost exclusive orientation towards the metropolis, one which serves to further isolate the islands from their Caribbean surroundings.

Finally, there is a fourth dimension: the ideological and psychological significance of the sheltered constitutional status of non-sovereignty. This is perhaps a moot point. The rhetoric of political nationalism invariably starts with the axiom that ending colonial hegemony is a prerequisite for 'real' national development. It is striking how in non-sovereign territories many politicians firmly opposed to independence still pay lip-service to the presumed ultimate objective of becoming an independent state. As a former Antillean prime minister once confided: "It is your pride, your dignity!" Such convictions, however, do not reorient the past or present actual performances by the political elite.

For all practical purposes politicians in the non-sovereign Caribbean aspire to maintain the many material advantages of the postcolonial bond, while at the same time securing maximum autonomy. This is a recipe for at times heated contestations over the thin dividing line between outside control and internal authority. Such contestations tend to occur not only in strictly administrative and political terms, but equally as an issue of a besieged national identity. All this becomes evident time and again, whether in Puerto Rico, Martinique, Curaçao or Montserrat. The enormous asymmetry inherent in metropolitan–(post)colonial relations is a permanent frustration on the Caribbean side, a frustration often experienced as a minor irritant in the metropolitan centres of power. This is not only a problem felt by local administrators. Certainly in the Caribbean context there is a wider collective ambivalence towards, if not outright distrust of, the metropolis. After all, the metropolis may be useful and accommodating today, but it started out in the region as a crass colonial power populating its plantation colonies with African slaves and Asian indentured labourers. Their descendants are as keenly aware of this historical background as of the fact that the metropolitan appreciation of said background is usually very limited.

It is obvious that there is no way – or need for that matter – to establish objectively which dimension or which combination of the four dimensions outlined above should be rated as decisive in assessing the costs and benefits of independence. The different actors in this postcolonial double bind – Caribbean governments and their individual citizens, Caribbean citizens as potential migrants and metropolitan governments – have widely divergent perspectives and interests. There is therefore no foregone conclusion, but there is one hard empirical fact: the overwhelming majorities within the non-sovereign Caribbean do not want to consider any change of status which would endanger the obvious advantages of their postcolonial dependency. Plebiscites, opinion polls and electoral processes have demonstrated time and again that the overwhelming majority of citizens in the non-sovereign Caribbean islands, and in the one continental territory, French Guyana, are adamantly opposed to a move towards full independence. The option of full independence for small territories remains widely resisted (Oostindie and Verton, 1998; Oostindie and Klinkers, 2003, pp. 220–221; Baldacchino, 2004).

Meanwhile the political legitimacy of the choice against independence, both for the Caribbean and world-wide, has become stronger over the years. The United Nations affirmed as early as 1960, and again in 1970, that any status including free association or integration within the metropolis was acceptable as long as this option was freely chosen by a former colony's citizenry (Oostindie and Klinkers, 2001, Vol. I, pp. 131–132; Vol. III, p. 77). The growing empirical evidence of the high costs of sovereignty for young micro-states provided additional argumentation. Indeed, as McElroy and Sanborn conclude for both Caribbean and Pacific islands, there is abundant "scientific basis for their [non-sovereign islands'] persistent choice to retain metropolitan linkages and the favourable benefits of the political economy of dependence" (McElroy and Sanborn, 2005, p. 10). Indeed, the findings of this scholarly work firmly coincide with common Caribbean sense!

This chapter will now review and analyse the past decolonization process of the Dutch Caribbean – initially comprising Suriname and the six-island Netherlands Antilles – and consider recent developments in the light of the dynamic relationship between the Kingdom of the Netherlands and its remaining Caribbean territories. A short conclusion will reflect on the wider relevance of this particular case.

THE FIRST PHASE OF DUTCH DECOLONIZATION: TOWARDS THE 1954 *STATUUT*

The core of Dutch colonialism was not situated in the Caribbean but rather in the Dutch East Indies. Here classic colonialism – based on economic and geopolitical interests combined with administrative zeal – was abruptly ended through a classical decolonization struggle characterized by bloody battles and protracted negotiations which would poison postcolonial relations. In only seven years – marked by the Japanese occupation in 1942, the unilateral proclamation of independence in 1945 and the transfer of sovereignty in 1949 – the Netherlands lost the Dutch East Indies, a colony which was, many thought, a mixed metaphor: both the cork which kept the Dutch economy floating, and the Dutch ticket to the status of player in world politics. At the end of the day the loss of Indonesia would turn out to be no economic drama but it did reduce the significance of the Netherlands in international politics.

Concurrently with this arduous process, The Hague developed a decolonization policy for its Caribbean colonies. The outcome was the *Statuut* or Charter of the Kingdom of the Netherlands, proclaimed in 1954. The *Statuut* defined the Kingdom as a voluntary relationship between three equal and internally autonomous countries, being the Netherlands, Suriname and the six Caribbean islands forming the Netherlands Antilles. A middle path had been chosen between the two extremes – full sovereignty for the former Caribbean colonies or, conversely, complete integration in the metropolis as provinces – neither of which was seriously discussed by any of the partners involved.

As stated in the preamble of the *Statuut*, the three countries would "take care of their own interests autonomously, manage communal affairs on an equal footing, and accord each other assistance". The Charter defined foreign policy, defence, citizenship, and the safeguarding of proper governmental administration as matters of common interest to be governed by the Kingdom of the Netherlands. This Kingdom government was simply delineated as the ruling Dutch cabinet, expanded to include one plenipotentiary minister for each of the two Caribbean territories. The initial concept to inaugurate a Kingdom parliament to which this Kingdom government would be accountable was eventually abandoned by all parties. At one point in the long-winded negotiations all parties agreed that this would be too complicated a structure, and too much of a drain on the limited Caribbean political and administrative resources. For pragmatic reasons the simpler variation was chosen, which up until today reflects the 'democratic deficit' of a government without a corresponding parliament.

The *Statuut* rests on notions of 'equality' and 'reciprocal assistance', which, because of the asymmetrical balance of power, are totally fictitious. That was already obvious in 1954. The initial formulae were actually not invented with an eye to Caribbean decolonization but, rather, to World War II conditions, where the exiled Dutch cabinet in London hoped to persuade the Indonesian nationalists to remain within a modernized postwar Kingdom of the Netherlands. There is a double irony here if we take the demographics into consideration. In 1940 the Netherlands had about nine million inhabitants, while Indonesia had 70 million. The Hague was therefore offering 'equality' to a population many times bigger than its own. At the same time Suriname had only 140 000 inhabitants and the Dutch Antilles 108 000. In the negotiating process leading to the Charter, West Indian politicians capitalized on the accommodations which The Hague had originally created specifically for the East Indies. Hence the fictitious 'equality' between two Caribbean nations and their metropolis, which, in reality, dwarfs them.

The *Statuut* has been the foundation of the transatlantic Kingdom for half a century. In the preamble it was stated that the Charter would not be an 'eternal pact'. In reality it seems to have been just that: a virtually unchangeable arrangement. Certainly its *membership* has changed, with Suriname attaining independence in 1975; Aruba seceding from the Netherlands Antilles and acquiring a separate status as a territory within the Kingdom of the Netherlands in 1986; and yet more changes in store. But the *contents* of the Charter have been preserved to the letter, just as they were in 1954. Unfortunately this absence of change can be attributed not to the constitution's luminosity but rather to its rigidity. As the Charter itself posits, no change whatsoever can be implemented unless all partners agree.

THE DUTCH PREFERENCE FOR A FULL RETREAT

Until the late 1960s all three countries of the Kingdom were by and large satisfied with the *Statuut*. For The Hague the turning point came in May 1969 with the revolt of Curaçao. A labour conflict with strong political and racial connotations ended with rioters burning down central parts of the capital, Willemstad. According to the Charter, the government of the Antilles had the right to ask for military help from the Dutch government, and the latter had to abide by that request. Within hours Dutch marines were patrolling the smouldering streets of Willemstad. This intervention sparked a new and unenthusiastic awareness in the Netherlands of its remnants of empire. The Hague now moved to the position that its relationship with the Caribbean parts of the Kingdom did not contain significant positive interests and implied many uncalled-for risks.

There are three main considerations behind this reluctance, which has since been characteristic of the Dutch attitude. Initially the most important concern was the awareness that the Charter, while entrusting the responsibility for guaranteeing good governance in the overseas territories to the Kingdom government, at the same time leaves this government little opportunity for preventive action in view of the domestic autonomy awarded in the same document. So, from a Dutch perspective, The Hague had little to do with the origins of the local discontent which sparked the 1969 riots, yet was obliged to intervene and ended up being unduly criticized for neocolonial behaviour. Dutch policy therefore needed to disentangle itself from similar future obligations by either simply terminating the postcolonial relationship, or conversely becoming ever more interventionist in order to prevent new potential embarrassments from developing. The first line was dominant until roughly 1990, the second ever since.

The second consideration lies in the economic realm. The expectation expressed in the Charter that mutual assistance would help narrow the gap in standards of living between the various parts of the Kingdom proved to be an illusion. Admittedly, the relatively generous Dutch development aid has helped Aruba to attain economic stability and hence its present very high *per capita* income. In contrast, neither pre-independence Suriname nor the contemporary Antilles has been successful in bridging the gap with the ever-richer metropolis. Today Dutch politicians complain of Antillean 'aid addiction' and claim that no country in the world receives as much *per capita* aid as the Netherlands Antilles. These are false exaggerations, and certainly the assistance extended to the islands is of no serious significance to the Dutch Treasury (Oostindie and Klinkers, 2003, pp. 222–223). Development aid is extended along with continuous reminders of the need for 'self-reliance'. Meanwhile, the reality is that Caribbean reliance on Dutch economic support has simply increased.

Over time, a third, mainly domestic, concern has gained ever more significance for Dutch politicians: unease with the unrestricted migration channel from the Dutch Caribbean to the metropolis. By the early 1970s some 40 000 people from the Antilles and Suriname had settled in the Netherlands. Today there are over 320 000 Dutch with Surinamese backgrounds and another 130 000 with Antillean or Aruban roots. The influx of migrants from Suriname has levelled out after open access was curtailed with independence. Antilleans and Arubans, however, enjoy Dutch nationality and have the right to settle in the Netherlands. As lower-class juvenile migration from Curaçao has created public order problems in Dutch towns over the past decade, this open channel has come under serious attack in Dutch politics. (There is a political divide over the question of whether free access of Antilleans and Arubans should be curtailed as such. A centre-right majority in parliament has urged the centre-right cabinet to devise such draconian legislation. This project led to draft legislation in 2005 but is likely to fail because of both juridical and pragmatic obstacles. Meanwhile, the whole spectrum of Dutch political parties, from the far right to the left, now favours tight controls on deviant Antillean youths. There is widespread support for unconventional policies. Thus in January 2006 the municipality of Rotterdam, claiming that young Curaçaoans are the most criminal group in the country's second city, presented a new project which will oblige young Antilleans to be either pursuing their education, in a job or in some sort of judicial trajectory.)

THE INDEPENDENCE OF SURINAME (1975)

With few overall benefits, little positive engagement, limited administrative powers yet many responsibilities, it is no wonder that the Netherlands has attempted since 1970 to disentangle itself from its Caribbean dependencies. There are decisive legal complications, however, since dismantling the Kingdom would imply changing the *Statuut*. To accomplish this, all partners involved would need to agree. This has proved to be highly problematic. The Dutch managed to strike a deal on this with Suriname, but failed to do so with the islands.

Suriname became independent in 1975 in a highly unusual and fast-track political process which defied all claims of the Kingdom government as a patron of good governance. Certainly there was a nationalist, pro-independence movement in the country, mainly catering to the Afro-Surinamese in a society deeply divided along ethnic lines. The mainly Afro-Suriname government headed by Prime Minister Henck Arron would celebrate the transfer of sovereignty as if it had been a hard-won victory, which it certainly was not.

The dominant sentiment in The Hague was no less anti-colonial, albeit especially with an eye for the Dutch image, and a Dutch weighing up of costs and benefits. This was really modern paternalism dressed up as progressive policy. The centre-left cabinet of Joop den Uyl managed to accomplish the transfer of sovereignty in just 20 months. The population of Suriname was never directly invited to offer its opinion on the transfer of sovereignty. Neither of the two governments had any interest in staging a referendum: both sides assumed, probably quite correctly, that a majority would oppose independence.

During these 20 months of negotiations, the mainly Hindustani opposition had little faith in either the process or its outcome. Meanwhile, the two governments watched helplessly as one-third of the population of Suriname voted with their feet, choosing to live in the cold European motherland rather than staying in the new republic. In the end the transfer of sovereignty was only achieved because at the critical moment in the parliament of Suriname there was a majority of just *one* vote in favour of independence. The Dutch parliament agreed wholeheartedly with this wafer-thin majority, while the Antillean assembly did not object as long as there were no implications for its own non-sovereign status.

In the three decades that have passed since the transfer of sovereignty, the hoped-for 'model decolonization' has proved to be a disappointment. Suriname received a relatively generous dowry of 3.5 billion Dutch guilders or about 10 000 guilders per capita (around €10 000 per capita at current rates). The continuation of development aid was pledged. Yet this largesse did not prevent economic decline: many politicians feel that it undermined the economy, and some economists lend credence to this (e.g. van Dijck, 2001). Current per capita income in Suriname is among the lowest in the Caribbean. Moreover, even if the dowry to Suriname has been much criticized as extravagant, since 1975 the Netherlands has spent twice as much on the six Antillean islands taken together, and per capita three times as much on the islands' population, as on the poorer Surinamese (Oostindie and Klinkers, 2003, p. 165).

This is not all. The demographic growth of the Surinamese population has been heavily concentrated in the Netherlands. The political and administrative history of the republic has had many low points, of which the military dictatorship of the 1980s was the nadir. Informal and illegal sectors have become pervasive in the economy and society, a development that successive governments have been either unwilling or unable to redress. Many observers already qualify Suriname as a failing state. It is indeed questionable whether, in the long run, Suriname will be able to survive as an independent state. The Netherlands, still the most important partner, is slowly disengaging itself. Suriname has been trying to strengthen its engagement with the

Caribbean Community and Common Market (Caricom) countries. But in the long run Brazil, which considers the Guyanas as its backyard, or even Venezuela, may well fill the void left by the Netherlands – possibly via informal dominion, or more likely through settlement and land clearances.

THE NETHERLANDS ANTILLES: DISINTEGRATION WITHOUT SOVEREIGNTY

In contrast to Suriname, the Antilles has never had a serious pro-independence movement. Over the past decades some political parties have rendered lip service to a parting with the Netherlands in a distant future, but in practice Antillean politicians have simply refused to discuss sovereignty. Much to the annoyance of their Dutch counterparts, they have consistently brushed aside threats that independence would be imposed upon them. After all, they maintain, the *Statuut* guaranteed that any change was contingent upon their cooperation; and no consensus on the subject of a transfer of sovereignty would be forthcoming from the islands. The predicament of the Republic of Suriname has only added to Antillean reluctance – and in the end induced the Dutch to rethink their stance.

Around 1990 The Hague finally concluded that it would be practically impossible as well as immoral and reproachable by international standards unilaterally to enforce independence upon its remnants of empire in the Caribbean. With this understanding the playing field changed yet again. The debate has since revolved around the question of the boundaries between Caribbean autonomy and the prerogative of the Kingdom – for all practical purposes, this meaning the Netherlands – to play a more active role in Caribbean administration. This is simply a means to a further end in the Dutch view. The Hague's perception is that the overseas governments have too often been incapable or even unwilling to meet international standards of good governance. There is uneasiness about fragile governments, about clear signs of corruption, about the threat of bankruptcy of the Antillean government.

As The Hague thus had to accept the impossibility of a full retreat from the region, the Dutch in the end also conceded to another unsolicited development, namely the internal disintegration of the six-island Netherlands Antilles. In 1986 Aruba received its much desired *status aparte*, a secession from the Dutch Antilles subject to the condition that the island would have to attain full independence 10 years later. The Netherlands had insisted on this condition, both in the vain hope of breaking the Aruban struggle for a *status aparte* and to keep the other islands from a similar separatism, which would most probably imply the end of the multi-island Antilles. The Hague at the time still hoped for a transfer of sovereignty to a six-island state of the Antilles. What really followed was predictable. As of 1 January 1986 Aruba started an all-out offensive in order to remove the fatal date of independence from the *Statuut*. It succeeded in 1996 with the attainment of a permanent separate status within the Kingdom. Henceforward the Charter once again binds three countries.

Much to The Hague's frustration, both the Antillean and the Aruban governments have been wary of complying with the pressure to trade in local autonomy in favour of a strengthening of governmental institutions at the level of the Kingdom. At the same time the Caribbean governments have relied heavily on Dutch support in helping them to resolve local problems. In the Aruban case this has worked reasonably well – actually, because of its vigorous liberal economic policy, the island has time and again been promoted as a shining example to the protectionist Antillean government. Over the past decade Willemstad has started to liberalize its economy as well, but a deep crisis remains. National debt by now is almost equal to GDP, unemployment in the formal sector is sky-high and, in spite of the overall, relatively high per capita income, there is outright deprivation in many parts of the Antilles.

Successive Antillean governments have blamed part of their problems on the complicated structure of the Antilles-of-five, a colonial construct which in practice is characterized more by island-centred visions, mutual distrust and chicaneries than by a genuine sense of belonging together. In the early 1990s the Dutch proposed a trade-off between the islands' preference for breaking up the federal Antilles against their own wish to secure a firmer grip on local governments. This Dutch policy rested on the unwillingness of local politicians to give up autonomy and led to what probably – in reaction – was a resurgence of pan-Antillean solidarity.

Debate over the *Statuut* has been revived since the year 2000. Large majorities of both political parties on the five islands and their electorates, who were given a chance to speak out in a national plebiscite, now opt for an end to the five-island state and want direct relations of each of the islands with the Netherlands. The forms these direct relations may take are multiple. One option is full integration of an individual island or of a combination of these into the Netherlands, as in a departmental or municipal status. Another option is for individual islands to acquire the *status aparte* Aruba already secured for itself in 1986, that is, the status of an autonomous country within the Kingdom of the Netherlands originally reserved for the six-island Netherlands Antilles only. The option of a continuation of a multi-island Netherlands Antilles is no longer feasible. And, to complete the picture, the option of a collective or insular choice for independence is still one without significant support (see Table 9.1).

Table 9.1 Results of plebiscites in the Netherlands Antilles, 2000–05 (%)

	Turnout	Status quo (Antilles-of-five)	Unilateral link with the Netherlands	Full integration into the Netherlands	Autonomous country within the Kingdom	Independence
Bonaire	56.1	15.9	59.5	n.a.	24.1	0.5
Curaçao	54.0	3.7	n.a.	23.6	67.3	4.8
Saba	78.0	13.0	86.0	n.a.	n.a.	1.0
St Eustatius	55.0	77.0	21.0	2.0	n.a.	0.6
St Martin	55.7	3.7	n.a.	11.6	69.9	14.2

Source: www.minbzk.nl

Note

The plebiscites were held on: 23 June 2000 (St Martin), 10 September 2004 (Bonaire), 5 November 2004 (Saba) and 8 April 2005 (Curaçao and St Eustatius). The available options were not identical, hence the blanks (n.a.) in the table. Full integration into the Netherlands was understood as some sort of special municipality status within the Dutch administrative apparatus. The option of a unilateral link presupposes slightly more insular autonomy, but always clearly short of the high level of autonomy presently applicable to both Aruba and the Netherlands Antilles.

On closer inspection the outcomes disclose some interesting contrasts. As expected, the drive for a *status aparte* within the Kingdom dominates in the two largest entities: Curaçao (with some 130 000 inhabitants) and (the Dutch part of) St Martin (nearly 40 000). Nominal support in these parts for full sovereignty has increased since the 1990s, but still represents a minority view only. In Bonaire (10 000), support for a country status within the Kingdom has more support now than before but, consistent with previous polls, a clear majority favours a direct link with the Netherlands. On Saba, with its 1400 inhabitants, an even more outspoken majority opts for this outcome. Surprisingly perhaps, the third Windward island of St Eustatius (2300 people) still harbours a clear majority for a continuation of the five-island Antilles. The only alternative option attracting significant support is, again, a unilateral link with the Netherlands.

The overall conclusion must be that the vast majority of the Antillean electorate have no confidence left in the five-island nation. In this they concur with their political leaders. Interestingly, they were not of the same opinion in 1993–94, when clear majorities in all islands still voted in favour of a continuation of the Antilles-of-five, even if the great majority of Antillean politicians advised them otherwise (Oostindie and Verton, 1998, p. 49). Then the proportion in favour of a continuation of the Antilles-of-five was over 85% for the three smallest islands, 73.6% for Curaçao and 59.4% for St Martin, while the independence option was chosen by less than 1% on all islands, except for St Martin (6.3%).

Why did patience with the federally structured Antilles wane? One reason advanced by many observers may have been that, in 1993–94, the electorate was largely expressing its lack of confidence in local leadership. Even so, while the character and quality of this leadership has not changed significantly over the past decade, Antilleans do feel today that each should go its separate way.

Basically this all started with St Martin, always the least enthusiastic partner in the Antilles-of-five. Once the St Martiners had in 2000 voted squarely in favour of separation, the rest simply followed, with only St Eustatius ('Statia') in vain opting against change. It should be noted that the argument in favour of a break-up centres on bureaucratic and political issues. All islands complain of the dominance of Curaçao, while Curaçao in turn feels the federation to be burdensome to its own development. Apparently the question of whether the colonial construct of a five-island nation over the centuries has really become a nation, or should work towards this, is no longer deemed relevant. This was very different after 1993–94, when the Antillean government made some efforts to restructure the five-island state and advocated concomitant nation building (Commissie Natievorming, 1996).

The Dutch have never been enthusiastic about the prospect of having to entertain separate relations with six small to absolutely tiny islands and only reluctantly agreed to the separation of Aruba first, and the further demise of the Antilles next. They have done so because they feel there is no willingness whatsoever left among the five islands to work together and that, moreover, inter-insular strife further diminishes the quality of Antillean governance. The Hague once again expects a trade-off now, in the form of a strengthening of the Kingdom's institutions within Caribbean government – for most practical purposes, this will mean more Dutch control, perhaps mitigated by partial repairs of the 'democratic deficit'. Whether this can be accomplished within the parameters of the present *Statuut* is still a matter of debate. A promising 2004 bilateral position paper on the subject suggests it can. But its lukewarm reception on the islands does not inspire much confidence (Werkgroep Bestuurlijke en Financiële Verhoudingen, 2004). Unfortunately, Aruba was not invited to participate in this commission, and therefore may have felt little obligation to contribute to its realization.

Arduous negotiations in 2005 led to a provisional agreement, which the islands hope will materialize in a permanent new status by mid-2007 (Hoofdlijnenakkoord, 2005). In the agreement The Hague only states that it is aware of the desire of Curaçao and St Martin to attain country status by 1 July 2007. The programme now is for both Curaçao and St Martin to attain autonomous country status within the Kingdom, while the small three will entertain direct relations with the Netherlands – Statia has explicitly agreed to what it now feels is inevitable, the full disintegration of the Antilles-of-five. Yet there is no clear conception as yet of what this arrangement would be like in practice. Curaçao and St Martin opt for a status equal to autonomous Aruba, but The Hague has strongly argued that autonomy needs to be limited in favour of more prerogatives to the Kingdom in the first place. The smaller islands could be some sort of municipalities within the Kingdom; but can there be municipalities without a provincial layer of government? To complicate matters, The Hague insists that any arrangement for a break-up of the five-island country should include a restructuring of the national debt, which now stands at a staggering 96% of Antillean annual GNP. And, finally, we have Aruba, distrustful of any change that might affect its own best-of-all-possible-worlds status, and which has the right to veto any changes to the Charter it feels them to be unfair or unwise.

THE ANTILLEAN PREDICAMENT

While the text of the *Statuut* has remained cast in stone for 50 years, contextual changes have been afoot. The major change is demographic. The numerical imbalance between the population of the Netherlands (now 16 million) and the six islands (180 000 in the Antilles and 90 000 in Aruba) has become even more pronounced. Moreover, with some 130 000 islanders having settled in the metropolis in the past two decades, the Antillean and Aruban population is now fully transatlantic. This has consequences for the islands and the migrants themselves, consequences that local politicians tend to ignore. What once were only Caribbean questions and problems – such as local unemployment, local criminality, local poverty – are now also Dutch problems.

The second changed parameter is the institutional setting. In 1954 the legislator spoke of self-governing partners under the umbrella of one Kingdom. Since then the small Caribbean partners have tenaciously hung on to their autonomy, while the largest partner has transferred a major part of its sovereignty to the European Union (EU). The progressive Dutch incorporation into the EU now obliges the islands to consider what further consequences they must draw from their refusal to opt for independence. In local debates on this question – such as on the possible choice for the status of an ultra-peripheral territory of the EU – one observes an anachronistic obsession with autonomy and an unwillingness to face up to the new geopolitical realities among most local politicians. This attitude seems self-defeating as well as risky. As observers in Brussels often remark, the more the EU spreads eastward, the more Brussels' willingness to accommodate the former West European colonies is likely to come under scrutiny.

Yet, in spite of the evident asymmetry of demographic, economic and geopolitical realities, the words of the original *Statuut* persist. The Caribbean partners continue to exercise the right to veto any changes proposed by the Dutch that they do not consider to be in their best interests. This deadlock may not continue indefinitely, however. The Hague is becoming weary of the many problems and few successes of its Caribbean policies, which in the Dutch press and in political circles alike are routinely characterized as an arduous 'muddling through'. The Dutch electorate too has become more aware of the Kingdom's bonds, and evaluates these mainly in negative terms. There is little sense of solidarity: clear and consistent majorities of the Dutch would prefer the islands to become independent today rather than tomorrow (Oostindie and Klinkers, 2001, Vol. II, pp. 38–39, 73–75; Vol. III, pp. 67–69, 231–232). In fact, one may well conclude that over the past half century Dutch politicians have been more accommodating of the islands than their own electorate would have liked. The recent attempts to curtail free immigration from the Antilles are a remarkable exception to this rule. Domestic problems connected with the lower-class Curaçaoan exodus to the Netherlands have only compounded this negative attitude.

Across the Atlantic the Antillean people and their political elites, aware of the Suriname experience, of the growing US influence in the region, and of the onset of a global climate more disposed towards 'free trade', do not want to lose their umbilical cord to the Netherlands. As was confirmed once more in the recent plebiscites, support for political independence is negligible on all islands except, to some degree, St Martin. Antilleans and Arubans fear the loss of their privileged position if they should agree to even the smallest of changes to the *Statuut*, let alone to a transfer of sovereignty. Yet their facing up to a common (former) colonizer does not imply mutual solidarity. In their encounters with The Hague Antillean politicians may readily emphasize the communality of their Antillean and wider Caribbean culture, but in their political behaviour, insularity rules.

While politicians on both sides of the ocean continue negotiations over the dismantling of the Netherlands Antilles and the formulation of a new balance between Kingdom institutions and Caribbean autonomy, a political backlash in the Netherlands is evident. The May 2005 Dutch decision to prepare legislation to restrict migration from the Caribbean territories to the metropolis is illustrative. Admittedly these restrictions, once legislated, would only apply to specific problematic groups of immigrants. Even so, and on very good grounds, Antilleans and Arubans, who value the right of abode in the Netherlands as one of the principal arguments for their adherence to the Kingdom, perceive this new policy as a slap in the face. As it is, both judicial and pragmatic objections may well prevent this intended policy from materializing (Oostindie and Klinkers, 2003, p. 196). It is ironic that the UK has moved in exactly the opposite direction.

Perhaps some Dutch politicians naively hope that the offence will provoke Antilleans to reconsider membership in the Kingdom. More probably the assertive Dutch policy on the migration issue will only poison the climate in which the delicate issue of a rearrangement of autonomies and overarching responsibilities within the Kingdom is discussed. The outcome of this new round of skirmishes is not yet clear.

Certainly the unilateral Dutch interventions have aroused animosity and provoked much anti-colonial rhetoric. The 'recolonization' concept has become an accusatory buzzword over the past decade. Antillean politicians are renowned for standing up vocally to The Hague and they may benefit from this, further complicating the arduous negotiations on a reform of the Kingdom and a planned break-up of the Antilles. But there is no indication whatsoever that this will translate into any significant support for a pro-independence nationalism.

So what may be expected? Independence is not on the agenda. Direct political subordination of the Caribbean islands (as in counties, municipalities or provinces) is a problematic option. Both Curaçao and St Martin are reluctant to let go of the present autonomy accorded to the Antilles-of-five. They prefer to inherit the same freedoms and competences Aruba did in 1986. Conversely The Hague is not really interested in transforming the Caribbean territories into fully integrated parts of the Kingdom. Dutch politicians are reluctant to return to the driver's seat after half a century of Caribbean autonomy. Moreover, they do not like the idea of possibly having to finance – as France does – a European lifestyle in the Caribbean.

Most probably The Hague will continue its policy of strengthening the institutions of the Kingdom and will in turn cooperate with the dismantling of the Netherlands Antilles as a single entity, a process that presupposes a modicum of mutual trust and pragmatism. From Dutch Caribbean politicians it requires the courage critically to assess what degree of autonomy really serves their islands' citizenry best. This is not necessarily the same degree of autonomy that matches their own personal interests and political convictions. Dutch politicians in turn may be expected to refrain from offering illusions to their own electorate wary of the Antilles in the first place. Thus, they will have to spell out that an eventual farewell to the Antilles is highly unlikely, that growth rather than a decrease in financial support is necessary, and that migration from the Dutch Caribbean will continue and should be accepted. This too requires a measure of courage.

Whatever the eventual political arrangements, the six islands will most probably experience a strengthening rather than a loosening of their transatlantic ties. While many Antilleans worry about the growing tendency for Dutch involvement as some kind of recolonization, the lack of any serious alternative to the present status precludes radical nationalist alternatives. This predicament translates into at times heated affirmations of insular patriotism which only underline the obvious paradox: much against their will, Antilleans today are more dependent upon the Dutch connection then ever before, a subordination only strengthened by their own choice of political insularism (Oostindie, 2005).

WIDER IMPLICATIONS FOR SUB-NATIONAL ISLAND JURISDICTIONS

Two broad concerns underlie this paper. The first, no longer controversial, is that there are a good many reasons why small, postcolonial territories may be wise not to opt for independence but instead to remain part of a larger state entity. For various reasons also the former metropolis may be expected to accept this decision to retain close ties. The second question is what degree of autonomy best serves the interests of these small, mainly island entities, non-sovereign 'jurisdictions' which, as Baldacchino (2006) argues, occupy the fuzzy middle ground between sovereignty and municipality. This second question, which incidentally refers not only to postcolonial territories, is both more complicated and more controversial than the first.

One refreshing and optimistic assessment of the advantages of maximum autonomy for such territories is Baldacchino's. He suggests that their status will stimulate flexibility among all parties involved. The metropolitan power – whether the UK, France, the USA or the Netherlands – offers an indispensable safety net and can exercise some form of 'soft imperialism'. But the Sub-National Island Jurisdiction (SNIJ) has "enough discretion to safeguard national identity, local culture and the general exercise of local power". For these SNIJs this apparent limbo is seen by Baldacchino (2004, pp. 77, 84; see also Baldacchino, 2006) as "a winning strategy in political economy". He therefore predicts that the next few decades will not witness "a flurry of independentist movements, but [rather] attempts by sub-national jurisdictions to carve out policy discretion on a specific number of areas in their favour".

My analysis of the Dutch Caribbean case supports this prognosis, but arrives at more ambivalent and indeed slightly more pessimistic conclusions. The major empirical evidence in favour of the 'winning strategy' argument is the dazzling economic development of Aruba after its *separashon* from the other Antilles. There is no doubt whatsoever that the new status at once greatly enhanced the island's flexibility and governmental efficiency and boosted local culture and identity. Aruba became a shining example both to Curaçao and to St Martin of what is possible with greater autonomy.

In contrast, there have been disturbing developments in the quality of governance itself on the islands, something that has clearly demonstrated the limitations of autonomous rule. Why is this? The central Antillean government's apparent unwillingness, or incapability, to redress corrupt governance on St Martin in the 1980s and early 1990s is one example. Similar problems emerged in Aruba in the 1990s, and they continue with the present dramatic debt crisis of the Netherlands Antilles (Oostindie and Klinkers, 2003, pp. 131–152). In these and other cases, The Hague saw itself as obliged to interfere – not from any nostalgic urge to 'recolonize' the Dutch Caribbean, far from it. Since local politicians have failed to live up to acceptable standards of good governance, the Dutch drive to strengthen the prerogatives of the Kingdom, and hence their own involvement, was less a matter of virtue or desire than of a sense of duty and necessity.

It seems to me that there are many parallels here with the British policy for its overseas territories as executed over the past decades. One is that the same regional and insular problems have demanded a stepping-up of metropolitan intervention quite in contrast to the earlier policy of retreat. Another is that this new policy may be welcomed on the islands on pragmatic grounds, but at the same time arouses much local concern over autonomy and identity issues. This postcolonial predicament is hard to solve and will undoubtedly continue to arouse much controversy – as it does in the American and French dependent territories in the Caribbean (Hintjens, 2004; Ramos and Rivera, 2001).

One final observation seems in order here. Perhaps other small, non-sovereign territories have fared better than the Antilles. Perhaps, indeed, other such entities do not suffer to the same degree from the vulnerabilities which seem to characterize the Dutch Caribbean. Their small scale – extreme in the case of these six island jurisdictions – has aggravated a specific clientelist political tradition resulting in deficiencies in the quality of local governance. The freedom of movement inherent in the postcolonial relationship is adding to this through the brain drain towards the metropolis. In addition, and this is sheer bad luck, the geographical location of the islands in a zone of narco-trafficking places them, literally and metaphorically, in between the centres of drug production and drug consumption. The problem is that the islands' internal capacity to counter the corrupting influence of the drugs business and its associated money laundering is very limited.

This is indeed one of the main arguments in favour of strengthening postcolonial constitutional arrangements. It is also a major argument for stepping up the level of intra-regional cooperation, both within the group of sub-national island jurisdictions and between this group and the independent states of the Caribbean. While history teaches us that genuine cooperation within this highly fragmented region is hard to accomplish, we might expect metropolitan institutions to give a positive impetus in this respect.

While the fight against narco-trafficking comes to mind here first, we may also think of the development of legitimate economic opportunities, such as economically sustainable tourism. As it is, tourism has become the most important legal sector in most Caribbean economies, thriving without subsidies or special protective measures. Yet the ecological effects of mass tourism threaten to ruin the very assets on which it is premised. This affects both the independent Caribbean and its sub-national island jurisdictions.

In conclusion then, yes, there are very good reasons to celebrate the opportunities enjoyed by sub-national island jurisdictions because of their intermediate status. But these obvious benefits should not keep us from critically assessing the risks that can arise from granting too much autonomy to territories that may be too limited in human resources and governmental capacities to handle such autonomy, or to cope with its risks. Tailor-made solutions will be needed for these jurisdictions. Blessed with the option of not having to struggle on their own, these unique entities are unlikely to find general models to fit them or show them the directions in which they should go.

Acknowledgements

I thank Godfrey Baldacchino and David Milne for their stimulating criticism on earlier drafts of this chapter, as well as the anonymous reviewers for *The Round Table* for additional useful suggestions. Much of the empirical matter presented in this chapter is based on Oostindie and Klinkers (2001, 2003). More elaborate analyses, references and background materials to this brief sketch of Dutch Caribbean decolonization may be found in these texts.

Note

1. The Caribbean is generally defined as all islands in the Caribbean Sea, plus the Guyanas and Belize. The three Guyanas, while located on the northern shores of South America, have traditionally been inhabited and developed mainly along the Atlantic seashore, looking outward across the ocean to Europe and subsequently the Caribbean and the USA rather than 'down' to mainland South America. For centuries these coastal zones were therefore virtual islands, isolated from their South American neighbours. Of course, the informal

regional expansion of Brazil and perhaps Venezuela may change this 'island status' over time. In fact, Belize, formerly British Honduras, initially shared much of this 'island orientation' across the Atlantic towards its colonial metropolis with the Guyanas. Over the past decades, however, both migration and political pressure from the surrounding Central American republics have broken this isolation, with mixed results for the local Anglophone population. This history may well repeat itself in the sovereign Guyanas.

References

Armstrong, H. W. and Read, R. (2000) Comparing the economic performance of dependent territories and sovereign microstates, *Economic Development and Cultural Change*, 48(2), pp. 285–306.

Armstrong, H. W., de Kervenoael, R. J., Li, X. and Read, R. (1998) A comparison of the economic performance of different micro-states, and between micro-states and larger countries, *World Development*, 26(4), pp. 639–656.

Baldacchino, G. (2004) Autonomous but non-sovereign? A review of island sub-nationalism, *Canadian Review of Studies in Nationalism*, 31(1–2), pp. 77–91.

Baldacchino, G. (2006) Innovative development strategies from sub-national island jurisdictions? A global review of economic policy and government practices, *World Development*, 34(5), pp. 852–867.

Bulmer-Thomas, V. (2001) The wider Caribbean in the twentieth century: a long-run development perspective, *Integration & Trade*, 15(5), pp. 5–56.

Commissie Natievorming (1996) *One People, One Effort, One Nation: Aanzet tot een beleidsplan voor de structurering van het process van natievorming in de Nederlandse Antillen* (Curaçao: Government of the Netherlands Antilles).

Hintjens, H. M. (2004) Governance options for Europe's Caribbean dependencies, *The Round Table*, 344, pp. 533–547.

Hoofdlijnenakkoord tussen de Nederlandse Antillen, Nederland, Curaçao, Sint Martin, Bonaire, Sint Eustatius en Saba (2005) mimeo, 22 October, Bonaire.

McElroy, J. L. and de Albuquerque, K. (1995) The social and economic propensity for political dependencies in the insular Caribbean, *Social and Economic Studies*, 44(2–3), pp. 167–193.

McElroy, J. L. and Sanborn, K. (2005) The propensity for dependence in small Caribbean and Pacific islands, *Bank of Valletta Review* (Malta), 31, pp. 1–18.

Oostindie, G. (2005) *Paradise Overseas – The Dutch Caribbean: Colonialism and its Transatlantic Legacies* (Oxford: Macmillan).

Oostindie, G. and Klinkers, I. (2001) *Knellende Koninkrijksbanden: Het Nederlandse dekolonisatiebeleid in de Caraïben, 1940–2000*, 3 vols (Amsterdam: Amsterdam University Press).

Oostindie, G. and Klinkers, I. (2003) *Decolonising the Caribbean: Dutch Policies in a Comparative Perspective* (Amsterdam: Amsterdam University Press).

Oostindie, G. and Verton, P. C. (1998) Ki sorto di Reino?/What kind of Kingdom? Antillean and Aruban views and expectations of the Kingdom of the Netherlands, *New West Indian Guide*, 72(1), pp. 43–75.

Payne, A. (2004) Small states in the global politics of development, *The Round Table*, 376, pp. 223–235.

Ramos, A. G. and Rivera, A. I. (Eds) (2001) *Island at the Crossroads: Politics in the Non-Independent Caribbean* (Kingston: Ian Randle and Boulder, CO: Lynne Rienner).

van Dijck, P. (Ed.) (2001) *Suriname: The Economy – Prospects for Sustainable Development* (Kingston: Ian Randle).

Werkgroep Bestuurlijke en Financiële Verhoudingen (Working Group on Governmental and Financial Relations) (2004) *Nu kan het . . . nu moet het!* (Now it's possible . . . now it should be done!) (The Hague/Willemstad: Ministry of the Interior and Kingdom Relations).

10 The rise and fall of sub-national island jurisdictions: the cases of the Galápagos Islands and San Andrés y providencia

Sandy Kerr

ISLAND TRAJECTORIES

Starting with Iceland in 1944, the emergence of many small sovereign island states has generated interest in the economic and political viability and vulnerability of small jurisdictions. This seemingly irresistible march to sovereignty proceeded for several decades after the Second World War, before waning considerably in recent years. Instead, many island jurisdictions today choose to operate as relatively autonomous units within a larger 'federal' framework encompassing larger states. Hence, recent island scholarship has taken a natural turn towards sub-national or non-sovereign jurisdictional powers and arrangements.

Globalization too has ironically appeared to create perverse incentives for both political fragmentation and economic integration. One side of this dynamic has led to a 'revolution in localism' (Bartmann, 2000: p. 52) unleashed in response to these simultaneous pressures. Three important trends facilitated this transition: (1) the advance of the principle of *subsidiarity* (which suggests that decisions are best made at the lowest appropriate level where these can be functional), combined with the championing of sustainable community-based decision-making (Wondolleck, 1985; Davos, 1998, van Hecke, 2003); (2) the proliferation of *information and communication technologies (ICT)* which facilitate social and economic networks that would otherwise be hard or impossible to establish; and (3) the coming into force of *international laws, designations and agreements,* agreed to by nation-states (and their regional units) which can therefore be used to the advantage of sub-national regions or groupings.

In the context of islands, these three developments reinforce trends to decentralization of decision-making towards local governance, and to collaboration among islands seeking to influence policy or engage in cultural, social or economic exchange. ICT increasingly allows the social structures of islands – which transcend their physical boundaries (Pitt, 1985; Veronicos, 1987) – to be both strengthened and deepened, permitting access to a wider audience and to niche markets. As a result, SNIJs may now be better able to exploit international agreements entered into by the parent country, to use these for their own advantage, or even in certain circumstances, to circumvent them.

CASE STUDIES

The case studies selected for this comparative study of sub-national island jurisdictions (SNIJs), the Galápagos Islands and San Andrés and Old Providence

(SAOP), are in many respects typical of islands around the world. Their respective economies, for example, are dominated by the primary and tertiary sector activities of fishing and tourism.

Both islands experienced periods of rapid population growth and economic development. In SAOP this started in the 1950s while, in the Galápagos, rapid development started in the 1980s. In both island groups, the development process led directly to a re-evaluation of, and change in, their SNIJ status. The trend worked, however, in two opposite directions for our case studies. Development in SAOP led to a contraction in its local autonomy, as the parent state increased its influence on the islands, whereas in the Galápagos politically aware local groups, supported by a local and international scientific lobby, were able to exploit the island's international status to expand and strengthen its autonomy. This chapter explores the development process on each of these island territories and seeks to explain why each island has arrived at such different destinations and jurisdictional outcomes. The analysis will show that, despite the contemporary political climate favouring greater localism, effective autonomy and resource management may be held back by internal island conflicts.

CASE STUDY 1: THE GALÁPAGOS

The islands of the Galápagos lie some 1,000 km to the west of mainland Ecuador. Reaching an altitude of 1,700 m, the islands comprise the top of a volcanic outcrop rising from the ocean floor at a depth of 3,000 m. The archipelago is spread over 45,600 km^2 of sea, with a land area of 800 hectares. There are 13 larger islands and over 100 smaller islands and outcrops. The mixing of cold water from the south and warm equatorial waters makes the marine environment highly productive. Isolation resulted in limited colonization by animals and plants, permitting then a unique evolutionary path. This unique ecosystem drew pioneers like Charles Darwin to its shores, just as surely as it now draws a lucrative eco-tourism industry.

Serious exploitation of the islands' resources first occurred in the nineteenth century with US and British whalers. In addition to whales, large numbers of tortoise were taken for food. The first animal introductions (rats and goats) occurred around this time. The introductions of new plants and animals continue to pose a major threat to indigenous flora and fauna.

Throughout the nineteenth and early twentieth centuries, there were failed attempts to establish settlements based on the exploitation of giant tortoise for tortoise oil, most notably by 2,000 Norwegians in 1929. Later the islands were used as a US military base during the Second World War, and as a penal colony on the island of Isabela between 1946 and 1959.

The Galápagos is of course most famous because of its association with Charles Darwin (1809–82). It was partly as a consequence of Darwin's observations in the Galápagos that he developed his theory of evolution through natural selection. Darwin's theory irrevocably changed the discipline of biology and is now almost universally accepted within the scientific and wider community. But Darwin's impact goes far beyond that of narrow science. Darwin's ideas directly challenged the conventional teaching of the monotheistic religions that claimed the earth was created, by God, for the overriding purposes of humankind. In Darwin's world, however, humankind was no longer separated from the natural world but was, in fact, an integral part of it. Without Darwin's vision, we would not have had the modern understanding and science of ecology. Possibly more importantly, Darwin's ideas helped change humankind's perception of itself and set in train a process whereby now much of humankind accepts a moral responsibility towards the earth and the environment. The evolution of environmental ethics builds on Darwin's view of the place of humans as integral parts of the natural world.

For our purposes, however, the islands of the Galápagos archipelago have grown in status and stature, hand in hand with the rising reputation of Darwin. They occupy a place of importance not only in the history of science, but also in the popular imagination and culture of the wider global community. As we shall see, this niche of intellectual and political capital has provided an important resource for asserting claims for the autonomy and jurisdictional entitlements of the islands against mainland Ecuador, particularly in relation to resource management and protection of the island's environmental heritage.

Population, migration and employment

Emerging economic opportunities particularly in tourism on the islands have been a powerful draw for immigrants from mainland Ecuador. The population has increased steadily, from just 1,346 in 1950, to 15,311 in 1998 (Erikson and Ospina, 1998; Borja, 2000; INEC, 1998). Based on the 1990–98 growth rate, the estimated population in 2001 was 21,000.

Ecuador is one of the poorest countries in South America with a GDP per capita of around US$2,000. In 1994, 35% of the population was living below the poverty line (World Bank, 2005). Per capita GDP is a good proxy for incomes, but of course tells us nothing about the distribution of that income. There are no official estimates of GDP in the Galápagos. However, a crude estimate, based only on tourism and fishing receipts, suggests a minimum GDP of around US$3,600 per head (based on year 2000 data) (Kerr, 2005). Moreover, the islands perform better than the mainland on key quality-of-life indicators (such as literacy, sanitation or infant mortality) (INEC, 1998; World Bank, 2005). The relative prosperity and better quality of life in the islands are an important attraction for potential migrants from the mainland.

Governance

The islands became part of the Republic of Ecuador in 1832. The Galápagos National Park was established in 1959. A marine protected area was declared in 1986, extending to 15 miles offshore. This was extended to 40 miles in 1998, as the Galápagos Marine Reserve (GMR). The Special Law for the Conservation and Sustainable use of the Province of the Galápagos (SLG), which established the GMR, was declared in March 1998. The SLG and the governance of the GMR are particularly important because they regulate access to the islands' key economic resources.

The SLG has delivered a heightened level of autonomy to the islands. This includes a restriction on immigration; the protection and confinement of fishing to locals using artisanal methods only, and restrictions on the number of tourist operators. Enforcement of the rules within the GMR is the responsibility of the Galápagos

National Park Service (GNPS). The SLG established two levels of decision-making bodies to manage the GMR: (1) an Authority for Inter-Institutional Management (AIM); and (2) a Participatory Management Board (PMB). AIM is the ultimate authority with responsibility for developing a management plan for the GMR. AIM members include four national government ministries (Tourism, Environment, Commerce and Fisheries and Defence) and three Galápagos-based groups (fishers, environmental group and tourism sector). Where necessary the AIM makes decisions by majority voting, thereby ensuring that in the event of conflict, the interests of mainlanders can outvote those of the Galápagos islanders. The PMB is formed by five local groups (Local Chamber of Tourism, fishers, the Charles Darwin Research Station (CDRS), the GNPS and nature guides). The PMB makes its recommendations to the AIM by consensus, providing stakeholder input into the establishment of each fishing season's catch quota and the regulation of tourist vessels. When consensus has been reached by the PMB, their proposals have generally been accepted by the AIM. However, when the PMB cannot reach consensus, AIM can take unilateral decisions, albeit within the general principles of the SLG, based on majority voting. As noted above, national rather than local bodies enjoy majority membership on the AIM. Under these circumstances, a failure to achieve consensus within the PMB can result in decisions made at the AIM that are driven essentially by off-island interests.

Although the PMB is a consensus-based decision-making body, there are serious tensions within its membership. The fishers, for example, have openly questioned the legitimacy of the CDRS within the PMB. The CDRS, essentially an international organization committed to the conservation of the islands, provides scientific and technical advice for conservation and pest eradication. Its scientific and conservation mandate may sit uneasily alongside the interests and preoccupations of fishers. Hence, consensus in the PMB is difficult to achieve, particularly where the 'best outcome' doesn't necessarily tally with the interests of an individual group, or where local and national interests and solutions collide in the nationally dominated AIM.

Fishers in particular have occasionally resorted to direct action in an effort to influence the AIM rather than rely on consensus decision-making. In this case promoting the objectives of the individual group, by any means, may take priority over wider social goals. This is even more of a risk in a relatively recently settled archipelago like the Galápagos, where social ties between socioeconomic groups are weaker than on islands with established communities, customs and social norms. In this respect, the Galápagos might be likened to a 'frontier society', with each social group only interested in securing its own claims on natural resources. These deficiencies in social capital can carry very serious consequences for island jurisdictions, and make their own contribution to failures in resourcefulness and consequently to lost opportunities.

The same challenge confronts the island–Ecuador dynamic since the SLG works in some respects against the interest of some mainland stakeholders – for example by excluding mainland fishers and controlling immigration. As a result, the SLG is certainly not universally embraced by the entire Ecuadorian political establishment. Mainland fishing interests have, for example, lobbied government and argued against the extension of the GMR, together with the Ministries of Defence and the Navy. In this kind of contest between local and national actors, it is clear that the locals draw upon the international status of the Galapagos and of international networks to counter national mainland interests and pressures that might otherwise prevail. Hence, these local–international actors and networks, building on Darwin's islands as the common intellectual property of humankind, cry out for protection, and have begun to establish a jurisdictional niche for natural resource protection of the islands and of their residents. In 1978, the Galápagos became one of the first locations to be conferred UN World Heritage status under the UN Convention Concerning the Protection of the World Cultural and Natural Heritage (1972). This status was extended in 2001 to include the marine reserve.

It is unlikely that the SLG, with its protections for the islands, would have existed had not the UN conferred World Heritage Status upon the Galápagos. After such a designation, any failure to protect the Galápagos would have received international condemnation. The SLG was passed in 1998 during a period of political and economic instability. Ecuador knew that it could ill afford to find itself out of favour with the world community, the UN, and such institutions as the World Bank. Hence, the SLG, though enacted into Ecuadorian domestic law, derives its real power from the sustained international interest in the Galápagos. The global status and appeal of the islands serve as anchor and leverage for local powers that would not have otherwise been devolved and granted by Ecuador. Moreover, without Darwin and the islands' global status, the islands would likely have remained a largely uninhabited, isolated, nature-rich archipelago just waiting to be consumed by the world's apparently insatiable appetite for sea food and resources.

Tourism

With this exalted status, the Galápagos could draw upon an assured niche in the international tourism market. Numbers of tourists, for example, increased threefold from 1985 to 1999. This achievement was assisted by improved communications, and heightened international awareness of the archipelago's ecological uniqueness, and growing interest in environment-based tourism. An important factor in this process has been a recent period of sustained economic growth, and the emergence of an increasingly wealthy and tourism-prone elite, in the US and Europe. In 1999, 66,000 tourists visited the islands, 82% of whom were non-Ecuadorian (GNPS, 2003). Galápagos tourism is oriented around island-based cruise vessels. Tourists live onboard, travelling from island to island. The activities of tourists are tightly controlled by officers of the GNPS, who accompany cruise vessels.

A questionnaire survey of 448 tourists who visited the Galápagos between January and March 2001 suggests that the largest group of visitors comes from the USA (44%), followed by Europe (32%) (Kerr, 2002). US visitors tended to be older, with most in the 56–65 age group. US visitors spent significantly more on their holidays than non-US visitors. There are two other illuminating results. Firstly, the majority of visitors (93%) were on their first trip to the Galápagos. There is a very low level of returnees. Secondly, most visitors (60%) had previous experience of nature-based tourism. Respondents had already visited a variety of global destinations on nature-based holidays (such as Costa Rica, Namibia, Kenya and Antarctica). Based on expenditure evidence gathered by the survey, annual tourism expenditure was estimated to be in the region of US$71.5 million (excluding external travel costs). Over 90% of this expenditure was attributed to European and US visitors.

Fisheries

The fishery in the Galápagos is split into three segments. There is the traditional fishery, open all year round, for fin-fish, which are dried, salted and sold to the Ecuadorian market. In 1999 this accounted for approximately 86 tonnes of dried fish with a value of US$0.3 million. The second component is a lobster fishery which grew rapidly in the 1980s and 1990s when refrigeration and air transport allowed the product to reach US markets. This is a dive fishery, with fishers typically using homemade surface supply equipment. Two or more divers will share a single air supply when underwater. In 1999, 55.4 tons of lobster was exported with an approximate value of US$1.0 million. This fishery is controlled by AIM and the GNPS with a quota, minimum landing size, and a four-month season. A permit is required to land and then export lobster. This makes illegal export difficult and provides the authorities with reliable catch data. The third and last segment is a dive fishery for sea cucumber (locally known as pepino). The pepino is processed before being exported to the Far East, where it is used as a medicine and a cosmetics ingredient. This is highly lucrative, with divers earning about US$1 for each pepino. Once dried, pepino are easy to transport and smuggle illegally (unlike lobster, which must be refrigerated). Prior to 1999, pepino fishing was prohibited in the GMR; however, there was an extensive illegal fishery. In 1999 the fishery opened, with a two-month season. It is estimated that in excess of 4.5 million pepino can be harvested in a season, with a local value in excess of US$3 million (year 2000 values). The retail value in the Far East is in the region of US$6–9 million.

The fishery sector in the Galápagos is artisanal, but not traditional. The ability to export product to external markets has allowed the sector to develop. Fishing incomes are determined by international markets in luxury fishery products (lobster and sea cucumber). Prices are maintained by demand from high-income economies (Singapore, Hong Kong and the USA) and a shortage of supply caused by unsustainable exploitation in other parts of the world (the Caribbean for lobster and the Far East for sea cucumber).

External and internal threats

It is widely recognized that the economies of many SNIJs are dependent on international markets, and hence are vulnerable to changes in external market conditions. The Galápagos is no exception from other islands in this regard. Its main exports are luxury products and services (lobster, pepino and tourism), targeted at wealthy countries. One would expect these markets to exhibit strong income elasticity of demand. Any serious economic downturn in the USA, Europe or the Far East would have a major impact on these markets. Added to this, there are other *external* threats:

- A change in international law in the trade of endangered species could have a major impact on pepino fisheries.
- A change in fashion for ecotourism in the USA or EU, or competition from new fashionable alternatives to the Galápagos could affect tourism numbers.
- Serious civil instability in mainland South America would have an impact on the number of US tourists (who are by nature reluctant international travellers, especially post-9/11).

The Galápagos islanders can do little to influence the above exogenous variables. However, there are also *internal* threats to the islands' economy. These include:

- over-fishing, causing a stock collapse;
- an increase in tourist numbers, destroying the exclusive quality of the holiday experience;
- ecological disturbance from tourist numbers, introduced species, pollution, waste disposal and land enclosure.

There is potential to address many of these issues at the level of the island itself using the vehicle of the SLG, though success will not necessarily come easily. Tourism can prove impervious to negative local feedback (McEachern and Towle, 1974; Carlsen, 1999). Moreover, it is difficult to control tourist numbers when outside interests own the infrastructure. If an exclusive resort begins to lose its status and tourism expenditure starts to fall, then the obvious way to maintain incomes is to increase the number of lower-paying tourists, thereby adding pressure on the environment. Fishery resources are valuable. Many SNIJs do not have control over their waters. National governments may regard the lease of fishing rights to third countries as a useful source of income. Controlling migration may be seen as an infringement of civil liberties by those wishing to migrate to an island or recent immigrants who want their family to join them.

In the Galápagos, the SLG provides autonomy to address many resource management issues. However, ensuring local control of resources requires consensus between the main socioeconomic groups. The development of the Galápagos has witnessed the emergence of three socioeconomic elites. There is a scientific/regulatory community with interests in the environment and conservation; a local fishing community; and a community of tourism operators and related interests. The scientific/regulatory community is global, well educated, and supported by a wider international network of conservation interests. The tourism community is politically well connected in Ecuador: after all, the Galápagos is the principal draw for tourists coming to Ecuador and an important source of foreign revenue. The fishing community is largely uneducated but it is unionized and prepared to take coordinated direct action to secure its goals. While the scientific/regulatory community was the main instigator of the process that led to the adoption of the SLG, each of the groups had a vested interest. Fishers saw the SLG as a way of excluding mainland boats from the lucrative fishery. Similarly, local tourist operators saw the SLG as a means of restricting new entrants, maintaining the natural environment, and raising the international cachet of the Galápagos.

Thus, the SLG served the purposes of each of the islands' elites. While each group has an egoistic interest in protecting the islands' resources, the objectives of the three groups regularly conflict. Fishers are happy to see mainland boats excluded but make regular demands for increased lobster and pepino quota. These protests have occasionally become violent, and have included the tragic massacre of giant tortoises (Larson, 2001). Fishers are mistrustful of the motives of fishery scientists and conservationists, a pattern seen the world over (Kerr *et al.*, 2006). Pepino and shark's fin are regularly taken illegally. In the Galápagos, it is the enforcement, rather than the creation, of laws that present the greatest challenge (Baldacchino, 2006, p. 193).

It also remains to be seen what will happen if there is a fall in tourism income, and operators make demands to increase tourist numbers. Despite these problems, the SLG does provide the mechanism to find island-based solutions to issues of resource management, and the Galápagos is without doubt in a better position than if the Special Law of 1998 had not been enacted.

CASE STUDY 2: SAN ANDRÉS AND OLD PROVIDENCE

Unlike the leverage provided by the undoubted iconic status of the Galápagos Islands on the international stage, fate has conferred no such strategic advantage upon the Colombian archipelago of San Andrés and Old Providence (SAOP). This archipelago, with its current economy also built on fisheries and tourism and surrounded by one of the largest coral reefs in the world, received no Darwin and no high international profile. Instead, SAOP suffered the more customary fate of a Caribbean island in the European age of empire whose political economy was dictated by outside forces. It became a classic farm and plantation outpost, finding its economy and system of governance conforming to that model (Warrington and Milne, 2007).

There are no definitive accounts of the 'discovery' of the islands. San Andrés first appeared on Spanish maps in 1527. The archipelago of San Andrés and Old Providence (SAOP), located in the western Caribbean Sea, approximately 770 km from the Colombian mainland and 240 km from Nicaragua, saw its first colonizers with the English Puritans who settled on the 18 km^2 island of Old Providence in 1629. There followed a train of subsequent colonizers from England, Spain, Argentina, Chile and France. The island of San Andrés, with an area of around 27 km^2, had by 1806 become a cotton plantation island, relying upon imported labour (Rosberg, 1975).

San Andrés has a spine of low hills, with a high point of 90 m. Natural vegetation is almost entirely absent, having been replaced by coconut plantations, farmland and urban development. This contrasts with Old Providence which has a rugged landscape reaching a height of 350 m. The low-lying land has been converted into farmland, while large parts of the interior remain covered by natural or semi-natural woodland. Two barrier reefs, with a series of atolls and smaller reefs, surround the island. The Old Providence reef is over 32 km long, the second largest in the Caribbean. The total marine area associated with the archipelago is approximately 300,000 km^2, representing nearly 10% of the Caribbean Sea (Coralina, 2000).

In 1822 the conference at Villa del Santa Rosa brought the islands officially under the control of the mainland and they have remained Colombian ever since. However, the English-speaking, Protestant islanders remained culturally distinct from mainland Colombia, and were essentially left as self-governing communities until well into the twentieth century.

The Baptist faith was brought to the islands in 1847. It has remained the religion most closely associated with the native islanders. The abolition of slavery in 1853 led to the introduction of sharecropping and a change in the main export crop to coconut. Fishing and crops supplemented incomes and diet. Exports of coconut oil to the USA began in 1855 and this remained the chief export for more than a hundred years. The 1930s, however, saw a major downturn in the fortunes of the coconut industry, with cheap alternatives to coconut oil, and recession in the USA depressed demand. Added to this, the plantations on the island were decimated by coconut blight. The predominantly black, English-speaking, Baptist population languishing upon this isolated and declining outpost of European empire shared strong cultural similarities with other Caribbean islands (e.g. the West Indies, Cayman and Jamaica) but relatively few cultural and economic similarities with the Latin parent state of Colombia to which they were tied. Such was the cruel and contrasting fate of this archipelago.

Free-port status

After the Second World War, following the cessation of the Colombian civil war (*La Violencia*), and partly in response to representations by islanders, the national government took a closer interest in SAOP. In 1953, San Andrés was declared a free-port. This marked the start of a period of radical socioeconomic change.

Free-port status might at first be thought to have been intended to encourage *entrepôt* trade and to set the islands upon a different and self-reliant foundation of political economy. The trade aspects of the San Andrés free-port, however, failed to materialize (and may never have figured genuinely in the government's intentions). In retrospect, it appears that the free-port designation of San Andrés was driven more by the internal economic and political interests on the mainland, providing as it did an outlet for wealthy Colombians to go on holiday and to buy luxury goods unavailable on the mainland, while generating tax revenue for the central government. This 'Colombianizing' of the Caribbean islands promoted angry nationalism in the wake of *La Violencia*.

The free-port allowed 'commercial tourism' to flourish. Mainland Colombians visited the island to purchase electrical goods, jewellery, watches, tobacco, perfume and exclusive alcoholic drinks. To take advantage of the free-port status, visitors were required to spend at least four nights on the island. This stimulated the development of shops, hotels, restaurants and night clubs. The emerging infrastructure helped stimulate further demand. In San Andrés, tourism became the mainstay of the economy, while Old Providence remained largely dependent on agriculture and fishing. The development of the free-port also led to an influx of migrants from mainland Colombia.

The demography of the islands, in terms of numbers and ethnic origin, underwent significant transformation over the latter half of the twentieth century. The population of San Andrés was just over 14,000 in 1964. The population rose rapidly as the free-port developed, mostly fuelled by migration of Hispanic Colombians from the mainland. Migrant Colombians arrived to take advantage of the opportunities presented by the free-port. During this time, incentives were given to mainlanders to settle on the islands. These included free passage, parcels of land, commercial licences, guaranteed jobs and business and home loans at low interest rates. In addition to mainland Colombians, small numbers of other nationals (mainly Lebanese and Syrians) settled on the islands and their descendants still play an important role in the island's retail sector.

The exact size of the population is a politically sensitive subject and difficult to establish. Even official estimates vary widely. Official data published in 2003 suggested that the population of San Andrés comprises approximately 73,000 (Mow *et al.*, 2007) even though the latest census data, that exclude illegal migrants, suggest that the population in 2005 was 55,426 (DANE, 2007).

Under the 1991 Constitution (Article 310), immigrants are required to hold residency cards, and illegal immigrants deliberately avoid the census. Illegal residents may number over 30,000, with no less than 33 shanty areas in San Andrés (Coralina, 2001). Continuing illegal immigration may be due partly to economic and partly to security concerns on the mainland. Population growth on Old Providence has been less dramatic with 2,318 inhabitants in 1964, up to 4,147 in 2005 (DANE, 2007).

Population growth has been, and continues to be, a key issue for the sustainable development of the islands and the cultural survival of its native community. Population growth results in various impacts, including:

- pressure on freshwater resources (such as increased demands on supply, and contamination from sewage);
- potential for disease and loss of environmental quality from poor sanitation, high volumes of waste production and inadequate waste disposal;
- over-exploitation of terrestrial and marine resources, leading to degradation of ecosystems, destruction of biodiversity, increasing poverty and loss of food security;
- continual pressure on land resources for urban development;
- loss of cultural identity of native islanders;
- ethnic tensions from inequity where specific groups dominate or are perceived to be unfairly economically advantaged;
- economic strain on local public service providers and infrastructure;
- urban development, shanty towns and sanitation problems, undermining the factors that make the islands an attractive tourist destination.

The rise in population has created tensions between different ethnic and social groups. On the one hand, native islanders – the Raizales – feel that over many years their culture and traditional rights have been taken over by Latin immigrants. On the other, tension also arises between established Latin residents and the new impoverished immigrants fleeing to the island in order to escape poverty and insecurity on the mainland (Mow *et al.*, 2007).

Prior to the 1950s, the islands were largely self-governing. This arose from a lack of interest on the part of mainland Colombia, then ravaged by civil war, rather than because of any expression of independence by the islanders. The islands were simply left to themselves and islanders got on with the business of survival. Both economic and cultural life on the island with its distinct black, English-speaking, Protestant Creole culture was largely separate from that of Colombia.

When mainland Colombia started to exert increasing control over all economic, social and cultural aspects of life in the 1950s, following civil war in Colombia, national politicians wanted to create a single unified state with one culture, one religion and one language. Consequently, the Creole culture and particularly the English language were suppressed. Catholicism was vigorously promoted on the islands. Public schools became Catholic and all Protestant schools were closed. Islanders had to convert to Catholicism to hold any public-sector jobs. In the late 1950s, Spanish was enforced as the language of the archipelago. Spanish-speaking teachers, predominantly Spanish monks and nuns, were unable to communicate effectively with the English-speaking native students, who were forbidden to speak English on school grounds. As a result, many children from that generation became illiterate in their native English language and also failed to develop adequate language skills in Spanish, the only legally recognized language in Colombia until 1991. All official business and legal transactions were conducted in Spanish. Thus, it was practically impossible for the native islanders to hold positions of authority or responsibility in business or public life.

Overview of economic activity

The establishment of the free-port in 1953 transformed the socioeconomy of San Andrés from one dependent on agriculture and fishing to one driven by tourism and commerce. In 1953, there were only four major commercial enterprises and some small home-based shops, and no hotels or restaurants. By 1962, there were 276 shops and 31 hotels (Toro, 1963). By 1997, the number of shops on the island had expanded to 2,077, with over 200 hotels, restaurants and bars catering for tourists (Diaz, 2000). Most of this development took place in the 1970s and 1980s.

The free-port created a sea-change in the socioeconomy of San Andrés. For almost a century prior to 1953, the economy had been based on the export of coconut oil, with incomes supplemented by agricultural fishing. The opportunities created by the free-port were in international trade, commerce and tourism. In the absence of any positive discrimination and training, there were few real prospects for islanders taking a leading role in this development. The disadvantaged position of islanders was compounded by discriminatory economic incentives, prejudice against non-Spanish speakers and racism.

Tourism in San Andrés

San Andrés currently attracts in excess of 350,000 tourists every year. However, there are few similarities between tourism in San Andrés and in most other Caribbean islands. Significantly, there are very few foreign tourists in San Andrés. In 1999, less that 5% of tourists were non-Colombian (Diaz *et al.*, 2000). A questionnaire survey of 240 tourists on the island of San Andrés in June–July 2000 and December–February 2000–1 revealed that over 60% of these Colombian visitors come from three mainland cities: Cali (27%), Bogotá (25%), and Medellin (19%) (Kerr, 2002). San Andrés is essentially a domestic tourist resort for the mainland state. This contrasts with tourism in most Caribbean islands, which is heavily geared towards North American and European visitors. For Colombians, San Andrés fulfils fairly conventional holiday needs. The main reason for visiting the islands is sun and sand (the Caribbean natural environment), and 76% of visitors stay with family or friends. San Andrés attracts repeat visits – 68% of Colombian visitors had visited before (many several times), and 95% said they would consider returning again. The small number of international tourists surveyed (30) indicated that value for money was the main attraction. San Andrés provides a small number of foreign visitors with an inexpensive Caribbean holiday.

The nature of tourism in San Andrés has changed significantly over the years. The initial model was 'commercial tourism' with wealthy Colombians visiting the islands to purchase luxury goods. Shopping is now a low priority for Colombian visitors and not a priority for foreign visitors. The tourist infrastructure grew in the 1970s and 1980s based on relatively small numbers of high-spending tourists. However, since the Colombian economy was liberalized, there is now no need for Colombians to travel to purchase goods, and other holiday destinations are available to wealthy Colombians. San Andrés now attracts middle-income Colombian families. As the 'exclusivity' of the resort has waned, the numbers of tourists have increased. High tourist numbers and over-population result in serious waste management problems. Raw sewage seeps into the sea, ground water is being polluted and there is a serious solid-waste disposal problem. When asked about problems on the island, both Colombians and non-Colombians repeatedly raised litter, sanitation, sewage and lack of toilets as significant problems.

There is a desperate need for investment in sewage and waste management facilities. The tourism industry on the island would like to attract higher-spending tourists and compete with other Caribbean destinations. However, poor infrastructure makes this difficult. Furthermore, overseas visitors, in particular North American visitors, are discouraged from visiting the island because of the poor security situation in Colombia. The islands are safe, but all connecting flights to San Andrés are via the Colombian mainland.

Fisheries

The fish and shellfish resources of the San Andrés archipelago are exploited by three groups of fishers: artisanal fishers on both Old Providence and San Andrés; legal industrial fishing, landing catch in both San Andrés and directly to the mainland; and illegal industrial fishing. The National Institute of Fisheries and Aquaculture (INPA) sets the quota for both artisanal and industrial fishers. The quota is heavily skewed towards the industrial fishery. In 2000, the industrial fishery received a quota of 197 tons, while artisanal fishers were awarded a quota of 3 tons (weight of lobster tail). It is widely accepted that this quota is exceeded by all fishers, with additional catches by illegal boats landing lobster in Central America.

Artisanal fishers tend to fish from launches which are generally 3–4 m long. They exploit a combination of fin-fish, lobster and conch. Lobster forms a greater proportion of the catch in Old Providence than in San Andrés. Fin-fish are generally caught using hand lines. Conch and lobster are gathered by free-diving without the aid of surface demand or scuba equipment. Free-diving limits the sea area available for exploitation by artisanal fishers. The artisanal fishers are almost exclusively native islanders (*raizales*). The fin-fish catch is sold locally. Lobster and conch are sold to local restaurants or to dealers. Lobster is exported to the USA (Miami or New York) via mainland Colombia. Fishing is particularly important on Old Providence, with 25% of households on the island reliant on fishing.

The industrial fishery exploits resources throughout the archipelago. It focuses on lobster, and to a lesser extent conch, using both traps and divers. Many industrial vessels are foreign-registered, obtaining fishing permits directly from Colombian authorities in Bogotá. Vessels may carry in excess of 20 divers, a large proportion of whom are native Central American. Twenty divers per boat is the legal limit set by INPA. However, there are regular reports of numbers in excess of this. An onboard compressor will supply air to several divers via a single pipe. As many as 600 people may be involved in this fishery. Industrial and artisanal fishers exploit the same stock and are therefore in competition.

A small number of boats land catch at a fish factory in San Andrés, but most of the catch is landed directly to the mainland before being exported to the US. Few, if any, islanders work on industrial vessels. The fish processing plant provides part-time employment for 25–30 people. Other minor benefits include the provision of services and supplies to the vessels themselves.

Autonomy: acquired by default, lost by design?

Prior to 1954, the islands of SAOP enjoyed significant autonomy. This was not a result of bilateral arrangements or protective legislation. Autonomy was essentially by default and purely a function of a lack of interest on the part of a parent state in the throes of civil war. A native population with a different language, religion, ethnic background and culture from that of mainland Colombia increased this sense of independence. The islands forged trade links with North America, resources were locally owned and controlled, and incomes were supplemented by small-scale agriculture and fisheries (Mow *et al.*, 2007). Yet it is dangerous to romanticize the past, for, like many other island economies, the economic situation in SAOP was precarious. The post-war collapse in the market for coconut oil, plus a coconut blight, brought real poverty to the islands. Initially, many islanders welcomed the increased Colombian involvement and investment that took place in the 1950s.

Post-1954, there was a dramatic loss of autonomy. Cultural autonomy was undermined with the imposition of Catholicism, and the use of Spanish in schools and official transactions. Economic autonomy was lost as outside interests bought property and controlled commercial activity. Political autonomy was lost as Colombians dominated the islands' administration. Control over marine resources was lost as the mainland administration limited the activities of artisanal fishers and leased lucrative fishing rights to outside industrial vessels.

The process of Colombianization created a new political class on the islands of SOAP. Mainland Colombians controlled all significant commercial activity and all positions of power in the islands' administration. These new groups were subservient to mainland interests and had neither cultural connection with nor empathy for the native population. The interests of this new business and political elite were best served by close links with the mainland and not by island autonomy. At first, many islanders welcomed development. Able to sell land to developers and find employment, many islanders felt increasingly wealthy. For a time, increasing incomes obscured the reality that only a fraction of the wealth generated on the island trickled down to islanders.

Fifty years later, San Andrés is now possibly the most densely populated island in the Caribbean, with significant environmental, housing, sanitation, and waste management problems. There is a crumbling tourist infrastructure unable to compete with other Caribbean islands. An industrial fishery exploits lucrative marine resources, with no significant economic benefit to the islands themselves.

Colombia is, however, not impervious to change. In 1991, it introduced a radical new constitution. The new constitution obliged the state to protect the diversity and integrity of the environment, recognize the right of people to participate in decision-making, and recognize all ethnic groups and their languages. The new constitution created 34 regional autonomous corporations (CARs) responsible for managing natural resources. Special rights were given to SAOP, allowing the introduction of population control measures. The CAR for SAOP is known as Coralina. In 2000, the archipelago was recognized as a UN Biosphere Reserve and the Seaflower Marine Protected Area was designated by national decree in 2005. Coralina has taken considerable steps towards developing a management regime for the reserve which involves all stakeholders. Encouragingly, a consensus has emerged across all the islands' ethnic groups concerning the need to protect the environment and marine resources.

The success of these measures will, to a large extent, be dependent on national institutions recognizing the legitimacy of this process. This requires a major psychological shift on their part. So far, national agencies have been reluctant to recognize local institutions and have not been prepared to share decision-making with islanders, particularly on the issue of fisheries management. Population control is an important issue but very difficult to address. While migration controls may prevent more refugees from mainland Colombia entering the islands, they cannot easily address the existing chronic over-population. Any positive measures to reduce population will be difficult and politically sensitive.

CONCLUSION

In some respects, SAOP and the Galápagos Islands were both 'discovered' by their parent states after years of neglect. The Galápagos were once considered to be little more than an inhospitable volcanic outcrop, with high ecological but low economic value. The advent of cheaper air travel and high-value nature tourism has transformed the islands into the wealthiest department in Ecuador. With this wealth came population growth, over-exploitation of marine resources, and the introduction of alien species. However, UN World Heritage Status, a high global profile, and an international climate supportive of subsidiarity have allowed the Galápagos Islands to gain considerable control over their internal resources.

The story in contemporary SAOP is very different. This archipelago went from benign neglect prior to the 1950s to repression and thorough consolidation with the Colombian mainland in political, cultural, and economic terms. Consequently all aspects of the islands' administration and resource management have been brought under central state control. The economy saw a rapid expansion and then decline of the tourism sector, with chronic over-population, severe environmental health problems, resource degradation, and the marginalization of native islanders and their culture. While a new constitution provides a glimmer of hope for an element of autonomy to SAOP and for international environmental protection under a UN Biosphere Reserve, successful resistance to a national administration with a strong political culture of centralized control is unlikely. SAOP's system of governance so far conforms to that of a classic fief, having never successfully managed the transition from dependence upon an earlier plantation economy, and hence found itself almost wholly subject to alien and outside control and manipulation (Warrington and Milne, 2007).

The lessons here are clear. The level of autonomy that SNIJs can aspire to is, often and to a large extent, determined by factors external to the island jurisdiction. The modern development of the Galápagos occurred within the context of a wider process of globalization, which has clearly facilitated the development of SNIJ status. At the start of the twenty-first century, with an increasingly globalized economy, the political *zeitgeist* is very much in favour of sub-national arrangements. Furthermore, the process of globalization has itself enhanced the international status of the Galápagos. Darwin's contributions to science are now widely accepted and have fundamentally changed how humanity perceives itself and its relationship with the natural world. As the status of Darwin increased, so did the profile of the Galápagos rise. Yet it is important to note that the political resource now enjoyed by the Galápagos is purely a function of chance. If Darwin had taken his father's advice and not accepted his position on the HMS *Beagle*, then the Galápagos would possibly be no more than a disadvantaged volcanic outcrop with its considerable marine resources being over-exploited by outside interests.

The development of San Andrés, on the other hand, happened at a time when the interests of the parent state demanded tighter control and this resulted in a dramatic loss of island autonomy. In the 1950s, there was international support for a small number of former Caribbean island colonies in their quest for independence. However, beyond this decolonization, there was little interest in autonomy for regions, or islands, within national states. Consequently, the anonymous SAOP archipelago enjoyed no external defence against the penetration of mainland interests, resulting in the complete loss of control over its own resources. Some external recognition has belatedly come in the form of a Biosphere designation. However, without the kind of celebrity status enjoyed by the Galápagos, resistance to Colombian authorities and to industrial fishing interests that threaten the Seaflower Biosphere Reserve brings no chorus of international condemnation. By contrast, the response by the international media to the recent minor *Jessica* oil spill in the Galápagos shows how uneven are the stakes between these two archipelagos.

With external factors so much a matter of chance, and with relative comparative advantages so temporary, the onus falls upon islanders to seize opportunities while they are still available. Yet even here, the role of internal factors cannot be overlooked, and history may not have dealt islands an equally benign legacy. SNIJ arrangements can only be developed if local elites and communities can function effectively and consensually in response to local needs. When development came to San Andrés in the 1950s, a new ruling economic and political class was effectively transplanted from the mainland. This group was strongly subservient to mainland interests and had no interest in developing local jurisdictional autonomy. By contrast, in the Galápagos, each of the key island groups had a vested interest in enhancing SNIJ status: principally, to exclude outside interests from gaining access to the island resources.

There are other lessons here. In addition to the requirement of a united local elite, intent on maximizing its SNIJ status, there must also be sufficient political and fiscal clout to manage this process. In the Galápagos, while each group saw an advantage in the development of SNIJ status, they have had difficulties in reaching agreement on the internal allocation of resources and on building stakeholder consensus. As a result, conflict remains endemic and the island remains weakened in its capacity to manage change in external circumstances. If, for example, the current 'fashion' for nature tourism amongst wealthy Europeans and Americans comes to an end, what will be the response in the Galápagos? Any fall in tourism incomes would inevitably lead to calls for increased numbers and a move towards a mass tourism model with increased numbers and increased environmental pressure.

The Galápagos and San Andrés were once backwaters, but are now exposed to the full force of economic development. In 1954, San Andrés was declared a free-port and the development that followed took place exclusively on that island. The island of Old Providence remains largely undeveloped. While San Andrés' population increased 1,600%, the population of Old Providence has barely doubled. On Old Providence the majority of the population is native and the local culture is vibrant. Most families rely on agriculture, and fishing. The island is covered by semi-natural forest, fringed by white beaches and palm trees, and surrounded by one of the largest coral reefs in the world. Old Providence is to western eyes the very epitome of the Caribbean island ideal. While San Andrés developed, the world ignored Old Providence. The Caribbean tourism boom has avoided Old Providence.

Conscious of what has happened on its sister island of San Andrés, Old Providence is wary of major tourism development and losing control to outside interests. It might be thought that perhaps Old Providence now has the chance to develop its potential without the environmental destruction, exploitation and cultural subjugation suffered by San Andrés; yet, without its own strong political resources and institutions, that outcome remains unlikely. Neither Old Providence nor San Andrés is as yet a fully fledged or genuine SNIJ, nor has either of the two been permitted to become so by their mainland masters. Unlike the Galápagos Islands, this Caribbean archipelago cannot muster sufficient leverage to win much beyond the barest rudiments of local institutions and jurisdiction. Without these, there can be no real protection from outside interests nor effective environmental management.

References

Baldacchino, G. (2006) Warm versus cold water island tourism: a review of policy implementations, *Island Studies Journal*, 1(2), pp. 182–200.

Bartmann, B. (2000) Patterns of localism in a changing global system, in G. Baldacchino and D. Milne (eds), *Lessons from the Political Economy of Small Islands*, pp. 38–55 (Basingstoke: Macmillan).

Borja, R. (2000) La migracion a Galápagos: una lectura desde los censos 1990 y 1998, *Informe Galápagos, 1999–2000* (Quito: WWF, Fundacion Natura).

Carlsen, J. (1999) A systems approach to island tourism destination management, *Systems Research and Behavioral Science*, 16, pp. 321–327.

Coralina (2000) *Caribbean Archipelago Biosphere Reserve: Regional Marine Protected Area System. Global Environment Facility Project Document* (Washington, DC: World Bank).

Coralina (2001) Slum areas (unpublished report) (San Andrés Island: Coralina).

DANE (2007) *Censo General 2005* (Bogota: DANE).

Davos, C. A. (1998) Sustaining cooperation in the coastal zone, *Journal of Environmental Management*, 52(4), pp. 379–387.

Diaz, M. A., Chavarro, E. H. and Barrios, J. H. (2000) *El turismo en San Andrés Islas en la Decada de los Noventa* (Bogota: Banco de la Republica).

Erikson, A. and Ospina, P. (1998) Estimated population, poverty, labour market, public policies and migration, *Galápagos Report 1997–1998* (Quito: WWF-Fundacion Natura).

GNPS (2003) Data supplied by Galapagos National Park Service, November.

INEC (1998) *Censo de Galápagos* (Quito: INEC).

Kerr, S. (2002) *The Socioeconomic Importance of Local Fisheries and Tourism in the San Andres Archipelago and the Galápagos Islands*. Report produced as part of research funded by the European Commission, Appropriate marine resource management and conflict resolution techniques in island ecosystems, ICI8CT980297.

Kerr, S. (2005) What is small island sustainable development about?, *Ocean and Coastal Management*, 48(3) pp. 503–524.

Kerr, S., Johnson, K., Side, J., Baine, M., Davos, C. and Henley, J. (2006) Resolving conflicts in selecting a programme of fisheries science investigation, *Fisheries Research*, 79(3), pp. 313–324.

Larson, E. J. (2001) *Evolution's Workshop: God and Science in the Galápagos Islands* (New York: Basic Books).

McEachern, J. and Towle, E. L. (1974) *Ecological Guidelines for Island Development* (Morges: IUCN).

Mow, J. M., Taylor, E., Howard, M., Baine, M., Connoly, E. and Chiquillo, M. (2007) Collaborative planning and management of the San Andrés Archipelago's coastal and marine resources, *Ocean and Coastal Management*, 50(3–4), pp. 209–222.

Pitt, D. (1985) Anthropological and social theories and microstates, in E. Dommen and P. Hein (eds), *States Microstates and Islands*, pp. 30–39 (London: Croom Helm).

Rosberg, M. (1975) *Social History of San Andrés and Old Providence* (San Andrés Island: Centro de Documentacion).

Van Hecke, S. (2003) The principle of subsidiarity: ten years of application in the European Union, *Regional and Federal Studies*, 13(1), pp. 55–80.

Veronicos, N. (1987) The study of Mediterranean small islands: emerging theoretical issues, *Ekistics*, 323/324, pp. 101–111.

Warrington, E. and Milne, D. (2007) Island governance, in G. Baldacchino (ed.), *A World of Islands*, pp. 379–428 (Charlottetown, Canada, and Luqa, Malta: Institute of Island Studies and Agenda Publishers).

Wondolleck, J. (1985) The importance of process in resolving environmental disputes, *Environmental Impact Assessment Review*, 5, pp. 341–356.

World Bank (2005) *World Development Indicators* (Washington, DC: World Bank).

11 'We are not ready': colonialism or autonomy in Tokelau

John Connell

Predictions of global decolonisation have waxed and waned. In the 1960s, during the first great wave of decolonisation, it was widely assumed that there would be distinct limits to this process and that numerous places were too small ever to become independent. At that time, only Western Samoa (now Samoa), Tokelau's nearest neighbour, was independent in the Pacific, and it was not until the 1970s that other Pacific island states followed. Even smaller states, such as Tuvalu with barely 10,000 people, did become independent despite warnings about their viability. In some there was local concern about uneven development, limited resources and infrastructure (as for example in the Solomon Islands), and many small states went to independence with trepidation as much as jubilation (Aldrich and Connell, 1998: 246). Nonetheless, the mood had shifted to the extent that it was loosely assumed that even the smallest colonial possessions would eventually become independent, or, at the very least, would take on a much greater degree of self-government.

Liberal academics, many of whom perceived colonialism with some degree of distaste, sometimes through familiarity with large continents, assumed that colonised peoples would eventually challenge and eject the colonial powers, as they had done throughout Latin America in the nineteenth century, and most of Africa and South-East Asia in the twentieth century. Indeed a wholly negative construction of 'colonialism' had become common parlance. Moreover, the United Nations Special Committee on Decolonisation had been set up in order to encourage the movement from colonialism towards independence, or something akin to that, under the assumption that colonialism would eventually be an anachronism (Aldrich and Connell, 1998: 156–161). By the end of the twentieth century, just sixteen territories remained on the formal United Nations list of 'colonial' territories.

However, it was becoming evident by the end of the 1980s that numerous sub-national (mainly island) jurisdictions, especially those that were relatively wealthy such as Bermuda (Connell, 1967, 2001), even though marked for decolonisation by the United Nations, were not anxious to challenge their colonial status, but rather preferred to remain within that framework (Aldrich and Connell, 1998). Despite relatively recent predictions of imminent decolonisation for a number of territories (e.g. Sutton, 1987), and the existence of the United Nations Committee, relatively little has subsequently changed. Even where there had been a violent struggle for independence, as in New Caledonia, there now appeared an 'infinite pause' in that struggle (Connell, 2003). And, as the era of decolonisation drew to a close, the only colony to be decolonised was East Timor, in spectacular, violent and unique circumstances (Hill and Saldanha, 2001).

In some respects this might have been predicted, at least in smaller Pacific islands and territories, where colonialism was sometimes belated, brief and superficial. It had long been evident, firstly, that only exceptionally had colonialism been as socially and economically problematic as it had been in some larger, resource-rich and more accessible states. Thus Simpson (1990) commented on colonialism in the Cook Islands, that the land escaped alienation and the material well-being of islanders increased as New Zealand provided welfare and protection. Knapman (1985: 83) wrote of the smaller outlying islands of Fiji that they had been 'spared – by geography – the journey through Hell of some African states', and similar statements were made of other possessions. Secondly, in contemporary decades, much of whatever prosperity existed in many remote islands and island territories came through overseas aid primarily from the colonial power and through international migration (almost always to the colonial 'power') and consequent remittances, and this migration was possible because islanders retained the citizenship of that country (Connell, 2007). Such circumstances in other very small Pacific islands held precedents for, and parallels with, Tokelau.

The political status of many colonies did evolve in the direction of greater independence and autonomy, but there were always limits. Thus both the Cook Islands and Niue moved to self-government in association with New Zealand, and came as close as seemed possible to independence, having a premier, diplomatic representation in New Zealand and membership of various international bodies, but the people never relinquished New Zealand passports, or the freedom to move (Aldrich and Connell, 1998). Nor did they gain seats in the United Nations General Assembly by maintaining a status that one journalist impolitely described as 'a kind of adolescent version of nationhood' (Parker, 2006: 68). This view, of course, presupposed that there was only one legitimate outcome of decolonisation, namely independence and a seat in the UN.

While small territories such as the Cook Islands and Niue (respectively with about 18,000 and 4,500 people when they acquired self-government) moved closer to independence, but chose not to take the 'final step', the third and smallest of New Zealand's overseas territories – Tokelau – invariably ignored their evolution, sought to retain the status quo and largely resisted any movement towards greater independence. This resistance seemingly culminated in 2006 when, in a referendum on moving to self-government in free association with New Zealand, the necessary two-thirds majority was not gained and Tokelau continued to remain the only overseas territory of New Zealand. This chapter examines political change and stability in Tokelau and the basis for its minority rejection of political evolution towards free association.

A BRIEF GEOGRAPHY AND HISTORY

Tokelau is the smallest administrative unit in the Pacific, after the tiny British overseas territory of Pitcairn Islands, with a population of under 1,200. It consists solely of three small coral atolls, Fakaofo, Nukunonu and Atafu, some 500 km to the north of Samoa, from where it was administered after 1925. It is only accessible by sea, almost exclusively from Apia, the capital of Samoa. Nukunonu lagoon was once seen as a possible flying-boat anchorage, being well placed between Suva and Honolulu, but that era came to an end before there was any possibility of such a connection. None of the three atolls are wider than 200 metres, no point is more than 5 metres above ground, and with a total land area of about 12 km² (though each has a large lagoon) population density is extremely high. None are within 60 km of another, thus they have had largely separate existences, despite sharing a language and a colonial history. Tokelau has historically never been a unified political entity and it was not until 1963 that there was the first official combined meeting of leaders from the three islands (Angelo, 2000).

Tokelauans are Polynesians who settled the atolls from elsewhere in Polynesia, mainly Samoa and Tonga. Atafu was unpopulated when first seen by Europeans in 1765, but inhabited at second contact in 1791, and the islands were probably some of the last in the Pacific to be settled (Hooper and Huntsman, 1973). Tokelauan social organisation is centred on extended families and is somewhat more egalitarian than the more chiefly, even royal, hierarchical structure of some other parts of Polynesia. This may be a response to the various relatively recent migrations of diverse Polynesians to Tokelau. Following settlement, there were acute tensions between the islands, warfare was long a problem and islands were often threatened by natural hazards (cyclones). One outcome of violence between the islands was the location of colonial administration in the 'neutral' centre of Apia in Samoa, an issue that had little importance until Samoa itself decolonised.

By the mid-1860s, missionaries had converted all the population of Tokelau. In the same decade the islands were devastated by the Peruvian labour trade, as half the population (almost all the men) were taken away and never returned. It was not until the end of the nineteenth century that Tokelau again reached its pre-raid population total of about 500. During the twentieth century the population increased steadily to a peak of 1,901 in 1966, when significant emigration to New Zealand began to have an effect. The population began to decline equally steadily, reaching a new low of 1,151 in 2006, its lowest population for sixty years.

Concern with population pressure on resources has been long standing: as early as 1926, it was suggested that the islands had a maximum sustainable population of 1,250 and that it would soon be necessary to transfer a surplus population to Samoa (Hooper and Huntsman, 1973; Connell, 1983). Tokelauans did choose to migrate to Samoa, and there were 500 Tokelauans there at Samoan independence in 1962. Afterwards, disadvantaged in Samoa (for example, in access to employment), many moved on to New Zealand, preceding the most important migration in Tokelauan history, and the most significant example of state-assisted migration in the Pacific. New concerns of overcrowding led to the Tokelau Islands Resettlement Scheme being formally approved by the New Zealand cabinet in 1965. The scheme initially took many young, single Tokelauans, and later families, to New Zealand, so that by 1975 some 528 government-sponsored migrants had left. In that year the scheme was suspended at the request of the people of Tokelau who feared the continued diminution of the economically active population, a real problem given the selectivity of migration. The original aim of the scheme had been to take the entire population to New Zealand to reduce the economic burden of supporting Tokelau.

Private migration, however, continued so that as early as 1971 there were more Tokelauans in New Zealand (1,195 migrants and 950 born in New Zealand) than in Tokelau (1,640), and those in Tokelau tended to be relatively old or young (Connell, 1983). In 2006, there were 6,849 Tokelauans in New Zealand (1,599 of whom were born in Tokelau) and 1,151 in Tokelau as the population balance had utterly shifted, with six times as many Tokelauans in New Zealand as in Tokelau – and others in the United States and Australia. Despite Tokelauans' longstanding wish not to experience a declining population like that of Niue, decline was now apparently established.

Most Tokelauans left for New Zealand for the same reasons as other Polynesians, centred on the limitations and marginality of the local economy but also drawn by the desire for modern secondary and tertiary education and health services, wages, and social mobility. That was accentuated for Tokelau by growing pressure on very scarce resources (most migrants coming from the two most densely populated atolls of Atafu and Fakaofo), and natural hazards (the 1966 cyclone being a significant factor, as was Cyclone Percy in 2005) and social pressures (Connell, 1983: 13–15; Wessen *et al.*, 1992). Migration was highly selective by age and also by education, resulting in the loss of better-trained and potentially trainable and educated islanders (Hoem, 2004: 79). A standard process of chain migration took the majority of Tokelauans to the Hutt Valley and Porirua, Wellington.

A TRANSNATIONAL ECONOMY?

Agricultural production is as limited as on most coral atolls, though islanders are also dependent on fisheries. The once almost wholly subsistence economy has never effectively evolved into an export economy but, rather, into one characterised by migration and remittances and a dependence on imports. In pre-war years there were trivial exports of copra and handicrafts and minimal imports, mainly of clothing, steel tools and fishing equipment. Copra exports continued in post-war years reaching a peak in 1975, but falling copra prices and new sources of income brought more rapid decline, and it is several years since there were exports. Efforts have been made to commercialise fishing; but income from fishing is almost entirely from the leasing of territorial waters. Isolation and inadequate infrastructure and communications have precluded tourism, one mainstay of several Pacific island states. Even the pretence of a self-reliant economy has been absent.

Tokelau is both a classic remittance economy and one of the prototypes of the MIRAB (MIgration, Remittances, Aid and Bureaucracy) economy (Bertram and Watters, 1985). Indeed, it is a 'copybook example' of the transition (Hooper, 1993: 242). During the 1950s, the administrative costs of the group, limited though they were, first exceeded locally generated revenue (Hooper, 1993: 244). At least since the 1970s, aid and remittances have been virtually the only two sources of income, with aid sustaining a large but limited public-sector economy. There is no private sector, other than one tiny hotel. By 1981 estimates suggested that remittances had already become the most important source of income in the islands (Connell, 1983: 15). New Zealand aid, mainly in support of wages and salaries, is about US$6 million a year. In 2001, a Tokelau Trust Fund, similar to that in neighbouring Tuvalu, was set up partly with aid income and partly with revenue from the leasing of fisheries waters (that generated NZ$0.7 million in 2001) to provide long-term support and to enhance self-reliance. By 2006, this fund stood at around US$16 million.

The Tokelau public service itself had 149 employees in 1979 including doctors, nurses, teachers and tradespersons. As in other remote atolls in the Pacific, such as the outer islands of Micronesia (e.g. Connell, 1992), their wages were a major source of shared income. From 1983 each atoll agreed to rotate these positions between households so that all households would have reasonable access to public service employment and wages. Incomes began to increase rapidly as more people gained wage employment (Hooper, 1982, 1993). Some form of government income reaches almost all adults; all men must make themselves available daily for the 'able-bodied workforce' which might then have such tasks as unloading a boat, fishing for the village or collecting garbage, and which entitles participants to around US$200 a month. Effectively the choice for a high school graduate is between emigrating to New Zealand and modern-sector employment or largely withdrawing from the labour market (Parker, 2006: 73). Hooper had earlier predicted that those Tokelauans without public-service jobs would simply migrate to New Zealand (1982: 100), a situation that has effectively occurred in New Zealand's other former colony of Niue (Connell, 2008), while government incomes in Tokelau are much smaller.

Dependence on outside incomes has brought a similar dependence on imported foods, which incidentally reduced the longstanding concern over population pressure on resources. Remittances have substantially raised the material standard of living in the islands, enabling access to a considerable range of commodities and consumer durables, improved housing, and a new diversity of consumption and entertainment. However, remittances and the new public-service employment brought a parallel transformation 'from a cohesive community based on traditional exchange and an established customary order, to one dominated by salary and wage incomes and two openly competing principles of social order' (Hooper, 1993: 242). These principles divided chiefly authority from the new authority stemming from employment in the Tokelau public service, where local control was absent, wages enabled new inequalities in income distribution and where the most talented and educated worked. Paradoxically, becoming more politically self-reliant meant losing local autonomy and control.

A BELATED POLITICAL HISTORY

In 1889, the islands were formally placed under an uninterested British protection and were nominally and loosely administered from Samoa (Huntsman and Hooper, 1996: 257–258). There was no overall political structure, and apparently no perceived need for one, and each island was administered separately (Hooper, 1993). In 1916 Tokelau, then known as the Union Group, became part of the new Gilbert and Ellice Islands colony, and, in yet another phase of labour migration, some Tokelauans were recruited to work on the phosphate island of Banaba. The distance from Banaba made administration difficult and in 1925 New Zealand agreed to administer the islands from Western Samoa, a decision that suited the Tokelauans who saw Samoans as having similar cultural traits and from where their missionaries had come. A few trading ships called each year, the missions provided basic education and Tokelau was ignored. In 1946, the islands were officially designated the Tokelau Islands and included in the territorial boundaries of New Zealand, in turn an unwilling guardian (Huntsman and Hooper, 1996: 264–269). It only officially became Tokelau, the name by which Tokelauans knew it, in 1976. Formal administrative colonialism was in every way tenuous, belated, superficial and conducted from Apia rather than from within Tokelau.

As decolonisation occurred in other parts of the Pacific, Tokelau made its own slight accommodations with new political landscapes. Occasional meetings were held in the 1960s and 1970s to discuss relations between Tokelau and New Zealand but they did no more than ratify the status quo, where rare critical decisions were taken by New Zealand officials. It was another decade before change more effectively involved the atolls themselves, and more rapid change came in the 1990s. Real change followed the success of self-government in Niue and the Cook Islands, the broader understanding by Tokelauans of the wider world (a function of travel, migration and education overseas), the appointment of a full-time administrator in 1992 and gentle encouragement from a generally benign and supportive New Zealand government.

From the 1970s onwards islanders told visiting United Nations missions that they were not yet ready to manage their own affairs and wished to maintain their close ties with New Zealand. The 1976 mission was informed that the people wanted no immediate change in their political status, but wished for more 'development' and 'progress' to improve local conditions before that might occur (Hooper, 1993: 252). Broadly, that position was taken by almost all other colonies that have similarly sought to delay independence: they were 'not ready' (Aldrich and Connell, 1998: 245). The same opinion was reiterated by the General Fono (see below) in 1987 and again in 1992, as the option was repeatedly posed in one form or another. When the Ulu o Tokelau (Head of Tokelau), addressed a UN Decolonisation Committee meeting in 1993 his address was entitled 'From the Lagoon to the Deep Ocean' and, using a familiar Tokelauan metaphor of canoes (*vaka*), he argued that Tokelau would be embarking on a venture that might take it from the calm waters of the lagoon to the uncharted and potentially stormy waters of the open sea (Kalolo, 2007). The future always posed multiple uncertainties.

By the 1980s, there was growing interest in the administration of Tokelau, with the Office of Tokelau Affairs and the national public service being transferred from Apia to Tokelau itself. The 1981 United Nations mission to Tokelau, one of a series of missions that broadly sought political evolution, also recommended that transfer. Constraints to such centralisation included the considerable separation of the atolls, and tensions and poor communications between them and the outside world, whether physical or electronic.

Each atoll has long had its own local government structure with, until recently, relatively little being decided at two or three General Fono (meetings) held a couple of times each year to bring together the three islands. The leadership rotates each year between the three islands. The chief representative of the New Zealand Administrator on each atoll is the highest elected official, the *faipule*, who exercises executive, political and judicial powers. The three *faipule*, who hold ministerial portfolios, along with the three *pulenuku* (island mayors), constitute the Tokelau Council of Faipule, essentially a cabinet. It is the nucleus of the General Fono and the highest advisory body, and must be consulted by the administration on all policy affecting Tokelau. Indeed, its establishment in 1993 effectively represented what might be seen as the first 'national' government in Tokelau. The position of Ulu o Tokelau is rotated annually between atolls.

Political change was trivial until the 1960s when New Zealand first came under the obligation to offer self-determination to its three island territories, Niue, Cook Islands and Tokelau, and it was further emphasised by the independence of Western Samoa in 1962. Tokelau was offered the possibility of becoming part of an independent

Samoa or the Cook Islands but had no wish to do so. Indeed, as Western Samoa and New Zealand disengaged, Tokelau drew closer to New Zealand (Huntsman and Hooper, 1996: 317–318). While Niue became self-governing in 1974 following the Cook Islands in 1965, this meant little for Tokelau where change scarcely seemed imminent. Though New Zealand has long undertaken and sought to assist Tokelau towards greater self-government, there has been little enthusiasm for it and, over time, dependence on New Zealand has effectively intensified rather than weakened, especially in a crucial economic sense.

However, following Niuean self-government, the New Zealand Ministry of Foreign Affairs assumed administrative control over Tokelau (taking over from the Department of Maori and Island Affairs) and 'the stage was set for the "decolonisation" of the atolls. The goal was self-government for Tokelau' (Hooper, 1993: 251). More income was expended in Tokelau in a revival and efflorescence of 'welfare colonialism' to boost education and administrative capacity.

A slow and parallel process of constitutional change took place in the 1990s, providing an expansion of, and a wider role for, Tokelau's political institutions. The relocation of the Tokelau Public Service from Samoa to Tokelau began in 1994 and by 1995 most government departments had been transferred. However the crucial Tokelau Liaison Office remained in Apia because of Samoa's more developed communications facilities. Significantly, two of the six other government departments were located on each of the atolls, rather than being centralised.

In 1994 the General Fono, now meeting relatively regularly in Tokelau, adopted a National Strategic Plan that outlined Tokelau's progression over the next decade towards increased self-determination and, possibly, free association with New Zealand. The executive and administrative powers of the administrator were formally transferred to the Fono and, when that was not in session, to the Council of Faipule. Two years later, in 1996, New Zealand approved a Tokelau Amendment Bill that gave the General Fono the power to enact legislation, to impose taxes and to declare public holidays. Though New Zealand retained the right to legislate for Tokelau, there was considerable uncertainty over the role of the General Fono, since there had never previously been a national institution. Nonetheless, it was an unprecedented phase of both decentralisation from New Zealand and Samoa and centralisation of power in Tokelau.

As limited power was slowly devolved to Tokelau the *vaka* (canoe) metaphor, that had accompanied and explained the acquisition of power, as elders (*taupulenga*) piloted the atolls towards a new destiny, gave way to a new metaphor: the 'modern house' of Tokelau. The planned 'new house' was equated with Tokelau's future self-governing status, and the posts that supported it were the institutions that would take Tokelau forwards – notably the General Fono (elected in new ways), the villages, the elders and the Tokelau Public Service (in reduced form) – so that the 'modern' house was simultaneously new, traditional and modern, 'marrying two or more cultural wisdoms' (Pio Tuia, quoted in Field, 2006).

Centralisation slowly continued. Management of the islands' public service was formally transferred to Tokelau in 2001, and in 2003 responsibility for the budget was transferred to the General Fono. In many respects this phase of restructuring was intended to be the prelude to Tokelau moving towards self-government in free association with New Zealand early in the twenty-first century, and the first stage in removing the 'colonial yoke'.

REFERENDUM 2006

Following the changes of the late twentieth century, pressure for political evolution in Tokelau intensified in the present century when a United Nations mission visited the islands in September 2002. It was once again told that the majority of Tokelauans wanted to remain part of New Zealand and that the territory was far too dependent on New Zealand to change its status. Nonetheless, New Zealand continued to direct and encourage some momentum for self-government. Late in 2003, New Zealand signed a *Principles of Partnership* with Tokelau, at which time the Foreign Minister predicted that 'It's pretty clear that most of the people on the Tokelaus [*sic*] will go the same way the Cook Islands and Niue went. They'll become a self-governing territory in free association with New Zealand' (*Pacific Islands Report*, 24 November 2003). The *Principles* were seen as yet one more move towards self-government. Pressure for change gradually focused on a referendum in February 2006 when the population of Tokelau voted on its political future, and specifically whether it wished to become self-governing.

As the referendum drew nearer, there were renewed concerns. Mounting fears among islanders that New Zealand was seeking to loosen its ties with Tokelau had led the New Zealand Minister of Foreign Affairs to state (back in April 2000) that New Zealand would not impose independence on Tokelau and any change would only come with the consent of Tokelauans. In 2004, the Ulu o Tokelau told a meeting of the United Nations Committee on Decolonisation that it was the UN and New Zealand rather than islanders that supported any transition: 'Life as a New Zealand colony has brought many benefits to the country. There is no poverty, no unemployment, and full literacy. Although electricity does not run 24 hours a day, all houses now have internal flush toilets' (quoted in *Sydney Morning Herald*, 31 May 2004). Material change and improved wellbeing were not inconsequential.

In preparation for the referendum, a Draft Treaty of Free Association between Tokelau and New Zealand was composed in 2005. This covered such issues as the retention and development of Tokelauan culture and language, recognised that Tokelauans would remain New Zealand citizens, noted that New Zealand undertook 'to provide ongoing economic support and infrastructure development to improve the quality of life of the people' and covered such themes as defence, international relations and the Tokelau Trust Fund (Kalolo, 2007). In anticipation of the referendum, numerous public education meetings were planned to discuss these issues and also such concepts as 'self-determination, democracy, good governance, accountability and transparency, which have no direct equivalent in Tokelauan' (2007: 258–259) and which had little direct relationship to past politics and government. The meetings were never held.

The referendum, 'arguably the most important event in recent years in Tokelau's political development' (2007: 256), finally took place in February 2006. The 615 registered voters chose between whether Tokelau would become self-governing in free association with New Zealand or would remain a non-self-governing territory of New Zealand. The two-thirds majority required for change was not achieved, with 349 (60%) voting for self-government and 232 against. Short of 46 votes, Tokelau opted to remain a colony.

One of the much touted benefits of moving towards self-government was the somewhat paradoxical argument that Tokelau would then be recognised by other countries who would offer assistance (Parker, 2006). Complex issues surrounding governance were also perplexing to many, in a context where many voters were elderly and poorly educated. Perhaps not surprisingly when voters were asked why they had voted 'No', many simply responded '*Ko au e he malamalama*' (I do not understand)' (Kalolo, 2007: 259). That same simple statement was repeated many times before the referendum, in terms of both the sense of the referendum and the voting conditions. One politician advised those who did not understand to vote against, and the local leaders had no consensus for change (Kalolo, 2007). Some people felt that Tokelau lacked the facilities required of a self-governing state: 'How can you love a country if it's without an airstrip or a ship?' and without other kinds of infrastructure and management skills (quoted in Parker, 2006: 71–72, 74). Others saw no reason to change: 'Only when I'm suffering, then I really want to change. I'm not suffering' (quoted in Parker, 2006: 75). Inertia offered greater certainty, as it had in earlier times; at the 2002 UN Decolonisation Committee meeting, the Ulu had pointed out: 'We are so small; we are afraid of any move to the future in case we make a mistake.' Finally, some of those who favoured self-government were seen as both self-serving and out of touch with Tokelauan tradition.

Voting was also caught up in the minutiae of island life and social issues that had more relevance to many than the seeming subtlety, complexity and irrelevance of political evolution. On Atafu, a bitter division emerged over a Congregational Church pastor who had earlier been caught up in a sex scandal and left the island, returning relatively recently to take up leadership in the church after a public apology. However, many islanders were unhappy and refused to attend the island's only church and part of the 'Yes' vote on Atafu probably came from those who felt that changing the political order would also mean changing the legal system (Parker, 2006). Bitterness was such that not only were there acute divisions within the island council but those who stopped going to church were referred to as Al Qaeda, houses were stoned and many left for New Zealand to wait for better times.

Overseas communities had no voting rights, having effectively been told that they had 'voted to leave' and so could not vote in Tokelau. This was deeply resented with overseas Tokelauans arguing that they supported Tokelau through remittances, and through their New Zealand taxes. Many Tokelauans in Australia and New Zealand lobbied for a 'No' vote, and visited Tokelau to support that position, mainly on the grounds that they feared losing New Zealand passports and more general contact with Tokelau (I. Hoem, personal communication, October 2006), and that self-government would place too much power in the needs of a few on the islands. Tokelauans in Samoa argued, as did many in Tokelau, 'Why change something that has worked well for Tokelau?' and, perhaps less frequently, 'I believe many people in New Zealand disagree with the referendum because if it is successful, unfettered power will be vested in a few people for their personal gain and not for Tokelau' (*Pacific Islands Report*, 1 March 2007). Such sentiments were similar to those in other places that had resisted the acquisition of more local political power. The notion that power corrupted held resonance. Ironically Tokelauan identity is minimal in Tokelau, and only significant in New Zealand (Hoem, 2004: 53). This in turn is ironic since Tokelauans perceive themselves as the 'real' New Zealanders amongst Polynesian migrants since they have always held New Zealand passports (Hoem, 2004: 54). The referendum forced new consideration of identity and nationality.

On the other hand, as the Ulu, Pio Tuia, said afterwards: 'We feel ashamed that we cannot stand up and determine our own future. That really hurts us, we cannot be free men. We continue being a colony of New Zealand; it is very hard' (quoted in Field, 2006: 30). Yet the subsequent Ulu, in his address to the UN Decolonisation Committee in 2006, took a rather different perspective on colonialism:

> Mr Chairman, in this context why then did Tokelau appear to hesitate in its February 2006 Referendum? One reason may be that Tokelau's situation is not a typical one. Tokelau is a colony, but has never known a coloniser's presence on its land. Indeed the strongest presence of that kind was when the New Zealand Administration of Tokelau was based in Samoa. Even that was distant and, to use the usual phrase, 'light handed'.
>
> (O'Brien, 2006)

The referendum thus failed to deliver a new political status and tended to emphasise divisions within Tokelau rather than establish a consensus in favour of a new status. Named 'the Union Islands' by the British, Tokelau was anything but united.

ETERNAL COLONY?

Tokelau offers a poverty of social and economic opportunity with few parallels elsewhere, and has one of the most dependent economies in the world. Isolation and fragmentation have heightened concerns over economic development, political evolution and security. Tokelau would have been the smallest state after the Vatican City. Here as in other relatively small islands, such as Bermuda, though none so small as Tokelau, there was almost constant repetition of the mantras 'we are not ready' and 'we need further explanation of the implications' (Aldrich and Connell, 1998: 245). There was constant concern over the necessity for capacity building to enable the effective continuity, management and delivery of services. Only reluctantly, because of its overwhelming dependence on a single larger state, has Tokelau gradually moved towards greater control over its destiny, and established basic institutions of governance. After all a form of 'welfare colonialism' had early protected Tokelauans from such depredations as the labour trade and later brought services and a standard of living that would otherwise have been unimaginable.

Tokelau depends on both migration and comprehensive government services and thus on New Zealand's willingness to provide both of these. Independence would probably reduce migration and threaten provision of services. Yet migration is a double-edged sword, as Niue has discovered. A visiting Tokelauan delegation in Hawai'i was told 'The only guarantee is integration. Look at Niue, what good is free association if you don't have people?' (Ickes, 2007: 2). Aid and remittances have massively changed local lives, improved housing and other facets of development and reduced problems of depending on subsistence safety nets, though remittances have never been as high as in other parts of Polynesia, probably because of the role of the public service and perhaps because most Tokelauans do not wish to return, and hence do not use remittances as social insurance. Indeed, few Tokelauans do return, other than for visits, hence modern skills are quite limited.

It is one of the quirks of the United Nations Committee on Decolonisation that so much time (and income) has been expended on taking one tiny state a few steps closer to an improbable independence, and then triumphantly celebrating this process. As one journalist noted in 2004, 'As if its role in Iraq were not onerous enough, the United Nations is seeking to impose "regime change" on a tiny speck of land in the Pacific Ocean' (Mather, 2004). Another journalist stated that Tokelau was 'cursed' by being listed with the UN Committee so that both New Zealand and Tokelau were constantly under pressure for evolution (*Pacific Islands Report*, 15 September 2004). Between 1976 and 2002 the Committee made five official mission visits to Tokelau, more than to any other listed territory. Tokelau has been the focus of UN Decolonisation Committee meetings simply because none of the other fifteen territories listed by the Committee have any programme aimed towards 'an act of self-determination', and other contemporary 'colonial' powers, including France and the United States, do not even allow the Committee access to the other listed territories. Equally ironically, there is limited evidence that UN involvement had any impact on political change. More generally, the most trenchant criticisms of colonial powers in recent years have been of their neglect.

Paradoxically, as political institutions evolved and self-government came a little closer to Tokelau, 'the external influences that created the possibility of self-determination in the first place are the very ones which have also worked to erode the legitimacy of those traditional institutions that are called upon to provide a basis for future development' (Hooper, 1993: 262). Political evolution simply threatened other forms of local autonomy, and necessitated complex and lengthy processes to build a House of Tokelau that somehow combined the past and the present. Tokelau has thus acquired a status quite different from that of other former New Zealand colonies as the definition, composition and role of the local agency, the General Fono, has emerged from the wishes of the local people rather than being a transposition from elsewhere, and that recognises local authority, rather than results from a transfer of 'western' power by the colonial government (Angelo, 2000). Indeed, voting in the referendum was much influenced by local values and issues of legitimacy and tradition. All that has occurred under the close scrutiny of distant exponents of decolonisation.

Conflicts in authority, heralded in the establishment of education, emigration and the MIRAB economy, subsequently accentuated by some return migration, emphasised the disharmony that often existed in small islands and isolated communities, masked by a seemingly idyllic landscape. Disharmony existed within and between atolls where high population density could lead to friction. A unity partly imposed from outside has failed to congeal. Such local social differences, divisions, tensions and fears in a geographically fragmented state, with little contact between the three islands, a slowly declining population, and growing fears of sea-level rise, enabled solace, certainty and continuity in New Zealand status and citizenship. Aid and remittances are powerful conservative forces.

As Niue and the Cook Islands struggle with the economic burdens of self-government, and a substantial bureaucracy, and have been bailed out by New Zealand on more than one occasion, dependence has obvious fiscal advantages. Welfare colonialism may say little about dignity, and may overwhelm nascent tendencies towards nationalism, but it enables survival. As in other small colonial territories such as Montserrat, 'the people ... regard continuing dependence as a safeguard against weak or corrupt government' (Taylor, 2000: 338), a guarantee of some degree of economic stability and standard of living, for which isolation, fragmentation and skill shortages offer little, and protection against the whims and uncertainties of global economic, political and environmental change.

Remarkably, another referendum was held a year later, in October 2007, and yet again Tokelauans rejected a change of status – with a marginal shift in favour of self-government, but again insufficient for the two-thirds majority required. Conservative fears have not been vanquished and the status quo may now remain for some time. In the end Tokelauans do and will have just as much self-government as they wish for. While Kofi Annan sent a message to the 2004 meeting of the Committee on Decolonisation that colonialism was 'an anachronism in the twenty-first century ... [and] ... decolonisation is a UN success story but it is a story that is not yet finished. We must see the process through to its end', that particular end is unlikely to reach Tokelau. Tokelauans accept 'anachronism', and are content to paddle the national *vaka* in the safe waters of the metaphoric lagoon with the certainty of overseas assistance, however much of a 'burden' this might seem to be to New Zealand. In its inflexibility, and its belief in the necessity of a particular form of evolution, it is increasingly the United Nations Committee on Decolonisation that appears the real anachronism. In this century, the apparent dichotomy between evil colonialism and virtuous independence is similarly an anachronism. Ultimately Tokelau has resisted the curious 'morality play' that seeks to shame players with doubts and uncertainties (however well-founded) into submitting inexorably to independence. The lesson from Tokelau is that real local choice and autonomy may lead to non-sovereign options, without the need to proffer excuses like 'not being ready' to ward off an insistent UN mantra of sovereignty and independence. The time when the constitutional choices of island communities need to be constrained by any such outdated 'morality play' is long past.

References

Aldrich, R. and Connell, J. (1998) *The Last Colonies* (Cambridge: Cambridge University Press).

Angelo, T. (2000) Establishing a Nation: Kikilaga Nenefu, *Indigenous Peoples and the Law*, www.kennett.co.nz/law/indigenous/2000/46.html

Bertram, G. and Watters, R. (1985) The MIRAB Economy in South Pacific Microstates, *Pacific Viewpoint*, 26(3), pp. 497–519.

Connell, J. (1967) Bermuda: The Failure of Decolonisation? University of Leeds School of Geography, Working Paper no. 492, Leeds.

Connell, J. (1983) *Migration Employment and Development in the Pacific: Country Report No. 17, Tokelau* (Noumea: South Pacific Commission and International Labour Organisation).

Connell, J. (1992) The Back Door of Bureaucracy: Employment and Development in Yap State and Woleai Atoll, Federated States of Micronesia, in R. Baker (ed.), *Public Administration in Small and Island States*, pp. 174–192 (West Hartford, CT: Kumarian Press).

Connell, J. (2001) Eternal Empire: Britain's Caribbean Colonies in the Global Arena, in A. Ramos and A. Rivera (eds), *Islands at the Crossroads: Politics in the Non-Independent Caribbean*, pp. 115–135 (Kingston: Ian Randle Publishers).

Connell, J. (2003) New Caledonia: An Infinite Pause in Decolonization?, *The Round Table*, 368, pp. 125–143.

Connell, J. (2007) Island Migration, in G. Baldacchino (ed.), *A World of Islands*, pp. 455–482 (Charlottetown, Canada, and Luqa, Malta: Institute of Island Studies and Agenda Publishers).

Connell, J. (2008) Niue: Embracing a Culture of Migration, *Journal of Ethnic and Migration Studies*, 34(6).

Field, M. (2006) Another Referendum for New Zealand's Last Colony?, *Islands Business*, 31(3), pp. 29–30.

Hill, H. and Saldanha, J. (2001) *East Timor: Development Challenges for the World's Newest Nation* (Singapore: Institute of Southeast Asian Studies).

Hoem, I. (2004) *Theatre and Political Process: Staging Identities in Tokelau and New Zealand* (New York and Oxford: Berghahn).

Hooper, A. (1982) *Aid and Dependency in a Small Pacific Territory*, University of Auckland Department of Anthropology, Working Paper no. 62, Auckland.

Hooper, A. (1993) The MIRAB Transition in Fakaofo, Tokelau, *Pacific Viewpoint*, 34(2), pp. 241–264.

Hooper, A. and Huntsman, J. (1973) A Demographic History of the Tokelau Islands, *Journal of the Polynesian Society*, 82(4), pp. 366–411.

Huntsman, J. and Hooper, A. (1996) *Tokelau: A Historical Ethnography* (Auckland: Auckland University Press).

Ickes, B. (2007) Tokelauan Delegation Seeks Support in Hawai'i for Free Association, *Pacific News from Manoa*, 1(January–March), pp. 2–3.

Kalolo, K. (2007) Tokelau, *The Contemporary Pacific*, 19(1), pp. 256–262.

Knapman, B. (1985) Capitalism's Economic Impact on Colonial Fiji, *Journal of Pacific History*, 20(1), pp. 66–83.

Mather, I. (2004) UN Cries Freedom to Contented Colonies, *Scotland on Sunday*, 23 May.

O'Brien, K. (2006) Statement, UN Pacific Regional Seminar on Decolonisation, Yanuca, Nadi.

Parker, I. (2006) Birth of a Nation?, *The New Yorker*, 1 May, pp. 66–75.

Simpson, G. (1990) Wallerstein's World Systems Theory and the Cook Islands, *Pacific Studies*, 14(1), pp. 73–94.

Sutton, P. K. (1987) Political Aspects, in C. Clarke and T. Payne (eds), *Politics, Security and Development in Small States* (London: Allen and Unwin), pp. 3–25.

Taylor, D. (2000) British Colonial Policy in the Caribbean: The Insoluble Dilemma – the Case of Montserrat, *The Round Table*, 89(355), pp. 337–344.

Wessen, A., Hooper, A., Huntsman, J., Prior, I. and Salmond, C. (1992) *Migration and Health in a Small Society* (Oxford: Clarendon Press).

Index

Names of contributors are in upper case lettering
References to their chapters are in **bold**